The
ELEPHANT
to
HOLLYWOOD

ALSO BY MICHAEL CAINE

What's It All About?

The
ELEPHANT
to
HOLLYWOOD

MICHAEL CAINE

St. Martin's Griffin
New york

www.stmartins.com

Designed by Meryl Sussman Levavi

The Library of Congress has cataloged the Henry Holt edition as follows:

Caine, Michael.
    The elephant to Hollywood / Michael Caine.—1st ed.
        p. cm.
    Includes index.
    ISBN 978-0-8050-9390-2
    1. Caine, Michael.   2. Motion picture actors and
actresses—Great Britain—Biography.   I. Title.
    PN2598.C15A3 2010
    791.430'28092—dc22
    [B]

                                          2010032863

          ISBN 978-0-312-60434-9 (trade paperback)

Originally published in hardcover format by Henry Holt and Company

          First St. Martin's Griffin Edition: November 2011

              10 9 8 7 6 5 4 3 2 1

To my family—

Shakira, Nikki, Natasha,

Michael, the father of my three grandchildren, Taylor, Miles and

Allegra—and to two of our closest and dearest friends,

Emile Riley and Danny Zarem

CONTENTS

ACKNOWLEDGMENTS

These are the people without whom I wouldn't be where I am, writing a book about myself. . . .

With everlasting thanks to Toni Howard, Sue Mengers, Jerry Pam and Dennis Selinger, who were not only my agents but were and are four of my closest friends. And in the UK, thanks to Duncan Heath and Kate Buckley.

With thanks, too, to all my wonderful friends at Hodder & Stoughton: Kate Parkin, Rowena Webb, Karen Geary and Juliet Brightmore. Without them this book would not have been written (or might have been one thousand pages long . . .).

PROLOGUE

Well, it's a long way from London's Elephant and Castle to Hollywood. And the shortest distance between two points is not always a straight line—as my story is going to prove. But then I've never been known for doing things the easy way. I wouldn't have minded easy, but things just never worked out quite like that. In fact—although I couldn't have known it at the time—they worked out a whole lot better.

Eighteen years ago I thought that my career as an actor was over, so I wrote my autobiography, *What's It All About?* to round off my professional life; and that, as far as I was concerned, was that. Fortunately, and not for the first time in my life, I was wrong. Very wrong. The best was yet to come—which, when I look back at my life—the crazy 1960s, the stardom, the glitz and glamour of Hollywood—is really saying something. The last eighteen years have been different—different style, different places and a different idea of happiness—but different has not only been good, it's been better than I could ever have imagined.

So this is the story of a man who thought it was all over, and found out it wasn't. It's the story of the last eighteen years—but it's also the story of where I came from and where I'm going. I know many people have read my first book, but you don't get to my age without looking back—and God knows I've been to plenty of memorial services—so I'm not going to apologize for telling some of the old tales. But there are plenty of new stories, too, because I've had the good fortune to work with a whole new generation of movie stars. And that puts me in a uniquely privileged position. There aren't many actors whose career has spanned nearly fifty years of moviemaking—from *Zulu* to *The Dark Knight*—and there aren't many actors who have had "Happy Birthday" sung huskily and Marilyn-like into their ear by both Carly Simon and Scarlett Johansson, twenty years apart.

Everyone gets lucky now and then, and I've had some lucky breaks. I've been lucky, too, with friends and agents and supporters who have all looked out for me. But if there's one person I feel I owe for the way the last eighteen years have gone, it's Jack Nicholson. In fact if it wasn't for him, I wouldn't be writing this book now. I have Jack Nicholson to thank for the resurrection of my movie career. I know he's not everyone's idea of a fairy godmother, but he did it for me. I'll explain how, later—but it could all have been so very different. . . .

This is not a serious tome by a pompous old actor—above all, I'm an entertainer, so please feel free to laugh. I want to share the joy and the fun and the good fortune I have had with friends, to tell you about the things I've done and the places I've been and about how when I got there it was never the way I thought it would be. In many ways this is an innocent's venture into the unknown, so I'm pleased you want to come along for the ride. To you and me—bon voyage.

The
ELEPHANT
to
HOLLYWOOD

CHAPTER ONE

THE TWILIGHT ZONE

When I finished my first autobiography, *What's It All About?* 1992 seemed like a good place to stop. I had a great film career, a worldwide bestseller, I owned some restaurants, a beautiful house and, most importantly of all, I had a loving family. Christmas 1991 and New Year's Eve 1992 were spent in Aspen, Colorado, as guests of Marvin and Barbara Davis, the Texan oil billionaires and socialites. My wife, Shakira, and I stayed at the Little Nell Inn (which Marvin happened to own) surrounded by friends, including Lenny and Wendy Goldberg, Sean Connery and his wife, Michelene, and Sidney and Joanna Poitier.

It was a fabulous group to spend a holiday with. I don't ski, but I have really worked hard at developing my après-ski skills and that is what Aspen is all about. As we sat around, enjoying the sunshine, gossiping about old times and eating fabulous food with this great group of people, I felt pretty happy with my lot. Everyone there had been part of my life since I first got to Hollywood, although in fact I'd met Sean in London back in the late 1950s at what was then called a "bottle party." If someone was giving a party in those days and couldn't quite afford it, the invitation would be to "bring a bottle and a bird." I was so broke then that I couldn't afford to bring a bottle, and so I brought two birds. And they were both very beautiful girls. I walked into this party and there was Sean, who seemed enormous compared with the rest of us weedy actor types, and he saw me with those two girls and I became his instant new best friend. That period, back in the 1950s, was a tough time for me—perhaps the toughest I've ever known—and I was living hand to mouth through much of it, owing small sums of money to people all over London and often having to cross the road to avoid creditors. Of course, what I couldn't have foreseen was that not so many years later, Shirley MacLaine would choose me to play opposite her in *Gambit* and give me a welcome to LA party, and in would walk Sidney Poitier. And that Sidney would become my instant new best friend.

Aspen with old friends was followed by a period back in Hollywood. I felt on top of the world. Things could only get better. I was completely oblivious to the downturn in store for me. Shakira and I had bought a small house with a fantastic view on a Beverly Hill but in the modest district of Trousdale. It was a holiday home, really—our main base was back in England but we wanted to be close to our dear friend, Swifty Lazar, whose wife, Mary, was very sick.

Apart from Mary's illness, there were no signs of impending doom. Our old friends were all in town. Just like our New Year at Aspen, the dinner we had one night at Chasen's restaurant in Hollywood with Frank and Barbara Sinatra, Greg and Veronique Peck and George and Jolene Schlatter seemed to sum up all that was good in our lives. It was a great Hollywood evening, full of in-jokes including a prime one from George that seemed to sum up perfectly the relationship between actors and their agents. George is one of the great TV producers, the man who discovered Goldie Hawn in his fantastic show *Rowan and Martin's Laugh-In*, and every bit as funny as the shows he's produced. I've been lucky—my agents have always been close friends—but the relationship between stars and agents is usually quite distant socially. As George told it, an actor gets a telephone call to say that his house has been burnt down and his wife raped. The actor rushes home and a police officer meets him outside and tells him that it is his agent who has come to the house, burnt it down and raped his wife. The actor's jaw drops and he turns to the policeman and says, completely astonished, "My agent came to my *house?*"

In fact, that dinner at Chasen's, and one the following week at Barbra Streisand's (all Art Nouveau, and sensational Shaker furniture), were to be the last high for quite some time. Looking back to this period I can see that the storm clouds, as they say, were gathering. A movie I had made the previous year, *Noises Off*, had come out and gone out just as quickly. I wasn't too bothered. Everyone has a flop movie now and then, I thought. But it was another little sign.

I took no notice. I had become part of Hollywood history. Completely out of the blue, Robert Mitchum, the great 1950s movie star, asked me to present his Lifetime Achievement Award at the Golden Globes. I loved Bob Mitchum and was honored that he should ask me, but I didn't know him and had never worked with him and I was curious. "Did you pick me because I had heavy eyelids like you?" I asked him. And he said, "Yes. You're the only one, you know. People were always talking about my eyelids and then I saw you in *Alfie* and I thought to myself: this guy's got heavy eyelids, too. They're not as heavy as mine, of course, but they're quite heavy. It's all to do with the eyelids." A charming story—and Bob was a charming guy—but I began to wonder if it was really because everyone else turned him down.

Whether or not that was the case, I've always liked the Golden Globes because you can sit at tables and get a drink and move around and talk to people. Burt Reynolds once pointed out something that everyone in the business knows but which is rarely mentioned: the class distinction. At awards ceremonies all the television people are seated at the back and the movie people at the front. It's absurd, really—you get TV stars like those on *Friends* who are earning a million dollars a week, and their tables aren't at the front. And I'm thinking—wait a minute—I've never earned a million dollars a week! I asked one of the organizers of the Golden Globes about it and he said simply, "Movies come first."

I was just about to find out how true that was.

Back in England, my book came out and went straight to Number One. And I embarked on a world tour to publicize it—what could possibly go wrong?

For a start, doing publicity on a book tour turned out to be just like doing publicity for a movie, which is something I have done and hated all my life. When I first went to America on a publicity tour for *The Ipcress File* and *Alfie*, it came as a big shock to be bundled out of bed at six in the morning by my press agent, Bobby Zarem, and told that I was appearing on the *Today* show at seven-thirty. "Seven-thirty?" I said. I'd only flown in the night before. "So why do I have to get up at dawn?" He looked at me pityingly. "It's seven-thirty this morning, Michael." "And who on earth's going to be watching at that time of day?" I demanded. This time Bobby was a little firmer. "Twenty-one million people," he said. "So if you want to be a star in America, you'll have to get up!" I'm used to the 24/7 publicity machine now, but it doesn't mean I like it and this tour was no different. It consisted of me giving jet-lagged interviews to journalists who hadn't even bothered to read the book, then getting on another plane and doing the same thing all over again in a different, equally fascinating and equally beautiful country that I only got to see from the car window to and from an airport.

I remember Chris Patten, the then governor of Hong Kong, sending an official to whip us through immigration and customs so we wouldn't be late for our first-night dinner with him. We stayed in the Regent Hotel and Shakira and I had a Jacuzzi together in the most romantic setting ever—in the middle of the roof of the penthouse apartment thirty stories up. There was nothing there but the Jacuzzi and a 360-degree view of Hong Kong. We spent hours in there. We must have been the cleanest tourists in the whole of Asia.

Spectacular though it was, that was pretty much all we saw of Hong Kong. We went on to Bangkok. As we came out of the airport we saw a Rolls-Royce with a police escort waiting for someone. That someone turned out to be us. It all seemed a bit over the top until we hit the traffic on the freeway—I had never seen anything like it. It didn't seem to matter to our policemen whether we went on the off ramps or off the on ramps, we just plowed our way into the city, doing what normally would have been a four-hour trip in under an hour. When we got to the Oriental Hotel we were ushered into the Somerset Maugham suite—more than a bit intimidating for a first-time writer.

On to Australia, New Zealand . . . and then to Los Angeles for the first stop in a whirlwind publicity tour, punctuated by something that was beginning to happen more and more frequently in my life: a memorial service.

I suppose if I'd been looking for signs that there was a downturn in store for me, I might have taken one from the death of John Foreman, a friend and the producer of one of my favorites among my own movies, *The Man Who Would Be King*. I gave one of the eulogies at his memorial service and others also got up and spoke, including Jack Nicholson. John Foreman was a very special kind of guy and I'd put him in the category of the "nearly greats"—I think he died just before he reached his full potential, although *The Man Who Would Be King* is more than enough to confirm his reputation.

Sitting in the packed chapel and listening as friends paid tribute to a wonderful man, I couldn't help thinking back to that film and what it had meant—and still means—to me. Not only was I working with a man I regarded as God—director John Huston, who had directed three of my all-time favorite films including *The Treasure of the Sierra Madre*, *The Maltese Falcon* and *The African Queen*—but I was playing the part of Peachy Carnehan, a part Huston had planned for Humphrey Bogart, my screen idol. I thought back to the first time I saw *The Treasure of the Sierra Madre*, that great film classic about a bunch of misfits searching for gold, a dream as impossible as mine to be an actor seemed then. As a teenager I had identified with the Bogart character completely and now I found myself in a movie directed by Huston, playing a part intended for Bogart. It seemed as if impossible dreams really could come true.

The other thing that made *The Man Who Would Be King* so special was that I was playing opposite Sean Connery. Working with him proved to be a real pleasure and we became even closer as a result. Sean, like me, felt he owed a great deal to John Huston and we were both very sad to hear the news, many years later, that he was on his deathbed. The two of us went to Cedars-Sinai Hospital in Hollywood to say goodbye. When we got there John was rambling. "I was in a boxing match," he was saying. "And it turns out the other guy had razors sewn into the gloves and that's why I'm here. He finished me off, that guy—that's why I'm here." He rambled on about this boxer for twenty minutes and Sean and I looked at each other and we were both in tears—and I've never seen Sean in tears. We left the hospital, very upset, and the next thing we heard was that John Huston had got up out of bed and made two more movies. When I saw him again I said, "The next time I come to say farewell to you, you'd better die or I'll bloody kill you." I added, "You don't know how upset we were." He said, "Well, Michael, you know how it is—people get upset. And people die." "Well, yes," I said, "but not twice."

Back at John Foreman's service, we had some laughs, told some stories and shed some tears and then it was on to New York for yet another book launch evening. This time it was at my friend Elaine's restaurant and guests included Gloria Vanderbilt, Lauren Bacall, David Bowie and Iman—these legends just floated in front of my jet-lagged eyes. I had a mind that couldn't think—not that it mattered, my tongue and lips were too tired to speak anyway.

If Chasen's symbolized my Hollywood life and was the meeting place for so many of my LA friends, then Elaine's was its New York equivalent for me. Elaine's is more than a restaurant: it's a New York institution, almost a salon. It was the perfect place to hold a book launch because it's always been a place where writers, actors and directors gather—from Woody Allen to the people from *Saturday Night Live*. Elaine herself would flit from table to table, making sure all her guests were all right. One night, there was a guy bothering me and she came over and grabbed him by the collar and threw him out on the pavement— all on her own. I protested. "That's a bit drastic—we could have got rid of him." And she said, "Nah—I don't like those sons of bitches!" Elaine is a close friend and I have lunch with her on a Saturday when we're in New York. It's always caviar, which she pays for in cash that she keeps in her bra. She says, "I'll get this," and she dives in and pulls out this wad of cash.

The party at Elaine's was the last of the tour and from New York I went back home to England. I was absolutely shattered, but scripts had arrived while I was away—it was time to get on with the day job. Eventually I picked myself up and sat down to read one. I was appalled. The part was very small, hardly worth doing at all. I sent it straight back to the producer, telling him what I thought of it. A couple of days later the man phoned me.

"No, no—you're not the *lover*, I want you to read the part of the father!" I put the phone down and just stood there, shocked. The *father*? Me? I headed into the bathroom and looked in the mirror. Yes, staring back at me was, indeed, the father. In the mirror was a leading movie actor, not a movie star. I realized the only girl I'd ever get to kiss in a film again would be my daughter.

The difference between a leading movie actor and a movie star (apart from the money and the dressing room) is that when movie stars get a script they want to do, they change it to suit them. A movie star says, "I would never do that" or "I would never say that" and their own writers will add what they would do or say. When leading movie actors get a script they want to do, they change themselves to suit the script. But there's another difference, and this was a difference I knew I could work with. A lot of movie stars can't act and so when the big roles dry up they disappear, insisting they won't play supporting parts. All leading movie actors have to act or they would vanish completely.

I had always known that this time would come. I was fifty-eight years old. Should I give up or keep going? The question stayed with me for months. Every morning as I opened the packets of coffee-stained scripts with the pencil markings that other, younger actors had made before they turned the parts down, I could see that things were going to be different now, more difficult.

I had reached the period of my life I called the twilight zone. The spotlight of movie stardom was fading and although the slightly dimmer light of the leading movie actor was beginning to flicker into life, it all seemed very gloomy. There were some bright spots. Out of the blue I was made CBE in the Queen's Birthday Honours List—a great honor and a beautiful medal. I was now a Commander of the British Empire and very proud of it, although an unkind journalist pointed out that I'd been made a commander of something that no longer existed.

CHAPTER TWO

THE ELEPHANT

I suppose the real question is not why the spotlight of movie stardom was fading, but how it ever got to shine on me in the first place. Beverly Hills is a long way from my childhood home in the Elephant and Castle in south London, and a Hollywood movie lot is a long way from the drama class I joined at the local youth club when I first had the spark of an idea that I might become a professional actor. That spark turned very quickly into a burning ambition for me—but to everyone else it was just a joke, a good laugh. When I said I was going to be an actor, they all said the same thing: "You? What are you going to do? Act the goat?" And they would fall about. Or if I said I wanted to go onstage, they would say, "Are you going to sweep it up?" I never said anything—I just smiled. In fact, I'd only been to the theater once, with school, to see a Shakespeare play, and I'd fallen asleep.

At the time, I was reading a lot of biographies of famous

actors, desperate to see how they had started in the business. It didn't help. The people I was reading about weren't anything like me. The first actor they ever saw always seemed to be playing at some posh West End theater and they got taken by their nanny. The story was always the same: as soon as the lights dimmed and the curtain rose, they simply knew they *had* to be an actor.

Things were a bit different for me. The first actor I ever saw was playing the Lone Ranger at a real fleapit called the New Grand Hall in Camberwell. I was four and I'd gone to the Saturday morning matinee, which was about as far from the West End as you could get. It was rough, very rough: Nanny would not have liked it at all. The ruckus started in the queue, which was all barging and shoving, and went on with missiles thrown round the cinema even after we'd all sat down. But as soon as the lights went down and the film began, I was in another world. I was hit on the head by an orange; I took no notice. Someone threw half an ice-cream cone at me; I just wiped it up without taking my eyes off the screen. I was so lost in the story that after a while I propped my feet up on the back of the seat in front of me and stretched my legs. Unfortunately, someone had taken out the screws attaching the seats to the floor and the entire row of seats we were sitting in tipped backward and landed in the laps of the people behind. They screamed; we all lay there, legs in the air. It was utter chaos. The film ground to a halt. The usherettes came running. "Who did this?" I was given up without a qualm and whacked around the ear. Order was restored, the film was started up again and as I watched it through a wash of tears I knew I had found my future career.

Of course I'd actually already been acting for about a year. My mother was my first coach and she gave me my first acting lessons when I was three. She even wrote the script. We were poor and my mother couldn't always pay the bills on time, so whenever the rent collector came round she would hide behind the door while I opened it and repeated, word perfect, my first lines: "Mum's out." I was terrified at first, but gradually I got more confident and eventually I progressed on to an even more discerning audience. Once I even convinced the vicar who came round to collect money for the local church. I wasn't always successful, though. One time, there was a ring on the bell and we got ready for the usual routine, but when I opened the door it wasn't the rent collector, it was a tall stranger, with long hair, a great bushy beard and strange, piercing eyes. I don't think I'd ever seen a beard before and I stood with my mouth open, staring at him. He reminded me of someone, but I couldn't think who. "I'm a Jehovah's Witness," he said, fixing me with his glare. "Is your mother in?" It was all I could do to stammer my lines: "Mum's out." He wasn't taken in. "You'll never get to heaven if you tell lies, little boy," he hissed at me. I slammed the door in his face and leaned against it, shaking. I'd remembered who he reminded me of: a picture of Jesus I'd once seen. As we climbed up the three long flights of stairs back to our flat, I asked my mother, "Where's heaven, Mum?" She snorted. "Don't know, son," she said. "All I know is it's not round here!"

My debut as an actor onstage was in the school pantomime when I was seven. I was very nervous, but when I walked on, the audience roared with laughter. I was delighted. This isn't so bad, I thought—and then I discovered that my flies were undone. Ever since, I've checked them automatically. Many years later when I was playing a psychiatrist in *Dressed to Kill* (that is, a murdering, transvestite psychiatrist, just to give the full flavor of the role), I read a number of psychological treatises and one of the conclusions that really struck home for me was the idea that we all become the thing we are most afraid of. I used to suffer from terrible stage fright and when I think back to my childhood and how shy I'd been, I think then how much this idea is true for me. I was never one of those kids who would perform for anyone—if a stranger came round I'd dive straight behind the curtains until they'd gone. I think I was the shyest little boy I've ever come across and it could be that I became a performer to overcome that fear of being in front of people. When you act, you project a part in public and you keep your real self behind those curtains. A journalist asked me recently, during a tour for *Harry Brown*, which character was most like me—Alfie, Harry Palmer or Jack Carter. I said, "I have never played anyone remotely like me." He couldn't understand that. "Those are all people that I knew," I said, "not people that I am."

My very first public appearance was on Tuesday, March 14, 1933, in the charity wing of St. Olave's Hospital, Rotherhithe, where I was born. I didn't have the easiest start in life—and I probably wasn't the handsomest baby, although my mother always said I was. I was named Maurice Joseph Micklewhite, after my father, and I was born with *blepharo*—a mild, incurable, but non-contagious eye disease that makes the eyelids swell. I never asked Robert Mitchum if he had the same condition, but like many things that seemed like a problem initially, it turned out to be to my advantage: my heavy eyelids made me look a bit sleepy on-screen, and of course sleepy often looks sexy. My eyes weren't my only problem in the looks department: my ears also stuck out. I know this didn't affect Clark Gable's career, but my mother was determined that I shouldn't have to go through life being teased and she used to send me to bed every night for the first two years of my life with my ears pinned back with sticking plaster. It worked, but I wouldn't recommend it.

So there I was with funny eyes, sticking-out ears and, just to round it all off, rickets. Rickets is a disease of poverty, a vitamin deficiency that causes weak bones, and although I was eventually cured of it, I've got weak ankles still. When I started walking, my ankles couldn't support my weight and I had to wear surgical boots. Oh, and I also had a nervous facial tic I couldn't control. I tell you, looking at me, acting would have been the furthest thing from anyone's mind.

We may have been poor, and I may have been shy and—at least in the early days—pretty ugly, but when I look back I can see just how lucky I was. I can never remember once being hungry, cold, dirty or unloved. My parents were both traditional working class and they worked their hardest to provide a home for me and my brother, Stanley, who was born two and a half years after me. Dad was part gypsy. Two branches of the family—the O'Neills and the Callaghans (two women with the names of O'Neill and Callaghan appear as signatures on my birth certificate)—came from Ireland originally and the reason they ended up at the Elephant was because there was a big horse repository there and they came over to sell horses. Dad didn't follow that line of business. He worked as a porter in London's Billingsgate fish market—like generations of Micklewhite men had done before him for hundreds of years. He'd get up at four in the morning and spend his next eight hours heaving crates of iced fish about. He didn't like the job, but although he was a very intelligent man, he was completely uneducated and manual labor was the only choice he had. Jobs at Billingsgate were highly prized and it was a real closed shop— you could only get in if a member of your family was already working there. Dad told me once with some pride that when I grew up he could get me a job there with no problem. I didn't want to tell him it would be over my dead body.

Dad may not have been educated, but he was one of the most brilliant men I've ever known. He built his own radio from scratch and he read biographies all the time—he was very interested in the lives of real people. He died when I was only twenty-two, so I never really got to know him as an adult, but we were very good friends and he was my hero. My mother always used to burst into tears at Christmas just looking at me and she'd say, "You are your father, aren't you?" And I'd say, "Yeah, I am." My whole character is based on him: he was a tough bugger, like me. When I look back at his life, what strikes me is the waste of talent—not just his, but the generations of his family and families like his—on manual unskilled labor. And although I know how much better it is now, that kids like my dad at least get a chance to go to school and have the opportunity to learn, I still feel we're failing a whole group of people who just don't fit into the educational mold. I should know: I didn't either.

Back then, Dad was part of a whole generation of working men who didn't think anyone or anything could help them; they were just trying to make the best living they could for themselves and their families. I was born right in the middle of the Depression and everyone was just trying to survive. Although Dad read the papers every day, I don't remember him ever discussing politics and he was certainly not a member of a union or a militant in any sense. In fact, he didn't vote at all. He regarded himself as outside the system completely and although he lived through the founding of the welfare state, and the National Health Service and the 1944 Education Act—all social policies designed to help the working class—his attitude was still that no one could help him but himself. He was socially disgruntled and a sense of this ran through everything he did. He had a relay wireless subscription, for instance, for which he paid two shillings and six pence a week, when he could have bought a wireless set for £5. Over the years he probably spent £100 on that relay wireless, but he just couldn't make the leap of faith and invest in something that would have saved him money.

One of the proudest moments of my life—even with the Oscars, and the financial success, and all the rest of it—was seeing my daughter Natasha graduate from Manchester University. She was the first member of our family for a thousand years to go to university—and for her children, my grandchildren, it will be a normal thing. Even though he was from a generation that didn't show a whole lot of emotion, I know my dad would have been so proud. He would have loved every minute.

Years after my father's death and in another world, I went to the birthday party of the son of my friend Wafic Saïd, the international business tycoon and founder of the Saïd Business School at Oxford University. It was held in a big modern banquet hall, which just happened once to have been Billingsgate fish market. As I sat there, sipping champagne and eating caviar, it suddenly dawned on me that I was staring across the room at the exact spot where my dad's fish stall had been and where I used to help him ice the fish every weekend. I was sitting next to Princess Michael of Kent who was chatting happily. "Did you ever meet President Putin?" she was saying. It sounded as if she was speaking from a very long distance away. "No, I haven't," I said. She leant forward and touched my arm. "Your eyes are watering," she said. "I've got something in them," I lied and grabbed a napkin.

The only thing my father liked about working at Billingsgate was the fact that he could come home at midday and get round to the bookies. He was a committed gambler and his steady run of bad luck on the horses was the main reason I began my acting career at the front door. It was my mother who held us all together. She devoted her life to my brother and me and made sure we never went without, but it was a secondhand world we lived in—secondhand clothes and (never a good idea with growing feet) secondhand shoes. By the age of four my rickets were cured—mainly from having to run up and down the five flights of stairs between our flat and the only toilet in the house, which was in the garden and shared between the five families living there. I also developed strong legs and a strong bladder but I was sorry to have to abandon my special boots. At least they fit.

By the time I got to school most of my physical problems had disappeared—or rather, they had reversed. No longer an ugly kid, I had turned into a very cute one—so cute, that my teacher at the John Ruskin Infants' School took one look at my curly blond hair and big blue eyes and christened me "Bubbles." Big mistake. After I had put up with two or three days of being kicked and punched by the other kids my mother came marching down to the playground. "Where are the boys who did this?" she demanded. When I pointed them out she beat the crap out of them. I had no more trouble after that, but I didn't want my mother to fight my battles for me, so I asked my father what to do. "Fight them," he said immediately. "There's no shame in losing, only in being a coward." And he got down on his knees and put his fists up and persuaded me to hit him. I soon got the idea—and no one at school tried anything after that.

Fighting at school was one thing, the Lone Ranger fighting the bad guys every Saturday morning was another, but some real fighting was just about to start. The first thing my brother and I knew about it was my mother sitting us both down and telling us that we were going to have to go and live in the country because a bad man called Adolf Hitler was going to drop bombs on our house. It didn't seem to make much sense to us. We didn't know anyone called Adolf Hitler so how could he know where we lived? But gradually the reality of war began to take over our little world. First there were the gas masks, made to look like Mickey Mouse and issued to us at school. We tried them on to make sure they fit and I ran about the playground just like the other kids—except for some reason my mouthpiece was blocked and I keeled over in a dead faint through lack of oxygen. I'd let the side down, it seemed, and I was sent home in disgrace, leaving me with a burning sense of injustice and a lifelong loathing of the smell of rubber.

I'll never forget Evacuation Day. My father had taken the only day off work he ever had in his life to come and say goodbye. Stanley and I were all dressed up in our best clothes, new prickly wool shirts that were the scratchiest I'd ever worn (until I joined the British army), ties choking our necks, and labels attached to our jackets. Right up to the time we got to the school playground, my mother was still pretending it was all going to be fun. But first one mother started sobbing, then another and eventually they were all at it—even ours—and we realized that this was no joke. As we marched off, me clutching Stanley's hand in an iron grip, I turned back for one last look at my mum waving her handkerchief and weeping—and promptly trod in a great pile of dog shit.

There was a lot of jeering and catcalling and I was made to go to the back of the line and walk by myself. As I walked on, tears streaming down my face, one of the teachers took pity on me and gave me a hug. "It's good luck," she said. I looked at her in disbelief. "It is," she insisted. "You'll see." Something must have stuck with me, because, years later, when the cameras were rolling for the opening shot of *Alfie*, where I'm walking along the embankment by Westminster Bridge, I did the same thing again. The director Lewis Gilbert said, "Cut!" and turned to me as I hopped about, changing my shoe. "That's good luck," he said. "I know," I replied. "My teacher told me." And we went on to do Take Two of the movie that would make me a star. You see? You should always listen to your teacher.

That first evacuation did not last long. Stanley and I were the last two children left in the village hall at Wargrave in Berkshire and had to be rescued by a very kind woman who whisked us off to a huge house in a Rolls-Royce. There we were showered with kindness and given unlimited cake and lemonade—it all seemed too good to be true. It was. The next day a busybody official came round and said we were too far from the school and we would have to be sent elsewhere and split up.

Stanley was sent to live with a district nurse and I was taken in by a couple who were just plain cruel. My mother couldn't come to visit straightaway because the Germans were bombing the railway lines. When she eventually managed to get down she found me covered in sores and starving. There was an allowance to cover the costs of taking in evacuees and my hosts were out to keep as much of it as possible; I'd been living on one tin of sardines a day. Even worse, the couple used to go away for the weekend and leave me locked in the cupboard under the stairs. I've never forgotten sitting hunched in the dark, crying for my mum and not knowing if anyone would ever come to get me out. That experience was so traumatic that it has left me with a lifelong fear of small, enclosed spaces and a burning hatred of any cruelty to children, and much of my charity work is aimed at children's charities. Anyway, back then I decided I'd rather risk the bombing than be locked up in a cupboard again. Happily, my mother agreed, and took Stanley and me straight back to London, determined not to be parted from us again.

By now the Blitz on London was happening in earnest and it seemed to me that Adolf Hitler had now found out our address. The bombs got closer and closer and when London was set alight by blanket incendiary bombing during the Battle of Britain, my mother had had enough. My father was called up to serve in the Royal Artillery and she took us to North Runcton in Norfolk, on the east coast of England.

Norfolk was a paradise for a scrawny little street urchin like me, coming from all the smog and fog and filth of London. I was a little runt when I went there and by the time I was fourteen I had shot up to six foot, like a sunflower growing up a wall. Or a weed. Wartime rationing meant no sugar, no sweets, no cakes—no artificial anything—but we had good food, supplemented with wild rabbits and moorhens' eggs. Everything was organic, because all the chemical fertilizers were needed for explosives, so I was given this unexpectedly healthy start in life. We lived with another ten families crammed together in an old farmhouse, with fresh air, good food and, best of all, the chance to roam free in the countryside. I went round with a gang of other evacuees; the village mothers wouldn't let their kids play with us because we were so rough and our language was a bit suspect, to say the least. Now I look back on it, we must have been a bit of a bloody nuisance—we raided the orchards, stole milk off doorsteps and got into fights with the local boys— but my experiences there changed my life. I appreciated the country because I went there and I appreciated London because I'd left it behind.

After six months in Norfolk, my father came home for a fortnight's leave. We wanted to hear Lone Ranger–type stories of fighting the Germans, but he was simply exhausted. He'd just come, he said, from a place in France called Dunkirk. It didn't mean anything to us at the time, but when I look back now I wonder at what sort of hell he went through there. When his leave was up, he was sent to North Africa with the Eighth Army to fight Rommel. We didn't see him again for four years.

By now the war had reached even sleepy Norfolk. With the entry of America, we found ourselves living in the middle of seven huge U.S. Air Force bomber bases and witnessing the war in the air at first hand. As we watched from the ground, we could see German planes attacking our own fighters—and we could see the deadly results as plane after plane spiraled out of the sky and crashed in the fields around us. I had never connected the fighting I saw in the movies with real life; now, when we reached the downed planes, often ahead of the police or Home Guard, I saw dead bodies for the first time.

Hitler may not have invaded us, but the Americans certainly did. The towns and villages of Norfolk were overrun by gum-chewing, laid-back, good-humored American airmen who seemed to think everything was a joke and amazed the locals with their generosity and sense of fun. Everything I knew about America I had learnt from my weekly cinema visits and these brave young men were the first real Americans I'd met. It was the beginning for me of a love affair with America and all things American that has lasted the whole of my life.

I'd also been very lucky in my elementary school teacher, a butch, chain-smoking, whisky-drinking, completely inspirational woman called Miss Linton. Looking back, I can see that I may have represented the son she'd never had. She saw something in me, encouraged me to read widely, taught me math through the unusual medium of poker, and one memorable day came flying across the village green in her academic gown to our house to give me the news that I'd passed the London scholarship exam to grammar school. I was the first child from the village school ever to do so. By now, my mother had got a job as a cook and we had moved into the servants' quarters of a big house called The Grange, on the edge of the village. After the Elephant and Castle, it had unimaginable luxuries—electric lights, a fully equipped kitchen, endless good food (we got the leftovers) and hot and cold running water. There was even a huge piano in the family drawing room, shaped like a harp on its side—nothing like the upright boxes I'd seen in the saloon bars in the London pubs.

The house was owned by a family called English whose money came from a timber firm—Gabriel, Wade and English. I'd always remembered the name, and years later Shakira and I decided to take a trip down the Thames on a sunny evening and we went past an old warehouse. I was surprised to see that name painted on the side. I think I'd somehow thought it wasn't a real firm. Mr. English was very kind to me and offered to pay for me to go to school and university, if I didn't pass the scholarship. I was a funny little boy, quite lonely, but people would catch on to me somehow and Mr. English used to take me through to the main house and give me tea in the drawing room. One day, I thought, I'm going to have all this—and the house I live in now in Surrey is really his home: I have replicated his life. It's even extended to food. Because we used to eat the leftovers from the Englishes' dinners, I got used to eating game—pheasant and partridge—as a young boy and that's had a lifelong effect on me, too. I eat like a country squire these days—albeit a country squire who's been to France a lot!

As you get older, you find yourself doing many things for what you are aware will probably be the last time. A couple of years ago I went back to North Runcton with my daughter Natasha. I had been invited to unveil a blue plaque on the village school where I had acted in public for the first time. We were given a great welcome and shown round the impressively modernized buildings, and then we drove to The Grange where the current owner let me in through the front door for the first time. The house, like the school, had changed—the quarters where we had lived was now a double garage—but the two bay windows in the drawing room looking out over the fields were just as they were when Mr. English used to have me in for afternoon tea. As I stood there, I realized that one major part of me had been shaped in this room, while another had been shaped by the school we had just visited. And as we drove away from North Runcton, I was conscious of saying goodbye to my childhood and, although they were long dead, once again to the people there who had been such an important part of it.

So, thanks to Miss Linton—and if I'd failed, it would have been thanks to Mr. English—I got to go to grammar school. The London school that had been evacuated nearest to us was a mainly Jewish school called Hackney Downs Grocers. I'd never met a Jewish person before, but my mother informed me that my father's bookmaker was Jewish and so was Tubby Isaacs, the man who used to sell Dad his jellied eels. Both these men were fat. Mum also said that Jews were clever because they ate a lot of fish (I hated the stuff my father used to bring home from the market before the war) and that most Jews had money, which made sense to me since Dad lost most of his at the bookies and spent what was left on jellied eels. So I was a bit surprised to get to my new school and find that although they were clever, the boys were not fat and they weren't rich—in fact they were just like me. We even shared a name. The name Maurice was a bit unusual round the Elephant, but at Grocers, everyone seemed to be called Maurice. In fact a lot of them had Morris as a surname, too. Very confusing. The only thing that set them apart from the kids I'd been to school with before was that they worked hard. They got this attitude from their parents. My best friend's parents were obsessed with the importance of his education and, yes, they ate fish at practically every meal.

We got back to London in 1946 and it was a miserable time. Many of the familiar streets of my childhood had disappeared and the landscape was littered with the rubble of collapsed buildings. When my father was discharged, having fought right through the war from El Alamein to the liberation of Rome, the council rehoused us in a prefabricated house. Years later, when I was in the movie *Battle of Britain*, I had lunch with General Adolf Galland, the former head of the Luftwaffe, who was acting as technical adviser. I didn't know whether to hit him or thank him for his successful slum clearance program, but it wouldn't have mattered: he didn't seem to have realized that the Germans had lost.

The prefabs, as they were known, were intended to be temporary homes while London was rebuilt, but we ended up living there for eighteen years and for us, after a cramped flat with an outside toilet, it was luxury. Outside, though, there was a constant smell of burning rubbish in the air as the authorities cleared the bomb sites, compounded by the thick smog produced by the coal fires. The shops were empty, everyone was queuing for the few goods that were available—and my only escapes were the cinema and the public library. For young working-class boys like me, America was really exciting. British war films were always about officers; American films were about enlisted men.

British authors wrote about officers; in the library I discovered Norman Mailer's *The Naked and the Dead* and James Jones's *From Here to Eternity*. Here at last were stories about the experiences of soldiers I could identify with.

I may have been a keen member of the public library, but I was not enjoying school. I'd had to move from Hackney Downs Grocers to a school nearer to us and it did not go well, either for the staff at Wilson's Grammar School or for me. The only subject I was remotely interested in was French—and that was only because of Mam'zelle whose short skirts offered a flash of thigh when she perched on the front of her desk—and I began to devote more and more of my creative energy to playing truant. Mum used to give me money for lunch each day and whenever I could I would spend half of it on a bar of chocolate to keep starvation at bay and the rest on a ticket to the Tower cinema in Peckham.

Where Wilson's was failing in its attempts to educate me, the Tower cinema was doing a lot better—and not just in the world of film. One day I turned up at the box office as usual with my chocolate bar and while I was buying my ticket, Doreen, the girl behind the glass, leant forward and whispered, "Give us your chocolate and I'll show you me tits." My jaw dropped. I sneaked a look at her torso. She was no oil painting, but when you're fourteen, most girls have a certain allure. "OK," I said hoarsely and pushed the bar across the counter before she could change her mind. She glanced around. The foyer was empty. "Here you are, then, Romeo," she said and slowly lifted one side of her jumper to reveal a slightly grubby bra. With one finger, she pulled up the left cup until first a nipple popped out and then a whole white breast. It was enormous! It quivered before my staring eyes for at most two seconds before she bundled it back inside her bra, pulled down her sweater, grabbed the chocolate bar and slammed the box office window closed. As I took the long lonely walk down the darkened corridor to the screen, a sense of injustice began to grow. She'd said "tits" plural! I'd only seen one. And now I was left with no chocolate. It didn't seem fair to me and I vowed that I'd never pay for sex again.

They say the average teenage boy thinks about sex every fifteen seconds. That wouldn't have got anywhere near it for me. But of course help was always at hand, so to speak. More constructive help was available at a youth club called Clubland in the Walworth Road, which offered a gym to keep our minds pure and our bodies exhausted. I did join the basketball team since I was already six foot tall, but I was a lost cause: the only thing I was really interested in chasing was girls.

I was obsessed with a girl called Amy Hood and one day as I was going up the stairs to the gym, I spotted her through a door, along with all the other best-looking girls in the club. I was standing there with my nose pressed to the glass, when the door opened unexpectedly and I fell into the room. I blushed, and the girls all tittered, but the teacher came over and grabbed me by the collar. "Come in!" she said, hauling me over to the group. "You're the first boy we've had all year." My lucky day; my twin obsessions—girls *and* acting! I had stumbled into the drama class.

I've never liked critics and it may well go back to my very first review in the Clubland magazine. I was playing a robot in *R.U.R.*, an obscurely intellectual play by Karel Capek. I didn't have a clue what it was about. I didn't even understand the one line I had. Even so, I understood fully the sarcasm behind the young critic's assessment of my performance: "Maurice Micklewhite played the Robot, who spoke in a dull, mechanical, monotonous voice, to perfection." Bastard.

Bad notice or not, I was on my way—or so I thought. From then on until I was called up for my national service, I was always in a play. I was also taken under the wing of a man called Alec Reed, a movie fanatic, who used to show his collection of 16-millimeter silent films at Clubland every Sunday evening. Not only did Alec teach me everything he knew about the history of film, but he also introduced me to the technical side of movie-making. Every summer the whole club would go on holiday to the island of Guernsey, off the south coast of England, and Alec would make a documentary of the trip. It was a proud moment for me when my name came up on the credits for the first time—"Maurice Micklewhite, Director." Once again, the audience laughed. Bastards. But I realized they were right. When I made it to the big screen it would have to be under a different name.

Even I had to admit, though, that my name was the least of my problems. I was a tall, gangly, skinny, awkward boy with blond hair, a big nose, pimples and a Cockney accent. All the movie stars of the day—Robert Taylor, Cary Grant and Tyrone Power, for instance—were dark-haired, smooth, sophisticated and very handsome. Even the ugly ones, like my hero Humphrey Bogart, were dark-haired, smooth, sophisticated and very handsome. It's easier now, of course, but back then people who looked like me would never have been cast as the hero. I remember Steve McQueen telling me once that if he'd been an actor in the 1930s he would have been the best friend.

So how did I make it in the end as a movie actor? I did a good ten years of hard work in the theater and TV, of course, before I got to *Alfie*, but even apart from the acting, you have to have the right face. Take a look in the mirror. Can you see the white on the top of the iris of your eye in relaxed position? Can you see your nostrils looking at your face straight on? Can you see the gums above your top teeth when you smile? Is your forehead longer than the space between the bottom of your nose and the bottom of your chin? If you are a man, do you have a very small head? If you are a woman, do you have a very big head? If you have any of these facial characteristics, you won't get the romantic leading roles. If, however, you have all of the above, you could probably make a fortune in horror films.

All those years I spent acting at Clubland and later in the

professional theater turned out not to be a lot of help ultimately. The art of cinema acting is the exact opposite of stage acting. In the theater you have to be as big and broad and loud as possible, even in the quiet scenes, which is a trick that only the best actors can pull off. Film acting, on the other hand, is about standing six feet from a camera in blazing light and not letting the tiniest bit of acting show. If you are doing it right, you make it look very easy, but it takes a great deal of hard work to accomplish. It's a bit like watching Fred Astaire dancing and thinking, *I could do that*—and you couldn't in a million years.

Of course there are some useful tips I've picked up along the way. . . . In a close-up, choose just one eye of the actor you're playing opposite, don't skip between the eyes or you will just look shifty; choose the eye that brings your face closest to the camera; don't blink if you are playing a strong or menacing character (and remember your eyedrops!); if you are playing a weak or ineffectual character, blink as much as you like—just look at Hugh Grant; and if you have to pause after another actor's line, always start your line and then pause—and you can hold that pause as long as you like. Last of all—full frontal nudity. Don't do it. Acting is all about control and the minute you are naked, you have lost control of what the audience is looking at. But if you absolutely insist on disregarding my advice on that last point, let me offer one final tip: don't move. When legendary ballet dancer Robert Helpmann was asked, as the notorious naked revue show *Oh! Calcutta* debuted in London, if he would ever do a naked ballet, he said, "Certainly not." When asked why, he replied, "Because everything doesn't stop when the music does." Wise man.

Even if you have got the right face, you still need to have a sense of humor about yourself. I think I'm a good dramatic actor, but I always look as if you could have a laugh with me. There's a connection between the actor and the audience that goes far beyond the part you play and it's got nothing to do with acting ability. Charisma—you've either got it or you haven't. Who's got it today? I'd pick Jude Law, Clive Owen, Matt Damon and of those, I identify most strongly with Jude Law. After all, he looks a bit like me—and he's remade two of my movies. I identify with him in another way, too. The press spends a lot of time attacking him personally. When we played in *Sleuth* together, one of the critics mentioned that he'd screwed the nanny and I thought—hang on a minute—he didn't screw the nanny in the movie! He's a wonderful actor, a great dad to his kids, and he's a bit of a jack-the-lad, like I was, although perhaps I was smarter at not being caught. But back when my friends and I were living the high life and dating a lot of girls, we didn't have to contend with the paparazzi or the celebrity magazines the way stars do now. We'd never get away with what we got up to then, these days.

CHAPTER THREE

LEARNING THE ROPES

People still ask me if the character of *Alfie* is based on me. Around the time the film came out, interviewers would say, "Alfie's you, isn't he? You're a young Cockney lad, you like girls.'" "Is that it?" I'd say. "I'm a Cockney and all Cockneys are exactly the same? All Cockneys who like girls are exactly the same?" What they misunderstood then—and some of them still misunderstand now—is that, yes, I'm a Cockney; Alfie's a Cockney. I like girls; he liked girls. But the way Alfie treated them is the complete opposite of the way I would treat a woman.

In fact I based Alfie on a guy called Jimmy Buckley who turned up one day at Clubland and made an instant impression on all the girls there. Jimmy had charisma. I didn't recognize it at the time (and I certainly couldn't have spelled it), but I could see that it worked for him and Jimmy Buckley became my new best friend. Unfortunately, none of his success with the girls rubbed off on me—although I was so desperate by now I would have taken even his rejects.

In the end it wasn't Jimmy Buckley who led me towards the promised land, it was another friend, who'd invited me to his sixteenth birthday party. I wasn't drinking at that point and I was sitting morosely in the kitchen, nursing my lemonade and watching all my friends get hammered, when the back door opened and my friend's auntie beckoned me out into the garden. She was drunk, too, but far from incapable, although mysteriously she did appear to have lost her skirt. I made a halfhearted gentlemanly attempt to help her find it, but after a bit it didn't seem to matter anymore. As I went back home with a whole new spring in my step, I couldn't believe my luck—so *that* was what it was all about!

I may have been gaining an education in some of the most fundamental aspects of life, but school continued to fail to capture my interest and I don't know who was more relieved, me or the headmaster, when I left Wilson's at the age of sixteen with a handful of passes in my final exams. I was free at last to pursue my show business dream.

My first job was as an office boy for Frieze Films—a highly specialized film company offering 8-millimeter tourist films of London and, on weekends, Jewish weddings. As a consequence, I was the only boy at Clubland who knew all the words to "Hava Nagila." One Sunday evening we were filming a wedding cabaret featuring a band called Eddie Calvert and His Golden Trumpet. Everything was going according to plan. We dimmed the lights, the bride clutched the groom's hand, a ripple of excitement ran through the guests and Eddie Calvert himself began to emerge from beneath the stage playing—yes—"Hava Nagila" on his Golden Trumpet. I was in charge of the lighting, and, anxious to capture this climax to the evening on film, I plugged in all the lights again. Every fuse in the building blew at once, the room was plunged into darkness and Eddie Calvert was left stranded in mid-ascent, chin at stage level, still blowing his Golden Trumpet. I was fired on the spot.

My next job lasted far less time. I was still an office boy, but I had moved a little closer to Hollywood. The J. Arthur Rank Organisation was the biggest film company in Britain and, surely, I thought, with all those producers and casting directors going in and out of their Mayfair offices, I would be talent-spotted. In fact the place was like a morgue and, even worse, it was a morgue with rules. When I first started, my boss took me aside and explained that Mr. Rank was a strict Methodist and consequently there was a long list of things employees were forbidden to do, including smoking. I'd just taken it up and wasn't going to abandon the pleasure for anyone, so I took to going down to the gents and lighting a fag whenever I had a free moment. A few weeks or so after I began, I was just sitting there, minding my own business, having a quick drag, when there was a sudden bang on the toilet door. "You! Whoever's in there! Come out—you're fired!"

After this episode it turned out that it would be me doing the firing for a while. The British government had established National Service in the aftermath of the war and every eighteen-year-old boy was required to serve his country for two years. I was subjected to eight weeks of boot camp courtesy of the Queen's Royal Regiment in Guildford, which involved hours of senseless drills and running around the barracks at the double or cleaning and polishing useless bits of equipment. This reached a peak of absurdity just before a visit by Princess Margaret when I was ordered to join a detail *whitewashing a pile of coal*. Mad, I know, but it will be no surprise to anyone else who's been through National Service. And it gets worse: just before the princess arrived, the sergeant in charge noticed that although we had swept the parade ground earlier, leaves were continuing to drift down from the trees. It was early autumn; this was not unexpected. "Get up them trees and start shaking!" the sergeant screamed at me. "I want every leaf off and on the ground and swept up before midday!" A lifetime later, I went to Princess Margaret's house on the island of Mustique for lunch, and when I arrived I found her scooping the leaves off the top of her swimming pool with a big net. I told her this story and she said with a wry smile, "I always wondered why autumn had come so early to Surrey." But I never found out what she thought about that unusual seam of white coal. . . .

After training, the government informed me that they desperately needed my help to occupy Germany, which I did for a year. They then informed me that unless I signed on for another year, I would be sent to Korea to fight communism and defend the capitalist system for a wage of four shillings a day. I couldn't help feeling that someone who was fighting to save capitalism should be paid more than four shillings a day, but more than that, I bitterly resented being bossed about. I was known as "Bolshie" (Bolshevik) by the officers because as well as helping the guys with reading and writing letters home (a lot of my fellow soldiers were pretty well illiterate), I was the person everyone came to for advice about the letter of the law—I knew every army rule backwards and forwards and I knew just how far we could go. As a result I spent over a year on more or less continuous punishment duty, including being made to scrape the guardroom floor clean with razor blades. Although it has turned me into the best potato peeler ever, the thought of another year of it was more than I could face, and so I took the Korea option.

Korea turned out to be the most frightening and also the most important experience of my life and I was lucky to stay alive. When I did get back, Dad welcomed me home, but we'd never talked about what he'd gone through in the Second World

War and he never asked me about Korea. Old soldiers never do. His attitude was, "Now you're a man, you understand," but it was unspoken. We were now on the same level. He didn't want to talk about his war because he would never have wanted to come across as the big hero, and neither did I. There are no heroes in war: it's just a question of doing a job and surviving. And all I know is that surviving Korea made me all the more determined to make my dream of becoming an actor come true.

Working in a butter factory may not seem the most obvious first step to stardom, but opportunities were few and far between after I was discharged. It was 1952 and butter was still rationed. I was put alongside a little old man and we were given the job of mixing the different qualities of butter together to make one big glob. God forbid you should have different qualities of butter available. One day we were mixing away and the old man said out of the blue: "You don't want to do this all your life, do you?" "No," I said. "Well, what do you want to do?" he persisted. "I want to be an actor," I said, and waited for him to crack up like they usually did. But he didn't laugh. Instead he said, "And how are you going to do that?" I shrugged. "Don't know," I mumbled, turning back to the butter. "You want to get *The Stage*," he said. "They advertise for actors in the back of the newspaper. My daughter's a semiprofessional singer and she gets a lot of work that way. Go down to Solosy's in Charing Cross Road—they stock it."

The next Saturday I was outside Solosy's when it opened. Five minutes later I was round the corner, sitting on a bench in Leicester Square looking at an advertisement for an Assistant Stage Manager ("plus minor acting roles") for a small theater company based in Horsham, Sussex. By Monday I had sent off my application (in what I hoped would be the more bankable name of "Michael Scott"), including a hastily taken photograph of me in which I appeared to be wearing lipstick. The following week I found myself sitting in the office of the owner and director of the company, Mr. Alwyn D. Fox. He seemed to be a bit disappointed. "You're nothing like your photograph, are you?" he said. Ah, I understood. I was twenty years old, six foot two, with long blond curly hair and the remnants of a tan I had acquired on the boat back from Korea, but I was categorically and unmistakably butch. "Edgar!" Alwyn D. Fox suddenly shrieked. From out of an inner office emerged a man even smaller and more delicate than Mr. Fox. The two of them stood side by side, hands on hips, gazing at me. "Oh, I think he'll *do*," said Edgar eventually. And I was hired.

My very first role as a professional actor was as the policeman who comes along at the end of the play to arrest the villain who has been discovered by the amateur detective. I can't remember the name of the play, or who wrote it, but I can remember my one line—"Come along with me, sir"—which is all the more remarkable after nearly fifty years, since I forgot it at the time. The problem was that—yes, again—I had forgotten to do my flies up and so when I went on, the audience fell about, which threw me completely. One of the actors helpfully whispered my words to me, but I couldn't hear what he said and asked, crossly, and in my normal speaking voice, *"What?"* Another gale of laughter—and I was banned from performing for the next three weeks.

Now I look back, I realize I learned a huge amount from Alwyn D. Fox and my time in Horsham. Of course I always now check my flies before each take, but I also always bring a pencil to rehearsals so I can take notes on the moves. ("The first thing you need to become an actor is a pencil!" Alwyn screamed at me the first day.) He also drummed into me the importance of speaking clearly. During my very first rehearsal he stopped me mid speech and pointed to the balcony. "The person sitting at the back there," he said, "has paid to hear every word you have to say and every gesture you have to make." He was right. He was right, too, about something else. In one play we did, I was playing a scene in which my character was not on speaking terms with the rest of the cast. I had to sit in a corner, downstage. One night, one of the old ladies in the audience took pity on me and leant out of her seat, over the footlights, and offered me a caramel. I took it and nodded my thanks. The minute we'd taken the last curtain call, Alwyn rounded on me. "How dare you break the fourth wall!" The fourth wall? What on earth was he talking about? "The fourth wall!" he went on, working himself up into a frenzy. "It's the invisible fourth wall between us and the audience and if you break it the magic of theater is *completely* destroyed!"

The sort of training I had in rep has more or less disappeared for young actors. TV is the training ground now, and that work just didn't exist when I started in the business. But I still think that if you're going to be any good at comedy you do have to do live theater, or you can't time laughs. When you make a movie or a TV series, there's no audience response to test yourself against, so I always make sure I speak as loudly as I can in rehearsal and then check the reaction of the technicians. If they laugh—and they've seen it all before—then I know I'm doing the right thing.

Although I was learning the craft of acting fast at Horsham, I still suffered from acute stage fright and kept a bucket in the wings into which I would throw up each time I went on. By now I had progressed to bigger parts, but I still felt sick and soon nausea was joined by violent attacks of shivering, which got worse and worse over the weeks. We were playing *Wuthering Heights* and in a spectacular piece of miscasting I was acting the weak, indecisive Hindley Earnshaw against Alwyn D. Fox's tiny and delicate friend Edgar, who had been cast as the powerful brute Heathcliff. The magic of theater remained surprisingly intact until it came to the fight scene in which Heathcliff has to beat Hindley Earnshaw to a pulp, when the fourth wall came crashing down spectacularly. The problem was that, by the end of a week of this I was shivering and shaking so hard that even if the roles had been reversed Edgar would have won hands down—and during the Saturday matinee, I collapsed.

It was cerebral malaria. Not something you would associate with Sussex, and you would be right. It seemed that Korea was determined not to let me go. When I was finally released from hospital and sent back home to my mother, I had lost over forty pounds, my clothes hung off my body and my face had gone a terrible yellow color. I had been told that my type of malaria was incurable, that I would have to take pills for the rest of my life and that that life would probably not last more than another twenty years. As it was clear that Hollywood was no longer a possibility, as soon as I could I rang up Alwyn. "Well—where have *you* been?" he demanded. "We thought you'd abandoned us!" I was so overwhelmed, I started crying. "I should warn you," I said, gulping back tears, "I don't look the same." "Oh, don't I know it!" he said. "I came to see you in hospital. Never mind—we'll do a season of horror plays."

In fact I had only been only back in Horsham a few weeks when I was summoned back to hospital. The army had found a tropical diseases expert who had come up with a cure for my particular type of malaria and I was to be part of proving him right. I wasn't the only one. When I arrived on the ward I found all my mates from the unit—and every one of them had turned the color of a daffodil. We were strapped to our beds for ten days because the medicine we were given made our blood so heavy that if we moved, we would knock ourselves unconscious. I never found out exactly what it was that Colonel Solomons gave us to put us right, but I'm still here, I'm no longer yellow and the reason I leave England in the winter is because I never want to shiver again.

As soon as I'd fully recovered, I rang Alwyn again to find out if the job was still open, but while I'd been in hospital, the company had folded. I never saw Alwyn or Edgar again—although years later, when I was in Beverly Hills, I got a letter from a social worker in Hammersmith, London. He said he had an old man called Alwyn D. Fox, lying destitute in one of his wards. Mr. Fox, he said, was claiming he had discovered Michael Caine. In all likelihood it was fantasy, but if there was any truth in it, would I mind writing Mr. Fox a letter and perhaps sending a small amount of money to make his last few weeks a bit easier? I wrote at once to confirm Alwyn's story and enclosed a check for £5,000. Two weeks later I had another letter from the social worker, returning the check. Alwyn had been delighted to get my letter, he wrote, and had spent the day he received it showing it to everyone on the ward. He had died later that night.

No Alwyn Fox meant no job for me, so I headed back to Solosy's to pick up another copy of *The Stage*. My time at Horsham meant that I had left the Assistant Stage Manager category behind and could now (with a certain amount of artistic license) call myself an "experienced juvenile." Unfortunately, my artistic license extended a bit too far and I added the part of "George" from *George and Margaret*, a popular play that would have been the next production at Horsham, to my list of parts. When I got to one audition, in a theater in the east-coast town of Lowestoft, I was taken aback to find that the seventy-year-old director seemed a bit hostile. "It says here, you played George in *George and Margaret*," he said. Something was clearly not right. "Well, I did," I retorted, determined to stick to the story. "Well, you're a bloody liar!" he roared. "You've never even seen the play—or you'd know that the cast spends two hours waiting for George and Margaret to turn up and they never do!"

In spite of this—perhaps he liked the way I'd acted so indignant—I got the job. I learnt a great deal from this wily old man. Three pieces of advice in particular have always stuck in my mind. In one play I did in Lowestoft, I was cast as a drunkard and at the first rehearsal I came rolling onto the stage and staggered about. The director held up his hand to stop proceedings. "What do you think you are doing?" he demanded. Feeling rather aggrieved, I said, "I'm playing a drunk." "Exactly," he said. "You are *playing* a drunk—I am paying you to *be* a drunk. A drunk is a man who is trying to act sober; you are a man who is trying to act drunk. It's the wrong way round." Spot on. Another time I was onstage, but not speaking. The director held up his hand and said, again, "What do you think you're doing?" "Nothing!" I replied. "Exactly," he said. "You may not have any lines, but you are onstage and you are listening to what's being said and in fact you have wonderful things to say, but you have just decided not to say them. You are every bit as much part of the action as the people who are speaking. Half of acting is listening—and the other half is reacting to what's been said." Spot on. I also remember a scene in which I had to cry. I thought it was going very well, but again the director stopped me with the line I was hearing rather too frequently for my liking. "What do you think you're doing?" he shouted. "Crying," I said, rather offended that he appeared unmoved by my performance. "No, you're not!" he said. "You're an actor trying to cry. A real man is someone who is trying desperately *not* to cry." Spot on, again.

I was keen enough to abide by the rules of theater when it came to acting, but I was determined not to let my lowly status as juvenile lead interfere with my love life. I had fallen in love with an impossible dream—Lowestoft's leading lady, Patricia Haines. Pat was absolutely gorgeous, two years older than me, light-years away in sophistication and a brilliant actress who didn't have to pad her CV. However, although she was always polite, she didn't seem to have really noticed me at all no matter how often I hung around casting meaningful glances in her direction.

Things went on this way for a couple of weeks and then, one night after the show, one of the actors gave a party. As usual, Pat was the center of attention. She acknowledged me with a brief smile and then ignored me. Realizing my love for her was forever doomed to be unrequited, I settled down to concentrate on getting thoroughly plastered. I sat there alone all night, mired in misery, until the party began to fold. Just as I was contemplating an unsteady return to my lonely digs, I heard a voice from behind me. "Are you shy?" I jerked round to see Pat standing there, all five feet nine of her (plus her three-inch heels). "Shy?" I lurched to my feet, spilling my drink down my trousers. "Me? What makes you say that?" She was a blunt Northern lass. "Because I can see you fancy me and you've not even tried to make a pass." A pass? Was she mad? Me, make a pass at Pat Haines? I wobbled there for a moment, intoxicated not just with cheap beer but by her closeness and the smell of her perfume, and then I took the plunge. What did I have to lose, after all? With all the confidence I could muster from all the Bogart films I had ever seen, I looked her straight in the eyes. "I'm in love with you," I said. There was absolute silence for a minute. The blood was pumping through my head so strongly I had to lean forward to catch her reply. "I know," she said with a smile. "And I'm in love with you, too." This time I knew just what to do. I leant forward and kissed her.

Pat and I were married a few weeks later in Lowestoft. Pat's parents, Claire and Reg, came down from Sheffield and although they made the best of things, it was clear that they thought the marriage wouldn't last.

And of course they were right. We left Lowestoft for London, but it was a very hard first few months. We were renting a small flat in Brixton from my aunt Ellen, the first person in our family to own their own house, and it was just as well she let us have it cheap, because neither of us was making it big. After a very dry period in which I only got a few walk-on parts in television, I gave up looking for acting work and took a series of dead-end jobs to support Pat while she pushed on with her career. It was soul-destroying—and it was about to get even more difficult because Pat became pregnant. Our beautiful daughter Dominique was born to a father who simply wasn't ready for her and couldn't support her and under the strain our marriage broke down and I walked out. Pat took Dominique back to her family in Sheffield and Claire and Reg took on the job of bringing her up. I was in despair: I had no money, I was out of work and I had abandoned my wife and child. At twenty-three, I felt I had failed my family and myself and I was almost suicidal with worry.

I moved back to the prefab. Things were bad at home, too. Dad had rheumatism of the spine and could no longer work so I got a job in a steelyard to bring in some money. It was mercilessly hard physical labor—the hardest I'd ever done—and bitterly cold. Meanwhile, Dad's back pain was worsening and the doctor told me (but not him) that in fact he had liver cancer and would only live another few weeks. I watched as this strong, vital man faded away in front of my eyes until the day I carried him out of the house to the ambulance waiting to take him to St. Thomas' Hospital to die.

I will never forget those last two days of my father's life. He was in agony. I begged the doctor to give him an overdose of painkillers. At first he refused but when I pointed out that death could hardly be worse than the living hell Dad was going through, he looked at me for a moment and then said, "Why don't you go now? Come back at eleven o'clock tonight." When I returned that night, Dad was much calmer and I sat with him holding his hand. I squeezed it now and again, and now and again he would squeeze back. We sat there like that for two hours, and just as Big Ben, which I could see from the window, struck one o'clock, Dad opened his eyes. "Good luck, son," he said, quite clearly, and then he died.

When they turned out my father's pockets at the hospital, all they found was three shillings and eight pence. Three shillings and eight pence was all he had after fifty-six years of hard manual labor. As I walked out of that ward I determined that I would make something of myself—and that my family would never be poor again.

———

Everybody gets a break now and again and it sometimes doesn't come the way you might expect. Who would have thought that it was my experiences as a soldier in Korea that would lead to my first exposure to the movie business?

My mum had had a small insurance policy—£25—on my father's life and seeing what a terrible state I was in, she cashed it in and told me to go and sort myself out in Paris. It was typically generous of my mum—who had so little money herself—and because I had fallen in love with the idea of Paris after reading a memoir called *Springtime in Paris* by the American writer Elliot Paul, Paris was where I chose to go. My return fare from London, Victoria, was £7 and with what I had left I managed to afford—at least to start with—a crummy hotel in the Rue de la Huchette, which was where Elliot Paul had stayed. Not having any money, I had to walk everywhere, but I was just out of the army and still very fit and in any case Paris is the best city to walk around in the whole world. For a couple of months I walked all over it, sat at cafés on the pavements just watching people go by and vowing that one day I would come back and do the whole place in style. My money soon ran out, but I survived on little bits of luck. I learnt to cook French fries on the pavement on the Boulevard Clichy, Paris's main street of vice at the time. The man who taught me sold hot dogs and I sold my "frites for a franc" next to him. After I could no longer afford the hotel, I slept at the old air terminal in the center of Paris. I had my bag with me and a discarded air ticket I had found so I looked like a passenger who had missed a flight. Breakfast was free, supplied by a sympathetic American student who ran the early morning shift in the terminal café, and he also kept my bag for me during the days so I could walk about unencumbered. I know you are supposed to fall in love in Paris—it is one of the most romantic cities in the world after all—but there didn't seem to be much enthusiasm for a sad, broke, unemployed, young Englishman among the women I met. I may not have fallen in love with a woman, but I did fall in love with Paris herself and my time there sparked in me a lifelong love of the city.

It also did the trick. I stayed there for several weeks until I felt able to go home, and when I did get back to the Elephant, it was to be greeted by my mother with a kiss, a cuddle and a tear and the news that I'd got a job. I started to cry myself because there was a telegram waiting from my agent offering me a small part, plus the role of technical adviser, on a film called *A Hill in Korea*. The film was being shot on location in Portugal and in the Shepperton film studios and they would pay me £100 a week for eight weeks.

This was untold riches! But there was a problem: the film was a month and a half away, Pat needed money to support herself and the baby and there was no chance of me getting a job for just six weeks. Once again my mum came to the rescue and took all her savings—£400—out of the bank. "You can pay me back later," she said. As ever, there was nothing she wouldn't do for Stanley or me.

Once I'd got past my dodgy debut performance I had never had any trouble remembering two hours of dialogue onstage. In my first film I managed to forget just eight lines—and I only had to deliver them at the rate of one a week. Filming a take is completely unlike acting in the theater; most of the time is spent coordinating the filming equipment. By the time the director, Julian Aymes, shouted, "Action," I was a complete bundle of nerves and it didn't help to overhear one of the cameramen muttering, "It's only one fucking line!"

If my film debut wasn't going as well as I'd hoped, I felt on much surer ground as a technical adviser. After all, I was the only person on the set who'd set foot in bloody Korea. No one understood what we'd been doing there in the first place—in fact it often seemed as if no one knew we had even been there at all. Whenever I've mentioned it to American friends, they are completely taken aback. "The British were in *Korea*?" And it wasn't just us Brits. I was in a division that also included Australians, New Zealanders and South Africans, not that anyone seemed to care. I've got a lot of sympathy for soldiers. I know what it feels like to be sent off to fight an unpopular war that no one at home really understands or cares about and then to come back and meet a complete lack of understanding—or, worse, indifference—to what you've been through.

I was only nineteen when I was sent off to Korea with the Royal Fusiliers and I'd never heard of the place. My basic national service training had consisted of learning to shoot a 303 Lee Enfield rifle (obsolete by the end of the Second World War), and how to fire a Sten gun. This machine gun had a major design fault: it either jammed after the first three rounds, or kept blasting even with your finger off the trigger. That happened to one of my mates at the firing range and the idiot turned around to ask the sergeant what to do, still holding his gun, spraying bullets in all directions. You've never seen a bunch of squaddies hit the floor so fast.

But no training could have prepared me for the real thing, for my first time on guard duty in a trench, for the absolute darkness of the Korean night, for the first time the flares go up— and above all for the first time I saw hordes of the enemy charging towards me. I felt far more hostility towards the rats that infested our bunker than I did for the Chinese soldiers we were supposed to be fighting. I will never forget standing on night duty daydreaming, as usual, that I was acting a major part in a heroic war film, when I was interrupted by the blast of a trumpet. "What the fuck is that?" I shouted at my mate Harry. Before he could reply with the obvious, the entire valley erupted with the sound of not just one but hundreds of trumpets, the searchlights sprang into life and there, in front of us, a terrifying tableau was illuminated: thousands of Chinese advancing towards our positions led by a troop of demonic trumpet players. The artillery opened up, but still they came on, marching towards our machine guns and certain death. The protective minefields we sheltered behind suddenly seemed irrelevant: the first wave of Chinese committed suicide by hurling themselves onto our barbed wire so their bodies could be used as a bridge for the troops following. Eventually they were beaten off, but they were insanely brave.

The closest I got to death—and the incident that still haunts my dreams from time to time—was a nighttime observation patrol in no-man's-land. Three of us—my platoon commander Robert Mills (who later became an actor, too), a wireless operator and me—were sent down the valley, faces blackened with mud and covered in mosquito repellent, to the very edge of the Chinese lines. Madness. It could have got even madder. As we squatted in a rice paddy, insects eating us alive, Bobbie Mills, who was the son of a general, had an idea. "I know," he said, "we'll grab ourselves a Chinese prisoner! I'll give you a fiver each." I stared at him. He'd spotted my mercenary streak, but he had seriously misjudged my interest in a futile gesture. "Are you off your fucking head?" I hissed. He looked hurt. "Does that mean you won't come with me?" "Too fucking right," the wireless operator and I said together. "In that case," he said as if he was depriving us of a great treat, "we'll just have to go back." We were halfway up the hill again, moving cautiously, when we suddenly caught the whiff of garlic—the Chinese ate garlic like chewing gum—and realized we were being followed. Just in time, we threw ourselves onto the ground as a troop of Chinese soldiers emerged from the long grass and began searching for us. I lay there, absolutely terrified, my hand on the trigger of my gun, with the enemy circling so close we could hear them talking. As I lay there, I was conscious of a growing fury—I was going to die before I'd even had a chance to live, before I'd had a chance to do all things I wanted to do, before I'd had a chance to realize even one of my dreams. I decided I had nothing further to lose; if I was going to die, then I was taking a lot of Chinese with me. Bobbie Mills said we would charge the enemy, all guns blazing, and take them by surprise. This time, we were all agreed. "I need a piss," said the wireless operator. We were all agreed on that, too, and knelt there in the undergrowth and all peed together. Then we got to our feet and hurled ourselves into the night. The Chinese began firing in all directions, but they had no idea where we were coming from and we just kept running towards the enemy lines until it felt safe to change direction and head back to our own. Somehow we got back in one piece—but it was a close thing.

A Hill in Korea was nothing like the real thing, but no one seemed to be interested in that. George Baker, now better known as Inspector Wexford in the Ruth Rendell mysteries, was sent into battle wearing an officer's hat and badges to mark him out as the star of the film. I pointed out that he'd have been marked out as a prime target by the snipers in a real war and wouldn't have lasted ten seconds in a proper advance, but I was ignored. I was ignored, too, when I suggested that the troops should fan out during the advance to maximize their fire coverage. No, they would have to huddle up, I was told, because the camera lens wasn't wide enough. I was about to venture the opinion that Korea actually looked more like Wales than Portugal, but held my tongue—after all, where would you rather film on location?

Once home I paid my mother back, moved into a furnished room and had enough money left over to get to Sheffield to see Dominique, who was now an enchanting one-year-old. Pat had gone back to acting and her parents were raising our daughter—and doing a superb job. Claire and Reg were very welcoming to me and I will always be grateful to them for all they did for Dominique. I felt relieved that they had stepped in to rescue us and promised to visit as often as I could. And on the train back to London I even allowed myself to relax and believe that my problems were over.

Of course, they weren't. My agent, Jimmy Fraser, saw the finished film of *A Hill in Korea* and promptly dropped me. To be fair, he'd seemed a bit reluctant to take me on in the first place. "You've got something, Michael," he said, when I first visited him in his grand offices on Regent Street. "For the life of me I can't see what it is, and I haven't a clue how to sell it, but I'll take you on for a bit and see if it becomes a bit clearer." Well, things did seem to have become clearer. If I didn't dye my fair eyelashes and eyebrows, he said, I'd never get anywhere. He wasn't right about that, as it turned out, but he was right about my performance in *A Hill in Korea*. In the few scenes of mine that had survived the cutting room, I was terrible. Not that anyone much ever got to see it: with superb timing it was released the night we invaded Suez.

After Jimmy dumped me I found another agent, Josephine Barton, but the jobs didn't exactly come thick and fast and I had to go back to living with my mum and Stanley. The next few months and years were very hard. I used to hang about a casting agency just off Trafalgar Square run by a man called Ronnie Curtis, waiting to see if I could get the odd walk-on part—play, TV, film, I didn't care. On one occasion I got a job just because

I happened to fit the policeman's uniform the film company had already got in their wardrobe. Every time I was rejected at an audition I had to pick myself back up and start again. As an out-of-work actor I couldn't rent a room, borrow money from the bank or get insurance. It's not surprising so many eventually decide they can't take it anymore. I was nearly one of them.

One night, when I really was on the verge of finally giving up the struggle, I placed my regular phone call to Josephine. Every evening at six o'clock, all of us young hopefuls would rush to the phone boxes in Leicester Square to call our agents to see if any jobs had come in that day. Usually there was nothing going, but this time Josephine had some good news: she'd managed to get me a small part in a TV play of *The Lark* by Jean Anouilh—courtesy of Julian Aymes, the director of *A Hill in Korea*, who had asked for me. There was one problem—I'd have to become a member of the actors' trades union Equity and there was already an actor on their books with my stage name, Michael Scott. Josephine said I'd have to change my name in the next half hour so she could send the contract back. I put down the phone and went and sat down on a bench in the middle of Leicester Square. It was—as now—the venue for all the premiere movie releases. I looked around at all the cinemas, at all the stars up there with their names in lights, and tried to imagine myself alongside them. Michael—? And then I saw it. Humphrey Bogart, my favorite actor, my hero, was starring in *The Caine Mutiny*. Caine—because it was short, because it was easy to spell, because I was feeling very mutinous at the time—and because, like Cain in the Old Testament, I, too, was outside Paradise. Michael Caine I would be.

CHAPTER FOUR

EVERYONE GETS LUCKY
SOMETIMES. . . .

I may have had a name that fit on a billboard, but billboards were pretty thin on the ground during the next few years. I got the occasional bit part in a film or TV drama, including a couple of episodes of a popular police series, but nothing like a breakthrough and I was forced to find other work just to make ends meet. I took on one job as a night porter at a small "hotel" in Victoria—easy money, I thought, the clientele was friendly—it was very popular with couples called Smith (Mr. Smith was usually an American soldier)—and it meant I would be free during the day for auditions, should I ever be invited to any. As always, things weren't quite as straightforward as that. One night I was settling down to my book as usual after escorting six tarts and a group of very drunk customers to their rooms when an incredible racket broke out on the floor above. Each to his own, I thought, and tried to ignore it, but after a bit I realized it was serious. One of the girls was being beaten up—and she didn't like it. With all the panache of my hero Humphrey Bogart, I rushed upstairs, shouldered the door open (it wasn't actually locked), hauled the guy off the girl and knocked him out. I was just putting the finishing touches to my knight in shining armor role by helping the girl—who was very frightened— back into her clothes and calming her down, when a bottle smashed down on my head and put me out cold. I'd forgotten about the guy's five friends—who were sober enough now— and they proceeded to kick the shit out of me.

Still no jobs—and with the unexpected and tragic death during a routine operation of my lovely and persistent agent Josephine Barton, I had lost one of the few professionals who really believed in me. My new agent, Pat Larthe, seemed to be having just as much trouble getting me the break and indeed unwittingly nearly pushed me to the very edge of despair. Initially, her news sounded so good. She had managed to get me an interview with Robert Lennard, the chief casting director of Associated British Pictures, one of the biggest movie companies in Britain at the time, which had a number of actors under contract. A contract would mean a regular income and maybe a chance to pay off some of the money I owed. I knew exactly how my mum had felt all those years ago when the debt collectors came to call—I was constantly dodging across the street to avoid my creditors and, even more worryingly, had by now fallen behind with my maintenance payments for Dominique. Mr. Lennard seemed a kind man, but he had a bleak message for me. He told me it was a tough business. Hardly news to me. He then said, "You will thank me for this in the long run, but I know this business well and believe me, Michael, you have no future in it at all." I sat there, trying to remain calm, but inside I was seething with fury. "Thank you for the advice, Mr. Lennard," I managed to say politely and left before I thumped him. On the way back I became angrier and angrier—and it was this that saved me from complete despair. I was going to try even harder; no one was going to tell me what I could and couldn't do.

Mr. Lennard, as it happened, turned out not to have the sharpest eye in the business. I wasn't the only actor finding it tough; the others who used to hang out with me waiting for work around this time included Sean Connery, Richard Harris, Terence Stamp, Peter O'Toole and Albert Finney. And all this while Mr. Lennard had dozens of people under contract whose names are entirely absent from the annals of movie history. Despite his advice, I picked myself up, yet again, and kept on going, surviving on the odd small part. I couldn't help noticing, however, that some of my friends were beginning to get the odd big part. Sean Connery, for instance, who had originally been discovered in a gym by a casting director looking for some slightly more convincing American sailors than the usual British chorus line for *South Pacific*, had got the lead role in the TV play *Requiem for a Heavyweight*. I came on in the last scene. Then my friend Eddie Judd got the starring role in the film *The Day the Earth Caught Fire*; I played the policeman—and I didn't even manage that very well. And Albert Finney, playing opposite the legendary Charles Laughton in *The Party*, was receiving rave notices for his performance—and rightly so. Meanwhile, I'd hit a new low. I turned up at one film audition, was called in, opened the door and the casting director shouted, "Next!" before I'd even opened my mouth to say hello. I really couldn't see what I'd done wrong—and it turned out I hadn't done anything wrong, except grow too tall. The star of the film was the famously short Alan Ladd and if you were above the height mark they had chalked on the door as you went into the room, you were automatically disqualified.

But slowly—certainly more slowly than some of my friends— bigger parts began to come my way, and more often. I did another episode of a TV show and then I was offered the job of understudy to Peter O'Toole in *The Long and the Short and the*

Tall, by Willis Hall, a play about a British unit fighting the Japanese in the Malayan jungle in 1942, one of the first British plays about ordinary soldiers. This was regular money and a chance to work with friends—Robert Shaw and Eddie Judd were also in the all-male cast. The play was a huge success, because Peter O'Toole was brilliant, but he—as we all did—liked a drink and he sometimes cut things pretty fine. Once he came hurtling through the stage door just as the curtain was about to go up, casting his clothes off and shouting to me, "I'm here! I'm here! No need to go on!" as he ran.

When Peter went off to make *Lawrence of Arabia*—the film that would rocket him to stardom—I took over his part in *The Long and the Short and the Tall* on tour. Playing one of the leads in a really good play with a talented cast was just what I needed to give me my confidence back and I returned to London after four months traveling the country certain, once again, that I was on the right path. When I got back I moved into a shared house in Harley Street with ten other guys, including a young actor called Terence Stamp—a fellow Cockney, like me—whom I had met on tour. I'd taken Terry under my wing and initiated him into some of the secrets of a happy touring life—including how to grab the best room in the boardinghouse and the rather more specialized significance of the Ivor Novello show *The Dancing Years*. This show was almost always on tour somewhere in the country and if you coincided with it, your luck was in. Set in Ruritania, it featured a large cast of village maidens and village lads and was known in the trade as *The Dancing Queers* as the village lads always seemed to be gay. This left a crowd of village maidens at something of a loss—although not for long if Terry and I were in town.

The year 1960 marked the lowest point of my life. Things could only get better—and they did. I began to pick up some more TV work and for the first time had a more or less steady income. Terrence Stamp and I moved out of Harley Street into a small mews house behind Harrods. Although work was coming in more steadily for both of us, Terry and I agreed that if one of us was "resting" (that great actors' euphemism), the other would cover the rent. It was a great location, but a little on the cramped side—there was only one bedroom, which caused us a few problems with our active love lives.

The year 1961 began well with a TV play, *Ring of Truth*, followed by a two-week run of a play called *Why the Chicken?* (don't ask—I did and was none the wiser) written by John McGrath, a theater and TV director who had become a good friend, and directed by Lionel Bart, also by now a friend. That was good, but I was very disappointed not to get the part of Bill Sykes when Lionel Bart went on to direct *Oliver.* I thought it was made for me and it would have been good steady work at a time when that was hard to come by. But it just goes to show you, you never know how things are going to work out. I can see now it was a blessing in disguise: the show ran for six years and was still running the day I drove past the theater in my Rolls-Royce, after a triumphant success not only in Britain but also in America with *Alfie.* I shuddered as I passed the billboard: that actor had been up there in lights since 1961. I'd have missed out on so much.

Although I couldn't see it then (and in fact it would have taken a genius to work it out), the pieces in the jigsaw that led to *Alfie* and stardom were beginning to fall into place. As a result of *Why the Chicken?* John McGrath cast me in his next TV show, *The Compartment*, a two-handed psychological thriller about two men—a posh twit and a Cockney—sharing a railway carriage. Now this really was made for me—the posh twit won't respond to the Cockney's friendly approach and by the end of the forty-five minutes the Cockney tries to kill him. Perfect— summed up everything I thought about posh twits. And perfect, ultimately, because a lot of influential people saw it and realized that I could carry an entire show. But even I hadn't quite understood the significance of *The Compartment*, until a few weeks after the play had been broadcast. Terry Stamp and I were walking down Piccadilly when someone called out to us from the other side of the road. We turned round—and it was Roger Moore. Roger Moore, star of *The Saint* and *Ivanhoe*, the ultimate debonair, suave, English hero. We looked around to see whom he was hailing, but he was coming over to us. "Are you Michael Caine?" he asked me. I nodded. "I saw you in *The Compartment*," he said, "and I want to tell you that you're going to be a big star." He shook my hand, smiled and strode on. I just stood there with my mouth open. If Roger Moore said so— perhaps it really might be true.

And Roger was not the only one. Dennis Selinger, the top actors' agent in Britain, had seen *The Compartment* and taken me on. Dennis knew that I was short of money, but he was determined that at this point in my career I should appear in the right shows, not ones that merely made money. It was he who steered me towards *Next Time I'll Sing to You* by James Saunders. It was clearly going to be a hit with the critics, which meant that the pay was terrible, but Dennis could see just what rave notices it was going to get—and he was right. It transferred to the Criterion Theatre in Piccadilly, our wages doubled and I finally got to the West End at the age of thirty. What's more, all sorts of influential people came to see the show, including Orson Welles who came backstage to congratulate me, which was a bit overwhelming. But even more significantly for me, one night, Stanley Baker, the star all those years ago of *A Hill in Korea*, stopped by my dressing room. Stanley was now one of Britain's biggest film stars and he told me that he was starring in and producing a film called *Zulu* about the 1879 Battle of Rorke's Drift between the British army and the Zulu nation, and they were looking for an actor to play a Cockney corporal. "Go and see Cy Endfield in the bar of the Prince of Wales Theatre tomorrow at ten and give it a try," he said, and wished me luck.

I've always thought that life swings on small, sometimes insignificant incidents and decisions. When I got to the theater at ten the next morning, Cy Endfield, a round, slow-speaking American director, said he was sorry, but he'd already given the part to my friend James Booth, because he thought he looked more Cockney than I did. I was used to rejection by now, so I just shrugged. "That's OK," I lied and turned and began to walk back towards the door. The bar at the Prince of Wales Theatre is very long—and that's why I became a movie star, because just as I reached the end, Cy called out, "Can you do a posh British accent?" I stopped just before the door and turned round. "I was in rep for years," I said. "I played posh parts many times. There's no accent I can't do. That's easy," I said, fingers crossed behind my back. "You know," said Cy, peering at me down the length of the bar, "you don't look anything like a Cockney. You look like an officer. Come back." I glanced in the mirror behind the bar. He was right. I was six foot two, slim, with blond curly hair and blue eyes. I came back—and I never looked back. "Can you do a screen test with Stanley on Friday morning?" Cy asked. "You'd be playing the part of a snobbish lieutenant, Gonville Bromhead, who thinks he's superior to everyone, especially Stanley. Do you think you could handle that?" Perhaps it was also something to do with Cy being an American; he had no inherent British class prejudice that might have made him think a working-class actor couldn't play an officer on the big screen. I thought back to national service; I thought back to Korea. I was quite confident I could handle that.

I wasn't so confident by the time Friday came around. I stumbled through the screen test, fluffing my lines, sweating with fear despite all Stanley's help and Cy's patience. At last we were done and I stumbled up the steps and set out to spend the weekend getting completely wasted before hearing the result on Monday morning. What I hadn't bargained on was bumping into Cy Endfield at a party on Saturday night. He seemed to be avoiding my eye. It didn't look like good news. Nonetheless, while he was still at the party I did my best to remain sober. Just as he was about to go, he finally came over to me. "I've seen the test," he said, "and you were appalling." I swallowed. It was going to be hard to bounce back from this one. "But you've got the part," he went on. "We go to South Africa in three weeks." I gaped at him. "Why did you give me the part if the test was so bad?" I asked. "I don't know, Michael," he replied. "I really don't know—but I think there's something there. . . ." He walked away and I threw up all over my shoes.

I had been a private in the army and I had my own experiences of officers and class prejudice and I was delighted to be able to get my own back.

But I did have a problem. I had known lots of officers and I knew exactly how they had behaved towards me, but I had no idea how they behaved towards each other and *Zulu* was a picture about a relationship between two officers. So in the weeks before I left for South Africa, I arranged to go for lunch every Friday in the Grenadier Guards officers' mess. The Guards were on the whole very tolerant of having this soppy actor hanging about, but I noticed that they gave the job of looking after me— which no one else wanted—to the youngest and newest member of the mess.

Perhaps I should also have asked the Guards for a bit of help with the horses. Riding lessons had been a bit hard to come by down at the Elephant and I'd told Cy Endfield confidently that I could ride. What I had omitted to mention was that I'd only actually done so twice and had fallen off both times. The first time I fell off the horse in front of a bus and on the second day I fell off the horse in front of a bicycle (with far more damaging consequences), and I didn't go back for the third. It wasn't that I didn't like horses—Lottie, the big old mare we'd had on the farm in Norfolk, used to follow me round like a dog—but I'd never done much more than sit on her with my legs sticking straight out at the side. Through some equine sixth sense the brute of a horse I was sitting on for my first shot in *Zulu* seemed to know this and took an instant dislike to me. The feeling was mutual. We were filming a long shot of me coming back alone to the British military encampment after a hunting expedition and I was told to walk the horse back towards the camera slowly. It sounded simple enough, but the horse refused to budge. "Kick it up the backside!" yelled Cy through the intercom and the prop man gave it a whack. The horse moved all right—just not forward. It reared up on its back legs and started prancing around with me clinging on the back of it for dear life. "Cut!" Cy shouted. "You're not auditioning for the fucking Spanish Riding School!" The prop man calmed the horse down and we started off again, walking along a path down the side of the hill. All was going according to plan until we rounded a bend. The horse, by now as much of a nervous wreck as I was, must have caught sight of its own shadow on the hillside and with an earsplitting whinny it leapt off the path and started hurtling towards a twenty-foot drop, with me yelling all the way. The prop man only just managed to catch up and grab the bridle and drag us both to a halt before we tipped over the edge. I'd really wrenched my back in the process and the prop man relayed this to Cy over the intercom. "Oh for God's sake!" I could hear Cy saying irritably. "We've got to get this shot today—the sun's going down. Can you ride?" he asked the prop man. The prop man could. And so my first appearance in my first-ever major motion picture is in fact not me at all, but a prop man called Ginger in my hat and cape.

I was a bit aggrieved that no one seemed bothered about my back at the end of that day's filming—or my knees, the following day, when the same horse, who had obviously really got it in for me, threw me into a pond. I brought this up with Stanley Baker. "Simple," he said. "You've only done two scenes and at this point we could replace you quite easily—almost more cheaply than we could replace the horse or your clothes." I opened my mouth to protest, but he went on: "The more shots you're in, the more careful we'll be about you—until the final scene when, once again, we won't care a shit. A golden rule, Michael," he said, "never do a dangerous stunt on the last day of a picture." And I never have.

Things went more smoothly after that, but even so I was dreading the initial rushes. The stakes were high; this was my big break. Eventually the big day came and I sat in the screening room surrounded by fellow actors and cameramen and the other technicians from the set. The projectors whirred into action, the screen flickered and suddenly a huge face appeared and began to drone on in a ridiculously clipped British accent. I broke out in a sweat, my heart pounding. I wasn't just bad—I was very bad. Career over, I thought. "Who told that silly bastard to pull his hat down over his fucking eyes?" I heard someone say just behind me. I was outraged—this was a skillful bit piece of characterization! I had worn a pith helmet that shaded the top half of my face and I would tip my head back to allow the sun to catch my eyes when I wanted to make a particular point. Not that it mattered anymore; I'd be on the first plane home. Once again I threw up all over my shoes and rushed out.

Next evening, determined to face the music like a man, I went down to the bar in the hotel we were all staying in, lined up a couple of drinks and waited for Stanley and Cy to come in from the day's shooting. "Hey—not bad, kid!" Stanley said as they breezed by. "Don't worry—you'll get better." I stood looking after them, mouth open. Did they really mean it? I downed the drinks and decided that I needed to work on my paranoia.

I wasn't too successful. A few days later, one of the secretaries from the production department beckoned me in as I was passing by. She was gorgeous, and thinking my lucky day had come, I followed her in to her office anticipating a bit of action. Instead, she rather nervously handed me a telegram. It had come from a senior executive in Paramount's head office in London. *"Fire Michael Caine doesn't know what to do with his hands."* Again I was outraged. Searching around for someone on whom to model the character of Lieutenant Bromhead, a man from an immensely privileged background, I had lit upon Prince Philip. The first thing I'd noticed about him was that he always walked with his hands clasped behind his back because, I realized, he never had to do anything for himself. He never had to open doors, he never had to use his hands to gain attention—he would always be the center of any conversation—and he was surrounded by bodyguards so he'd never have to use his hands in self-defense. This was yet another piece of skillful characterization wasted on an unappreciative audience! Was I doomed always to be misunderstood?

I was certain that Stanley really would have no alternative but to fire me this time and I hung about miserably for the next two days waiting for the ax to fall. The problem was that I couldn't reveal I had seen the telegram without getting the secretary into trouble. Eventually I cracked and confronted him. "I know you're going to fire me," I began, concocting some wildly improbable tale of having accidentally seen the telegram in his office, "and I completely understand and I'll go at once." I finished in a rush. He stood there for a moment and I realized he was actually angry. "I am the producer of this movie, Michael," he said. "Have I fired you?" "No, Stan," I said. "Then get on with your job—and stop reading my fucking mail or I *will* fire you!" So I really was going to be in the movie. This time I managed to get to the gents before I was sick on my shoes.

The landscape of the Drakensberg Mountains was powerful and the wildlife was incredible, but it was the African people who really made the filming of *Zulu* so memorable. *Zulu* tells the story of the Battle of Rorke's Drift between a small detachment of a Welsh regiment (hence Stanley Baker's interest in the incident) and the Zulu nation, in 1879. We were fortunate not only to have Chief Buthelezi, the head of the Zulu nation, playing the Zulu leader, but a Zulu princess as our historical consultant, which meant that the battle lines of the Zulu forces were drawn up exactly as they had been. This level of authenticity made a huge difference to the impact of the film—I still think the battle scenes are some of the best I have seen in any movie. Certainly my first sight of those two thousand Zulu warriors coming over the hills and into the valley where we were filming was unforgettable. They wore their own battle dress with high headdresses and loincloths made of monkey skins and lions' tails and as they approached they began beating their spears on their shields and singing a slow lament mourning the dead in battle. It was an incredible sight and sound. What it must have seemed like to the handful of British soldiers holding down their position at Rorke's Drift I can only begin to imagine. Their bravery resulted in the award of eleven Victoria Crosses in one day—a unique event in British military history. Of course, as anyone who knows their British military history will have instantly spotted, the final Zulu assault on Rorke's Drift didn't involve just two thousand warriors—there were six thousand. Stanley and Cy were four thousand short. Cy Endfield, ever resourceful, had the solution. In the last scene, the camera pans round to show the Zulus lining the hilltops in the distance, looking down on the British below. It's an awesome sight and you would never guess that each of the two thousand warriors up there was holding a bit of wood with two shields and headdresses stuck onto the top, instantly trebling the numbers.

South Africa was still in the grip of apartheid. I hadn't known anything about the politics of the country when I arrived, but it made me increasingly uncomfortable to see how badly the foremen treated the black workers on the set—uncomfortable, and then plain angry. One day, one of the workers made a simple mistake, but instead of telling him off, the brute of a foreman drew back his fist and smashed him in the face. I couldn't believe it—and started running over, shouting as I went. Stanley got there before me and I have never witnessed fury like it. He fired the foreman on the spot and got all the other white foremen together. "From now on," he said, "on this set, no one treats their workers like this." We all shared his outrage, and it was fueled by another incident. One of our English foremen had "gone native," as you might say, and had taken up with three Zulu wives. We thought nothing of this—he seemed to be having a good time—until one day filming was interrupted by the sound of helicopters overhead. It was the police. They were going to close filming down. Our foreman had committed a crime under the South African miscegenation laws, which forbade sexual contact between blacks and whites. Unbelievably, punishment was either a long prison sentence or twelve lashes with a whip—or both. We realized that one of the Afrikaner foremen must have informed on us. With diplomatic skills that wouldn't have disgraced the UN, Stanley brokered a deal: the foreman would leave the country that night and we would stay to finish the film. It left us all with a very nasty taste in our mouths—and me with a determination never to go to South Africa again while apartheid still ruled.

Of course, *Zulu* represents the biggest piece of luck I personally ever had in show business, but it's also a movie that has withstood the test of time. In fact it has achieved near-cult status, both in the UK and America, despite the fact that it didn't have any sort of general release in America originally. I think that one of the reasons for its lasting success is that it was one of the first British war films to treat a native enemy with dignity. Yes, the heroism of the British troops is celebrated, but so too is the heroism of the Zulu nation, whose forces are depicted as the disciplined, intelligent tacticians and soldiers that they undoubtedly were. The lack of jingoism means that it resonates for a modern audience in a way that other British war films just don't any longer. It has never dated—and I remain very proud of it.

CHAPTER FIVE

HELLO, ALFIE

There's precious little to spend your money on in the Drakensberg Mountains and I got back to London with my £4,000 earnings almost intact. Now was my chance to put things right. I went straight up to Sheffield to see Dominique. She was eight years old and mad about horses, according to her grandmother, Claire (that was obviously not something she'd inherited from me), and for the first time I felt I could do something for her. The pony I bought her from the proceeds of *Zulu* turned out to be the first step in what would prove to be a very satisfying career for Dominique.

Then there was Mum. She was still living in the prefab with Stanley, but he was out all day at work and she was lonely without my father. My solution was to suggest she move to the flat in Brixton that Pat and I had had when we were first married. The house was owned by family and there were other people her own age all around her; it was safe and she had good company.

Meanwhile, the final touches were being put to *Zulu*. I knew that there was no chance I would get another film until it came out, but I had been given a seven-year contract by Joe Levine, the president of Embassy Pictures, and I was confident that he would hold to his side of the bargain. The problem with my contract was that it was entirely one-sided: they could renege on it whenever they wanted; I was stuck with it. Nonetheless, when I was summoned to Joe's office I was pretty certain that everything would be fine. Joe Levine was straight out of central casting, everybody's idea of a movie producer: short, fat and with a big cigar. "Siddown, Michael," he said when I came in. "You know I love you, doncha?" I nodded, stomach plummeting. I could tell where this might be going. "I said to you, Michael, I said: 'Michael, you'll be dripping with diamonds.' Didn't I?" I nodded again. He had said that—and I had seen Mrs. Levine so I knew he knew all about diamonds. "Well, I still believe that's gonna happen"—he paused and I held my breath—"just not with Embassy Pictures." I breathed out finally. I had gone very dizzy. Time for another performance. I was getting very good at nonchalance. "Didn't you like me in *Zulu*?" I asked. "*Loved* you, Michael," Joe said warmly. "But there's one thing I gotta tell you." He seemed to be bracing himself. "I know you're not, but you gotta face the fact that you look like a queer on-screen." I sat there dumbfounded. Me? Queer? "I know you're *not*," Joe said again hastily, "but there's a lot of queer stars out there who look butch, and that's fine—but you're the other way round and it's the *wrong* way round. You'll never be a romantic lead." I got up. "Thanks, Joe," I said, and left. I found out later that he'd given my contract to James Booth.

To my surprise, Dennis was not fazed by this. As ever, he used the opportunity to get me some work that would enhance my reputation and extend my range. In my one and only classical role ever I played Horatio to Christopher Plummer's Hamlet in a film for television. I'd had no dramatic training and had always felt Shakespeare was not for me, but I soon found myself caught up in the story and I decided that if my on-screen appearance was going to be an issue, then I would use it to bring out all Horatio's ambiguous sexuality. It was a great experience and an opportunity to play alongside my old friend Robert Shaw—and to meet a new one, Donald Sutherland, who was playing Fortinbras.

Back from location in Denmark, things were building up for the premiere of *Zulu*. Jack Hawkins, who played the missionary Otto Witt in the film, had been interviewed for the advance publicity. "Watch out for a new actor called Michael Caine," he advised, which was good of him. I got another star rating the next day from the writer Edna O'Brien who was doing an article on the five most attractive men in London—one a day. I was Mr. Friday. I felt like cutting it out and sending it to Joe Levine.

As the premiere neared I had to decide which girl to take. There were plenty of candidates, but no one special, and then it dawned on me that I should take Mum. I rushed over to Brixton and was very taken aback when she refused point-blank. "Why not?" I demanded. I was hurt. After all, it was she who had kept me going all these years and I wanted her to see me in my moment of triumph. But there was no persuading her, so eventually I gave up and promised to come back the next day to tell her all about it.

Most of the evening went by in a complete blur—so much so that I'm ashamed to say I can't actually remember whom I did take to the premiere. What I do remember is that when I emerged from the Rolls-Royce I'd hired, girl on my arm, the crowds cheered and the flash bulbs went off and as the smoke cleared and I made my way up the red carpet I saw a familiar face in the crowd. There was my mum, in her old hat, being held back by a burly copper, trying to catch a glimpse of her own son. I've never forgotten that moment.

The moment *Zulu* was released, things started to happen. I was sitting with Terry Stamp having dinner one night in the Pickwick Club, one of the new trendy restaurants that popped up all over the place in the 1960s. I liked it—for a start you didn't have to wear a tie, which had been one of the rules English restaurants used to enforce at the time to keep the likes of me out of them. This particular evening, Harry Salzman who, with Cubby Broccoli, was responsible for the James Bond movies, came in with his family. Just as Terry and I were finishing dinner, he sent a note asking me to have a quick coffee with him. I went over and sat down. They had just come from seeing *Zulu*. "We all think," said Harry, "that you're going to be a big star." I thanked them. Joe Levine's opinion was beginning to feel like a minority one. Then Harry changed tack abruptly. "Have you read Len Deighton's *Ipcress File*?" "Yes," I said. And it was true—I really was in the middle of it right then. "Good," said Harry. "Would you like to star in the movie I'm going to make of it?" "Yes," I said again. "Would you like a seven-year contract?" "Yes," I said. "Would you like to have lunch with me at Les Ambassadeurs tomorrow?" Unsurprisingly, the answer was again—and unoriginally—"Yes!"

I staggered back to my table in a daze. "What was that all about?" asked Terry. "I've got a starring role in a movie and a seven-year contract," I said, still not believing what I was saying. "But you've only been gone two minutes!" said Terry. I looked down at the remains of my supper, now congealing on my plate. Had I really heard right? Just then, the waiter came over with a bottle of champagne. He opened it and poured Terry and me a glass and as I looked over at Harry to thank him, he and the rest of his party toasted me. "Congratulations!" "Thank you," I said, just to prove that my vocabulary was more extensive than "yes." When the time came to pay the bill,

I decided to treat Terry, who had always been so generous to me. But Harry Salzman had already paid. "Thank you," I said again to him as we passed his table on the way out of the restaurant. Harry smiled. "And tomorrow?" he said. "Wear a tie."

The night was yet young and Terry and I went on to Ad Lib, a club owned by the American art dealer Oscar Lerman, who was married to Jackie Collins, and run by the brilliant Johnny Gold, who was to become—and remain—one of my closest friends. Ad Lib was the best disco I had ever seen and that night was the beginning of my "night life" (which I only gave up ten years ago . . .). And even here it felt as if extraordinary things were happening. As we moved onto the dance floor we saw all the Beatles and all the Rolling Stones were out there with us.

Lunch at Les Amabassadeurs was a somewhat different occasion. I was the only unknown in the whole place. Harry ordered champagne and caviar ("It's only the high life for you from now on, Michael!") and I lapsed into silence; I was completely out of my depth. Harry cast me a sudden glance. A smile broke out over his features. "I wonder what the rich people are doing today?" he said. I laughed and relaxed. It was the beginning of a very different life.

Even with a contract under my belt and money in my bank account I still felt that I was in the middle of a dream I would one day soon wake up from. Just in case, I stuck close to Harry Salzman and before long found myself invited to his family house—more like a mansion in fact—every Sunday for good food and even better conversation. Although we always had a great time, Harry also used these gatherings professionally and it was here that a lot of the decisions about *Ipcress* were made. Harry had made it quite clear that he wasn't looking for James Bond as his central character. The whole point about Len Deighton's antihero was that he was deeply ordinary—so ordinary he could always be underestimated. Deighton had never given him a name and that was our first challenge. "We need something dull," said Harry. There was a long silence while we all pondered. "Harry's a dull name," I ventured brightly. The silence became very chilly indeed. Harry Salzman gave me a level glance. The room held its collective breath. Harry started to laugh. "You're right!" he said. "My real name," he said, turning to me, "is Herschel. Now for the surname." When I had stopped shaking I tuned in to the rest of the discussion, but decided to avoid any more clever suggestions. Nothing seemed to be right. Harry, as always, had the last word. "I met a dull man once called Palmer," he said. And Harry Palmer I became.

Harry was always working, always thinking. I'm shortsighted and I've always worn glasses. Over dinner one Sunday, I noticed Harry staring at me. "You know what to do with your glasses," he observed. "I wear them because I need them," I pointed out a bit defensively. "No, no," he said. "It's good. Let's have Harry Palmer wear them, too. You'll make them look good." He was right again and he'd also laid to rest a worry I'd had—which was, at the time, a bit presumptuous, to say the least. My mate Sean Connery was vastly successful as James Bond but he'd said to me a few times recently that he feared being typecast and so identified with the character that he'd never get another part again. If *Ipcress* took off and there were sequels (I told you this was presumptuous!), I wanted the glasses to be the character, not me. If Harry Palmer wore glasses, then Michael Caine could hide behind them and emerge if the opportunity presented itself—which it did. . . .

Even with this level of advance preparation, things didn't go entirely smoothly. On the first day of shooting I was picked up by a chauffeur and settled back to be driven in luxury to Pinewood Studios, on the northern outskirts of London. "You the star of this film?" the driver asked. I said I was. "Biggest piece of shit I've ever read," he announced. Not a good start. It wasn't about to get much better. When I walked onto the set for the first rehearsal, the director, Sidney Furie, asked me for a match. I handed him one, he put the script on the floor and set it alight. We all stood round in silence watching as it burned into ashes. "That's what I think of that," said Sidney. We all shuffled our feet and mumbled a bit. "Now," Sidney said to me. "Can I borrow your script?" I handed it over. "OK," he said, "let's get to work."

It was a stormy beginning and it didn't get much easier. A lot of the dialogue in the movie is ad-libbed—especially by me—and although it was great fun, it was pretty stressful. Sid and Harry Salzman argued all the time about everything and tempers became so frayed that one day Sid walked off the set. We were on location in a run-down area of Shepherd's Bush in west London when Sid had finally had enough—and he ran down the road and jumped on a number 12 bus. "Get in the car!" Harry Salzman screamed at me, and the two of us leapt into his Rolls-Royce and took off in pursuit. It must have been an extraordinary moment for the other passengers as this huge Roller pulled up alongside their bus and this fat man leant out of the window shouting, "Get off the fucking bus!" The conductor stopped the bus at the next stop, Harry and I got on and by the time we'd got to Marble Arch (four pence) we'd persuaded Sidney to come back and finish the film.

In the end *The Ipcress File* was one of the best movies Sidney Furie—who would later become a friend and neighbor in Beverly Hills—ever made. It was certainly the most commercially successful. It still ran into the old movie executive problem, though. After the first rushes, we got a cable from Hollywood. *"Dump Caine's spectacles and make the girl cook the meal."* This is not the exact message—I've cleaned it up a bit—but the implication is clear enough. We had deliberately gone anti-Bond and as well as the glasses, we'd decided that Harry Palmer should be a cook, which was admittedly risky stuff in Britain in 1964, but we made it work. So when Harry goes shopping in a super-market and pushes his trolley round, it turns into a fight with the trolleys as weapons. And when Harry seduces the girl, he doesn't wine and dine her in a fancy restaurant, he takes her home and cooks her dinner—making an omelet by breaking two eggs at once in one hand. (I could see how seductive this would be, but I never mastered it and so in the movie it is writer—and fantastic cook—Len Deighton's hand you see doing the trick.) And as for the glasses, when the girl (played by Sue Lloyd) asks if I always wear them, I reply, "I only take them off in bed," and she reaches over and takes them off. It's now seen as one of the great moments of movie seduction, so I'm glad we stuck to our guns.

My next major film role would finally nail the idea that I looked gay on-screen once and for all: Alfie is one of the movie industry's great womanizers. I wasn't first choice for the part; the director, Lewis Gilbert, wanted Terence Stamp, who'd played Alfie in Bill Naughton's stage version, and I spent three hours trying to persuade him to do it. But Terry had taken the play to Broadway, where it had flopped, and wasn't keen to repeat the experience. Thank God.

I found *Alfie* a surprisingly straightforward movie to make. I was growing in confidence with every new role and I found Lewis Gilbert—who came from a similar background to me— great to work with. Unlike some directors, he actually worked with his cast and took their opinions into account, even asking me whom we might cast as the middle-aged married woman Alfie seduces. I immediately thought of Vivien Merchant, with whom I'd appeared in Harold Pinter's *The Room* at the Royal Court. She was a brilliant stage actress, but she'd never appeared in a film before and Lewis wanted her to do a screen test, which she refused to do. It looked as if that was that, but Lewis took a chance on my judgment and we cast her anyway. She turned out to be a huge success and was eventually nominated for an

Oscar. Lewis and I also came up with a way to have Alfie address the audience without making it seem as if he was delivering a long declamatory speech: I spoke instead as if I was talking just to one person, so the audience felt as if they were an intimate friend of the character.

In spite of all Lewis's encouragement, however, and my gut feeling that things were going well, I still refused to see any of the rushes. I'd learnt from my experience with *Zulu* that if you see them you'll just screw up the next day's shooting worrying about yesterday's. It's a lesson in life—don't look back, you'll trip over.

"Why not just wait outside?" Lewis said to me kindly one day when he was about to go into the screening room with the latest reels. Feeling decidedly queasy, I hung about nervously— and was immensely relieved to hear gales of laughter coming from inside. Maybe, just maybe, this was going to be a hit.

Lewis certainly thought so. We were having lunch in that twilight zone in between finishing filming and awaiting news of a release date, and he said to me: "You know you're really very good in this. I think you could be nominated for an Oscar." I just sat there dumbly, gaping at him. I'd never imagined that *Alfie* would have any traction in America whatsoever. Alfie himself spoke in such a heavy Cockney accent that Shelley Winters, my costar, told me that she hadn't understood a single thing I'd said to her during the course of the movie and had resorted to just watching my lips to know when to come in on cue. I'd had to lip-synch a clearer version of my lines onto the original take, in case we did get an American release (if you ever see the American version of the film you'll think I can't do a Cockney accent, but you will get to hear the end closing titles sound track "What's It All About, Alfie?" because Burt Bacharach only wrote it after he saw an American preview), but I hadn't really thought it was likely to happen. Just shows how much I knew. . . . And Lewis was right. I did get nominated for an Academy Award by the people in my boyhood dreamland, Hollywood. I didn't go to the ceremony and in the end it was just as well. The Oscar was won by my favorite stage actor (and friend) Paul Scofield in the movie version of my favorite stage play, *A Man for All Seasons*. I asked his wife later where he was when he heard the news. "On the roof of our barn," she said, "mending it." "What did he say?" I persisted. "Oh—you know, 'Isn't that nice, dear?'" I have been nominated many times for an Oscar and won it twice, and whenever I see the tears and tantrums at today's ceremony, I always think of Paul and smile.

But all this was in the future. I had filmed *Ipcress* and *Alfie* back to back, and was first waiting for the release of *The Ipcress File* and the verdict of the critics. It didn't look too promising. Harry Salzman and I sneaked out of the low-key premiere to gauge the reaction of the audience and the first man we spoke to told us he thought it was the biggest load of crap he'd ever seen. I was immediately plunged into the depths of gloom and went off and got very drunk. I woke up the next morning with a stinking hangover and went off to get the papers.

The first review I read confirmed my worst fears: it was awful. But the next one was good, the one after that was even better and after that the good notices began to pile up so consistently that even I could see that I had made it. I began to cry— not just quietly, but great heaving sobs I couldn't control. After all this time, after all the knock-backs, the rejections, the struggle—I really was a success. Without quite realizing what I was doing, I scrunched up the papers and started throwing them out of the window, howling as I did so. "Oi!" a voice from the street below shouted. "What do you think you're doing?" An old charlady was standing there looking up at me, hands on hips. "Come down here and pick these up!" she shrieked and, then, seeing my tearstained face staring down at her,

"You don't need to cry," she said more kindly. "It's time you grew up."

I took a deep breath and looked around me. She was right: I did need to grow up. I was thirty-two. I had been so focused on work that I hadn't had a chance to sit back and take stock. I went down to the street and picked up all the paper and vowed that from now on I'd take things a little more calmly.

I couldn't have got away with sneaking out of the premiere of *Alfie* as I had after *The Ipcress File*. This was the real deal. It was held a year later in March 1966 at the Plaza in Piccadilly and was a massive event. It seemed as if anyone who was anyone in the '60s was there—from all of the Rolling Stones and the Fab Four Beatles to Barbra Streisand and Tippi Hedren, who fainted during the abortion scene and had to be carried out. This time I did take my mum as my date. When I look back, I can see that she hadn't wanted to go to the *Zulu* premiere because she was terrified she might make a mistake and screw up my career at such a delicate stage—that was the way she thought. I think it was probably a class thing and she was intimidated by the thought of all those people in evening dress. She was completely devoted to what I was doing—mind you, she wasn't quite sure what it was—but she trusted me. She hadn't wanted to go to the premiere, but she still wanted to witness it.

Things were different at the premiere for *Alfie*. The party afterwards was in a pub called The Cockney Pride and she almost had to be forcibly removed at two in the morning. It was a great night, but best of all was sharing it with the person who had done so much to make it all possible. Not that she was going to let any of my success go to her head. She still worked as a charlady, getting up at six in the morning to clean people's houses, and no matter how often I told her that I had enough money for her never to work again, she stubbornly refused to give it up. I didn't know what to do—but eventually, I hit on the right solution. "Mum," I said, "what do you think the press would say if they knew you were still scrubbing floors when I was earning all this money? They'd crucify me!" She saw the sense in that at once. As I said, there was nothing she wouldn't do for her boys.

She never let me see how important my success was to her, or how proud she was of what I'd achieved. In fact she hardly mentioned it at all—unless it was to take the piss out of me. But when she died in 1989, her friends and members of the family all told me that she'd spoken of me with tremendous pride. She was just very careful not to let me get too big for my boots.

Meanwhile, there was something she was keeping from me. She'd lost touch with my brother, Stanley, and she was very upset about it. None of his friends seemed to know where he'd gone and I began to get worried too as all my efforts to trace him failed. I'd almost given up when one day I was in Heal's, the classy furniture store, ordering a new sofa and I asked to see one they had out the back. Two blokes in overalls heaved it into the showroom for me and as they maneuvered it into place, one of them turned in my direction and I saw it was Stanley. I was really shocked to see him looking so shabby and felt terrible that he was working so hard to keep his head above water while I was ordering sofas without a second thought. In the end, it worked out brilliantly. I took care of things for Stanley and as I was about to go away to the Cannes Film Festival where they were showing *The Ipcress File*, he moved into my flat to take care of things for me.

It was in Cannes that I finally realized what my life had become. Harry Salzman put me up in a very grand suite at the Carlton Hotel and I reveled in the luxury of it, but as soon as *Ipcress* was shown I saw that my days of freedom were over. I couldn't leave the hotel without being mobbed by the press. Sean Connery was also in town and he hated it so much—he couldn't even get to the hotel dining room in peace—that he left the same day. I stuck it out and went to the reception given by the British Consul. The Beatles were also in the lineup and I was next to John Lennon. After the fiftieth person had shaken our hands and asked who we were and what we did, John and I changed our names—his to Joe Lemon and mine back to Maurice Micklewhite. It didn't seem to make much difference, but it cheered us up. John and I made a nice little drinking team for the couple of days we were in Cannes and toured the parties together. He was a tough, no-nonsense man and completely indifferent to the glamour of our surroundings. At one party, we found ourselves both needing a pee and all the lavatories occupied. We roamed round some great palace of a house and eventually I found an en suite bathroom upstairs and rushed in. When I'd finished, I came out to find John rather unsteadily peeing out of the bedroom window. "John, you've got it on the bloody curtains!" I said. "Who cares?" said John in that unmistakable voice. "They're rich—fuck 'em!"

If Cannes seemed like impossible glamour, then New York, where I was off to next, was in another league all together.

CHAPTER SIX

TO HOLLYWOOD

Alfie had opened in the United States and had been such a hit that it went on general release, which was a rare event for a British-made picture. So the plan was that I too would go on general release along with it and do my first-ever American publicity tour from New York. When I got there, I discovered that *The Ipcress File* had been bought by Universal and was also on general release, and I was overwhelmed by the response I got. A year ago I had been a complete unknown, here I was with two hit movies playing to packed houses across the States and I was hailed everywhere as a star. In fact I was the one who was starstruck—at parties given for me and in restaurants, night after night, I found myself next to one movie legend after another. At the "21" Club I sat next to Kirk Douglas and Maureen O'Hara; at Elaine's (soon to become a fixture of my New York life) I knocked over Woody Allen's wine glass and trod on Ursula Andress's foot; and at the Russian Tea Room I sat in between

Helen Hayes and Walter Matthau. If anyone had told that little boy sitting in that dark, smoky cinema in the Elephant all those years ago that this was where he'd end up, he'd have thought they were mad.

But perhaps the most memorable encounter of all during that whirlwind tour was with the legendary Bette Davis. People had been so generous to me during my trip that I asked Paramount if they would let me host a cocktail party the night before I left to say thank you. My new friends, the wonderful theatrical couple Jessica Tandy (who went on to win an Oscar at the age of eighty-two for *Driving Miss Daisy*) and Hume Cronyn, asked if they could bring Bette Davis along as well. I could hardly believe what I was hearing and when the evening came, I couldn't wait to introduce myself to her. "You know," she said, in that unmistakable drawl, "you remind me of the young Leslie Howard." I'd heard this before but this was from Bette Davis! She went on, "Did you know that Leslie screwed every single woman in every movie he made—except me?" I had heard this, I said. "Well," she said, "I was not going to be just one on a list of conquests— but when I look at you I was just wondering what difference it would have ever made if I had." She sounded almost wistful. I blurted out, "Will you have dinner with me tonight?" She looked at me for a minute. "I was *not* making a pass at you," she said, rather severely. "No, no," I said hastily. And I didn't think she was. But she was trying to tell me that she had been there and that sometimes you can have regrets. "We could have dinner together with Jessica and Hume," I went on, "just the four of us." She smiled and relaxed. "That would be nice," she said, "as long as I can go home in a taxi on my own."

I wasn't back in England long before I got the call from my agent that would truly change my life. Shirley MacLaine had seen me in *The Ipcress File*, Dennis said, and as her contract stipulated that she could choose her own leading man, she had chosen me for her next film, *Gambit*. Of course the fact that I was a relative unknown and therefore cheap was a bonus for the production, but nonetheless she had picked me out and wanted to take the chance. They had sent the script and I thought it was great, but that was completely beside the point. This was Hollywood—and I would have done anything to make a movie there. I had made it at last.

So off I went to the land of my youthful dreams. My expectations were so high I thought the reality would be a disappointment. I was wrong—it was better than the wildest of those dreams. I arrived at LA airport and was whisked off in a Rolls-Royce to a luxury suite at the Beverly Hills Hotel. Then there was a bit of a hiatus, a glamour blip for a few days as Shirley was delayed and so I sat there in the hotel in splendid isolation awaiting her stamp of approval and the welcome party she had planned for me. To pass the time, I took to star spotting in the hotel lobby. I didn't know it, but both *Alfie* and *The Ipcress File* were doing the rounds of the luxury home cinema circuit in Beverly Hills and going down very well—and my face was beginning to become known around town. The first famous person to recognize me was Jane Russell, the gorgeously sexy star of Howard Hughes's *The Outlaw*. She was passing through the lobby and came over to have a chat and invited me to lunch. Lunch with Jane Russell—it might seem the very essence of glamour, but by this stage Jane was *une femme d'un certain age* to put it politely and the lunch was hosted by the Christian Scientist Church, of which Jane was a member. Not my most stunning Hollywood moment.

The next lobby encounter made up for it. As I was sitting there I heard the sound of a helicopter landing in the gardens opposite the hotel, which, a porter told me, was strictly illegal. We stood at the door to see who had dared break the law so flagrantly and out of the swirling cloud that had been whirled up came the figure of John Wayne. He strode into the lobby and up to the desk, wearing a full cowboy costume and hat. He was covered in dust. I just stood there, mouth open, while he waited to be handed his room key. Suddenly he turned round, saw me looking at him, pointed at me and said, "What's your name?" I could barely get the words out, partly from nerves and partly because I'd hardly spoken to anyone in days. "Michael Caine," I croaked. "Are you in that movie *Alfie*?" "Yes," I said again, still hoarse. "You're gonna be a star, kid," he said, "and if you want to stay one, remember to talk low, talk slow and don't say too much." "Thank you, Mr. Wayne," I said. He put his hand out and I shook it. "Call me Duke," he said and, putting his hand on my shoulder, he guided me round the lobby with him. "And never wear suede shoes," he said confidentially. This threw me. "Why not?" I asked. "Because I was taking a piss the other day and the guy in the next stall recognized me and turned towards me and said, "John Wayne—you're my favorite actor!" and pissed all over my suede shoes." And with that he was gone. I was to meet the legend many more times in Hollywood and he was always full of advice. I was even with him when he was dying of cancer in 1972. Shakira was in the UCLA Medical Center and when I visited her I found John Wayne in the next room. Every time I visited Shakira I would join him on his long, slow, painful walk up and down the corridor. I don't remember what we talked about—old times, I guess, people we knew—but I remember his bravery as he faced up to the terminal illness he'd been fighting for so long. "It's got me this time, Mike," he said to me. When Shakira was well enough to go home I went in to see him for the last time. "I won't be getting out of here," he said as I got up to go and then, seeing I was close to tears, "Get the hell out of here and go and have a good time!" I left before he could see me cry.

When Shirley MacLaine arrived, my real Hollywood life started. I couldn't believe my luck in having this powerful, gorgeous woman on my side. I had wondered what she and Ronald Neame, the director, saw in me that made them think I was right for *Gambit*, and I think it was the sort of nefarious charm I projected with Alfie. Alfie's a bit of a villain, but charming. I've still got the poster for *Gambit* and the blurb says, "Alfie's on the go again," and that's just right for my character in *Gambit*. Once Shirley had decided I was the one, she backed me all the way and I became her protégé—although to this day she claims she made a mistake. She's a great joker and whenever I see her now she always says: "Are you still doing it? When are you going to give it up? How many movies are you going to make this year?"

It's all a tease because she knows and I know that my life in Hollywood all began with the incredible welcome party she threw for me. The first person to arrive was Gloria Swanson—who looked just like Gloria Swanson, only smaller. The next person to arrive was Frank Sinatra. I simply couldn't believe it—Frank Sinatra! Then came Liza Minnelli, and then star after star. Of course they all walked straight past me and went to say hello to Shirley, but I didn't mind. She was very generous and took them all over to meet me. Almost everyone had seen *Alfie* by now and they were very complimentary and after a while I started to feel I really had arrived.

Of all the movie stars and producers and celebrities passing before my dazed eyes, there was one man in particular who was destined to play an especially important role in my new life. And he was the smallest man in the room: at just over five foot tall, I could easily have missed him. But his size was the only small thing about Irving Lazar. He was one of the greatest agents of all time; his clients included Noël Coward, Gene Kelly, Ernest Hemingway, Cary Grant and my idol, Humphrey Bogart. In fact it was Bogey who gave him his well-known nickname of "Swifty," because he once got him three movie deals in one day. Swifty—no one ever called him "Swifty" to his face, he was always "Irving," except when he answered the phone, which he would do with a very clipped "Lazar here"—was the first person to get a million dollars for a script (for *My Fair Lady*) and the first person to get a million dollars for an artist (Elizabeth Taylor for *Cleopatra*). And it was he who would persuade me, years later, to write my first autobiography. So I've got a lot to thank Swifty—sorry, Irving—for.

Later, when I got to know Hollywood better, I realized that Shirley had really indeed pulled in the A-list that night. It was a dazzling event and among the whole host of people I met were many who would go on to become some of my closest friends, including Swifty and Sidney Poitier. "Who is this party really for?" I asked Shirley about halfway through. She smiled her wonderful smile and said, "You, Michael, only you!" but only she could have pulled it off in that town: she was so loved.

The night after the party, I was invited to a quiet Chinese dinner in Danny Kaye's kitchen. It really was a kitchen, and Danny Kaye really did do the cooking himself, with the help of a Chinese chef. I didn't know it then, but these were famous evenings and I would end up going to many of them, but that night was my first time and it was a memorable one. We went into the kitchen and Shirley introduced me to the other guests: two English naval officers and a bald American who was wearing dark glasses, which was odd inside a house and at night, to say the least. I was completely mystified—and then in walked the Duke of Edinburgh and it became obvious that they were his security. And then, as if the guest list didn't feature enough surprises, in walked Cary Grant. I was overwhelmed and sat almost silent throughout the meal, only speaking when I was spoken to. I had actually met Cary Grant in Bristol while he was visiting his mother and I was on location, but I was too shy to remind him of this or to talk much to him. Many years later when we moved to Beverly Hills we would become good friends, but on this evening he was still one of my idols and I was very much in awe.

Feeling a little more in command of myself by the end of the evening, I escorted Shirley home. As we approached her house I saw clouds of smoke pouring out from it. I pulled the driver up. "Shirley," I said, "I'm very sorry, but I think your house might be on fire." "Oh, Michael," she said. "That's just the steam from the swimming pool." Welcome to Hollywood, I thought.

———

Dinner in Danny Kaye's kitchen with Prince Philip and Cary Grant seemed a strange idea of a quiet relaxing night off, but when Shirley invited me to dinner with her family the following evening I felt sure that this really wouldn't present any surprises. I couldn't have been more wrong. When I walked into the restaurant, there was Shirley, her mum and dad—and Warren Beatty. Now, Warren and I had knocked about together in London a couple of years earlier. He'd heard what was going on there in Swinging London and had come over to see what it was like. I knew he was a bit of a jack-the-lad, but I had no idea he was dating Shirley. And of course he wasn't—he was her brother and this really was a quiet family dinner. He was just as surprised to see me as I was to see him and as I wasn't sure how much his parents knew about Warren's London exploits, we didn't do too much reminiscing about what we'd got up to.

We used to have a competition for a fiver a time. It went like this (sexist, I know, but it was the '60s): we'd see a woman from the back and one of us would say, "Ugly or beautiful?" And the other would choose and then when she turned round you would either win or lose. One day we were out together and we saw a girl with her back to us buying one of the London newspapers. "Ugly or beautiful?" Warren asked, quick as a flash. "Ugly," I said, and he said, "All right—beautiful." And she turned round and it was Candice Bergen, one of the most beautiful women in the world. I felt such a putz I nearly paid double—but then Warren always did have an eye for the ladies.

The day after dinner with the Beatty family I took myself off to explore my new surroundings. Back then, Beverly Hills, which now features some of the world's most expensive and luxurious boutiques, was quite a sleepy place with just a few shops including, bizarrely, a hardware store on Beverly Drive. I once nipped in there for a ball of string and there was Fred Astaire looking for sandpaper and when I was lining up by the till, I found myself behind Danny Kaye who was buying a single lightbulb. It was in that store that I had what still ranks as my most terrifying experience in America: I was browsing through the power tool display when I popped my head round the corner and there in the next aisle was Klaus Kinski buying an ax. Never has a shop full of DIY aficionados cleared so quickly. . . .

Rodeo Drive contained two places that were destined to play a big part in my future social life. The first was the Luau, a Tahitian bar and restaurant where everybody who was anybody in the young and gorgeous A-list set in town would meet at the beginning of the evening to find out the who, what, why, where and when of the night's social activities. On the other side of the street was the Daisy, the first discotheque in Beverly Hills. Shirley took me to the Daisy one evening early to have a drink before dinner and it was practically empty, but as we sat there, the door flew open and in burst about forty girls who all looked just like Doris Day. It turned out that this was no accident—they were all competitors in a Doris Day lookalike competition, "Doris for a Day," and were being shown round the haunts of the stars at a time when it was unlikely there would be any stars in the haunts. Tonight, however, they had struck lucky. When they spotted Shirley, they all started screaming at full pitch, two of the girls fainted and several of them burst into tears. In the pandemonium that followed we made our escape. Welcome to Hollywood!

By the time I started work on *Gambit* I had begun to get a bit more familiar with the high life—but I still had to pinch myself to believe it was all real. On my first day's filming, a limousine picked me up to take me to Universal Studios. When we got to the gate, the guard smiled at me and said: "Good morning, Michael. Your parking space is down on the right by your bungalow. It's got your name on it." The driver pulled up outside this luxurious bungalow and it did indeed have my name on it. Even more exciting for me was the name on the bungalow next door: Alfred Hitchcock. And when I went into mine, I discovered that my first dressing room in Hollywood was bigger and more luxurious than anywhere I had ever lived until then.

The filming of *Gambit* went so well—largely thanks to the calm genius of its English director, Ronald Neame—that I was able to focus much of my energy on my new social life. It centered largely on the Luau and the Daisy and I owe much of the good time I had there to Steve Brandt, a new friend and reporter from *Photoplay*, who seemed to know everybody in town. The very first night I walked into the Daisy I couldn't quite believe what—or who—I was seeing. Paul Newman was playing pool at a table just inside by the entrance and once I'd recovered from that and wandered inside, I realized that the song they were playing—"Mack the Knife" by Bobby Darin—was being sung along to by the *real* Bobby Darin, who was at the next table. I stood there gaping until Steve nudged me and introduced me to Mia Farrow whom I took onto the floor to dance. And as we were dancing, I looked over my shoulder and there was Sammy Davis Jr. dancing next to me. It really was that sort of place.

After a few weeks of this, I had just about got over my shock at the casual proximity of major stars when late one night at the Daisy, Steve was called to the phone. He came back to our table to tell Mia, who was with us, and me that we were going round to Rita Hayworth's place. Now this really would be Hollywood glamour, I thought, but when we got to the house, I was in for a bit of a shock. Rita Hayworth greeted us at the door wearing a grubby dressing gown and slippers and with a half-empty bottle of whisky in her hand. She appeared to be drunk. So was I, by now, and I proceeded to get even drunker as I watched the screen legend drag Mia round the room in a parody of a dance to the theme music to Rita's greatest-ever movie, *Gilda*. Drunk as I was, it was a sobering moment. In fact I found out much later that although everyone always thought Rita was a drunk, she was already suffering from the dementia that would eventually kill her.

As the new boy in town I found myself in great demand as party fodder. Luckily I quickly acquired three mentors who helped me navigate my way through the social minefield. One of them would always be on the phone telling me what was going on. And then it was just party after party. As well as the incomparable Swifty Lazar, who always had his finger on the Hollywood pulse, there was Denise Minnelli, the second wife of Vincent Minnelli, Liza's father, and Minna Wallis, sister of the great movie producer Hal Wallis. Minna may have looked like a sweet and harmless old lady, but like Miss Marple, you underestimated her at your peril. Minna had been an actors' agent and her greatest discovery was Clark Gable. In fact she had discovered his talent in more ways than one, she told me confidentially, and once—just once—they had gone to bed together. I never heard the precise details so I can't share with you the secret of Clark's success, but I can tell you that Minna never got over it.

Minna saw it as her job to marry me off and steered me in very short order towards three amazing women: Natalie Wood,

Barbra Streisand and, finally, Nancy Sinatra. Although all three became good friends, I've always insisted on sorting out my own love life and in the end Minna had to give up on me.

For a young man who had always dreamed of Hollywood and wondered what it would be like, it turned out to be a continuous stream of being shown an exhibition of all the best bits of life with no real life intervening at all. In fact, my days on the set of *Gambit* seemed like the most normal experiences I was having. Universal had just started what would become its world-famous studio tour in which tourists got to be driven around the movie lot in an open bus. In those days you didn't go to a big separate exhibit like you do now; people would actually stand at the back of the soundstage and watch the actors during the shoot. One of the drivers was particularly clever and always seemed to have worked out where we would be, and he would drive by slowly so his busload always got to see the stars—Shirley or Hitchcock in our case. It was a bit disruptive, because if they did catch up with you, you had to stand around signing autographs, but I had to admire his initiative and I got friendly with him—at last, I thought, an ordinary guy! Wrong again—that driver was Mike Ovitz, who went on to become one of the most powerful agents in the business, the head of CAA.

One of the things I'd read about before I arrived was the Hollywood homes of the stars, but in fact no stars live in Hollywood, and it took me a while to work this out. Some stars live in and around Beverly Hills—Frank Sinatra did and, as far as Frank was concerned, so did everyone else who he thought mattered. Frank had a twenty-minute rule. If he was invited to dinner and he was in his car for more than twenty minutes, he would simply demand that his driver turn round and go home. "I'm twenty minutes," he would call out. "Turn around. It's too far."

Beverly Hills took me by surprise, too. For a start, there are hardly any hills there—and the most expensive area of all is the Beverly Estate, which is in fact a very deep valley. Stars who want bigger estates than can be found in Beverly Hills—and for less money—live in Beverly Hills Post Office, or BHPO. It's not actually Beverly Hills, but it is according to your address. Just to complicate things further, most of the stars don't live in Beverly Hills at all; they live in the surrounding glitzy areas like Bel Air (which has its own security guard force and guard posts), Holmby Hills (where the Playboy Mansion is), the Hollywood Hills, or in luxury apartments on the Wilshire corridor, the bit of Wilshire Boulevard between Beverly Hills and Westwood where my friend Billy Wilder lived. (I went to the toilet when I went round to his apartment for dinner once, and stacked up against the walls in the corridor were what must have been about fifty paintings. I kicked over a couple by accident on the way back from the bathroom and when I bent to pick them up I nearly had a nervous breakdown. They were a Klimt and a Hockney). Some people live by the sea at Malibu (where the richest people in Hollywood live closer to each other than any other wealthy people in the world). Confused? I certainly was.

I did, of course, eventually sort it all out and when Shakira and I moved to LA in 1979 we chose BHPO. The house we bought was originally built by Barbara Hutton, the Woolworth's heiress, as her son Lance Reventlow's twenty-first birthday present. (Hmmm—I think all I got for my twenty-first birthday was a bollocking from my dad for being an out-of-work so-called actor.) It had been built in the shape of an L, which takes personalized gifts to a new high, but although this made it an awkward fit on the site, we loved it. The swimming pool stretched from the outside, right into the living room, which sounds very Hollywood, but as I didn't want to be woken in the night by a wet burglar—or a dry one, come to think of it—I had to have it blocked up.

Buying and then selling the house turned out to be a real

lesson in Hollywood real estate. It cost $750,000 in 1979, which was a fortune to me at that time, and I thought I was being very clever when I sold it eight years later when we decided to make Britain our permanent base again, for $2.5 million, which was another fortune. But, as often happens in areas where real estate changes hands for this sort of money, the original was then torn down, and rebuilt and offered back to me a few years ago for $14 million. And now I hear it's been re-rebuilt again, the swimming pool has been moved and it's being offered at $26 million. I'm not surprised—I've checked out all of them and it does have the best views in the whole of Los Angeles. (Rupert Murdoch lived in the house behind and we had to keep cutting our eucalyptus trees so it didn't block his views.)

In 2006 I came back to Los Angeles to make the thriller *The Prestige* for Christopher Nolan and rented the only really "Hollywood" house we have ever lived in. It was billed as having previously been rented by the Artist Formerly Known as Prince and also Mariah Carey, who had apparently run up massive heating bills because she sat in the heated outdoor swimming pool all night. It was just off Mulholland Drive, near Jack Nicholson's, and I realized just what circles I was moving in when I turned into the road and saw a sign which read: "Your license plate has just been photographed and stored for future reference." I'm a bit ambivalent about heavy security: on the one hand I'm pleased that it is there, but on the other I always think that something bad must have happened to make them so keen. At the entrance to the drive were two of the biggest real palm trees I have ever seen. I've been around a bit and I've seen a few palm trees in my lifetime and these were gigantic. They were just a sign of things to come: the house itself was also absolutely enormous, too—when we eventually moved in, it was too big to find each other so when the phone rang and wasn't for whoever answered it, we just had to take a message. The sitting room entrance hall had over one hundred museum-quality tribal masks from all over the world hung on one wall, and a thirty-foot-high ceiling. It was a bit like being in a cathedral dedicated to some pagan religion and I never felt entirely comfortable passing through late at night. The dining room seated thirty-two. When the estate agent showed us round he said in that enthusiastic way they have, "You could have some *great* dinner parties here!" "I'm planning on opening a small bistro," I said and I could see that he wasn't sure if I was joking or not. I wasn't surprised to find that he came back later to check. When we went into the bedroom, I paced it out and it was thirty foot long and fifty foot wide: bigger than the whole of the house I grew up in. There were "his and her" dressing rooms and "his and her" outdoor patios—I began to feel that Shakira and I would never see each other again—and bizarrely, given the climate in Los Angeles—"his and her" *fireplaces*. Perhaps strangest of all, the bedroom featured something I had never seen before: nine small trees. I suddenly remembered that when I'd been in hospital with malaria all those years ago, someone had brought in a bunch of tulips and the nurse had whisked them away because, she insisted, they "sucked up all the oxygen in the air." "If a bunch of tulips can do that," I said to Shakira, "what on earth will nine trees do to us? We'll suffocate during the night!" She gave me a long look and went over to examine the trees more closely. "They're plastic, Michael," she said kindly.

Glamorous as this house was, there are many far more luxurious in and around Beverly Hills. Our friends Marvin and Barbara Davis had one that seemed to define the term "Hollywood mansion": the driveway didn't just go in and out, it was a whole dual carriageway. . . . We were in the middle of dinner there one night when a slightly embarrassed butler brought in the telephone and whispered in Marvin's ear. Marvin shrugged and took the phone. "Yeah?" Pause. "Sixty." Another pause. "I told you: sixty." Further pause. "That's it. Yeah. Bye." He gave the phone back to the butler and someone—not me—had the courage to ask him who was on the other end. "Michael Jackson," said Marvin. "He keeps ringing me wanting to buy this house for forty-five million dollars and I keep telling him it's sixty." There didn't seem much to add to this, so we went back to our dinner.

Marvin was a real wheeler-dealer and a bit of a rascal and I adored him (I've got a soft spot for rascals, being a bit of one myself). His father, a Polish Jew, was a boxer known as Fighting Joe Davis and he'd landed up in London before signing up to the British merchant navy and then jumping ship in America. Marvin made all his money in Texan oil and ended up buying Fox and selling it to Rupert Murdoch and buying the Beverly Hills Hotel and selling it to the Sultan of Brunei. He was very interested in art and the art market and I recall one evening round there when David Hockney came to dinner. Marvin spent a long time trying to get David to tell him how much his paintings cost and how much they might be worth in the future. David didn't have the faintest idea—it was fascinating to watch art meeting commerce and both finding the other completely incomprehensible.

If Marvin had been unable to ascertain the value of a David Hockney from the man himself, he was on surer ground with his Renoirs and Picassos. He showed me round once and there in the middle of all this incredible art was a still of Sly Stallone and Dolly Parton in *Rhinestone*, the 1984 movie Marvin backed and that was released with, shall we say, indifferent results. When I pointed out the incongruity of this photograph hanging side by side with some of the world's greatest paintings he pretended to look surprised. "But that's the most expensive picture in the house, Michael," he said. "It cost me forty million dollars!"

Marvin had everything and knew everybody. You could turn up to dinner there and find yourself one evening—as we once did—at a political fund-raiser for Bill Clinton being sung to by Barbra Streisand, or, on another occasion, sitting next to Ronald Reagan. For some reason, President Reagan seemed to think I was a friend of his and he greeted me with a hug and asked me how my sons were. And he did that from then on whenever we met. He never actually used my name and as I don't have any sons I never actually found out who he thought I was—and after a bit it would have become been too awkward to put it right. He was a funny guy and had a great way with words and a knack of getting to the nub of things, which really appealed to me. He once told me that California was not a place to live but a way of life—and I think he got that absolutely right. Another time he said to me that he didn't mind at all no longer being president. "You know"—and I waited for him to say a name, but he adroitly avoided it—"I'm very happy living in a private home after eleven years in a public house." I wonder if he realized how funny that was to a Brit.

Ex-presidents, presidents-in-waiting—there was nothing you could do socially for Marvin, nothing you could give him that he couldn't buy, but I did once do something for him that no one else could have done and that even Marvin, with all that money, couldn't have done for himself. Shakira and I were friendly with Prince Andrew and Sarah Ferguson while they were married and introduced Marvin to them. Sarah really liked him and when we asked if Marvin and Barbara could join a dinner party she was organizing at Buckingham Palace, she kindly agreed. It was something Marvin never quite got over—I guess he had finally found a mansion he really couldn't afford.

CHAPTER SEVEN

NO HOLLY, NO WOODS

Back when I arrived for the first time, it didn't take me long to work out that a lot of what I had thought about Hollywood was wrong. Looking back, I was a wide-eyed innocent and I spent months thinking to myself, "I guess Hollywood just isn't really like that," every time I made a new discovery about the reality of the place. Even my grasp of the geography and history was off, never mind the power politics. For a start, I'd assumed Hollywood was the biggest center of filmmaking in the world, but I soon discovered that very few films are actually made there. . . .

The founder of the original Hollywood was a man named Hobart Johnstone Whitley. He and his business partners were land developers and built more than one hundred small towns all over the western United States. In 1886 they bought several hundred acres at the foot of the Cahuenga Pass and decided to build a new town there. It was Whitley who came up with the name. The hillside above was covered with toyon, a plant also known as Californian holly, because it's covered in red berries in the winter. It wasn't until 1910 that the movies came to the town, with D. W. Griffith who was looking for a location for a picture called *In Old California*. Although they were able to shoot under electric light by that time, they found the bright Californian sunshine was perfect for the primitive film stock. Griffith and his crew went back east to New York and New Jersey, where most of the infant film industry had settled, and spread the word about the sunshine and light they had found in Hollywood.

The first movie studio built in Hollywood was called the Nestor Studio and it was on the corner of Sunset Boulevard and Gower Street. It was opened by David and William Horsley, two brothers from Bayonne, New Jersey. In 1913, Cecil B. DeMille and Jess Lasky bought a barn on the corner of Selma and Vine Street and turned it into a studio and in 1917 Charlie Chaplin opened his studio on the corner of Sunset and La Brea. After that, the rest of the movie industry came swarming in from the east and the myth of Hollywood was born.

Although the studios started there, most of them have since moved out and these days only three are left: Paramount, Chaplin and Goldwyn. Paramount, founded by Adolph Zukor in 1912, is the oldest working studio in America—and it certainly was paramount for me. This studio financed *Zulu*, my first major film, and even though it didn't get a U.S. release to begin with, Paramount followed it up with *Alfie*, my breakout film, which they gave a major release in America where it got me my first Academy Award nomination. And my next Paramount film became *The Italian Job*. So I have a lot to thank Paramount for. *Zulu*, *Alfie* and *The Italian Job*, three of the biggest films in my life. In fact I had a chance to thank Adolph Zukor personally when I was a guest at his hundredth birthday party in 1974. He was in a wheelchair, looking very frail, and I went up to him, shook his hand, wished him a Happy Birthday and said a big "thank you." He looked at me blankly for a moment and said, "For what?" He clearly had no idea who on earth I was. Bob Hope was the compère of the event and in a toast to this tiny old man all bundled up in his chair, he said, "If Adolph had known he was going to live to be a hundred, he would have taken better care of himself!" And indeed it seemed touch and go as to whether the birthday boy would last the evening. I asked Bob what the protocol was in the event of sudden death. "The studio has thought of everything," he told me solemnly. "A hundred magicians stand ready in the kitchens, one for each table. Should Mr. Zukor be unexpectedly taken from us before the festivities are over, at a prearranged signal from me, they will run in, whisk the white tablecloths off and reveal the black ones that have been laid beneath as a precaution." He kept a straight face longer than I did.

The Chaplin studio, which Charlie Chaplin built in 1917, is, to me, a sign that he was a little homesick for England. It is built to look like a street in an English village, complete with manor house and village green. It takes authenticity to the extreme: all the buildings have chimneys, which don't get a lot of use in sunny Hollywood. I suppose it's not surprising that Chaplin should want to re-create his version of England as a rural idyll: he grew up very close to where I did and no one would have wanted to re-create those slums as they were then. Once, years ago, I bumped into Charlie Chaplin walking round the Elephant, quite anonymously, unnoticed by the crowds. Like me, he had come to pay a visit and he seemed to feel quite nostalgic about it and sad about the way it had been destroyed—first by the Luftwaffe and then by the developers. He didn't have a clue who I was, but we talked for a little while and he pointed out the ruins of the south London music hall he had appeared at in his last show before he went to America. It was only about three hundred yards from the prefab I had grown up in. I once asked my mother where she went for her honeymoon. She laughed drily and said, "The south London theater to see Charlie Chaplin in *Humming Birds* with Stan Laurel." Small world. . . . He was beautifully and expensively dressed, but even in his overcoat and hat—a trilby, not a bowler—I couldn't help seeing the echo of the Little Tramp as he walked away.

Samuel Goldwyn's studio is the third and last studio still actually in Hollywood itself. It was originally built on land owned by Mary Pickford and Douglas Fairbanks on the corner of Formosa and Santa Monica Boulevard known as "The Lot," until it was renamed when they formed United Artists with Charlie Chaplin and D. W. Griffith. Goldwyn eventually took it over and named it after himself, after a lengthy legal battle with Mary Pickford, who owned the lease and wanted to name it after herself—an early Hollywood story but one that strikes a chord. Now the studio is called The Lot once more and is still used for independent filmmaking—I made the Austin Powers *Goldmember* movie there myself, with Mike Myers.

Next door to one of the most prime areas of real estate in the world, Holmby Hills, is the city that *Cleopatra* built. Century City was once the back lot of Twentieth Century Fox, which now sulks in a small corner of its formerly great property. Fox had a string of movie disasters in the late 1950s and early 1960s, most notably *Cleopatra*, the biopic starring Elizabeth Taylor and Richard Burton notorious for costing $44 million rather than the original $2 million budgeted, and in 1961 they were forced to sell their 180-acre back lot to the Alcoa company who turned it into the Century City you see there today. To be a city in Britain, you have to have a cathedral, but this is Hollywood and it has its own cathedrals: skyscrapers full of the archbishops, bishops and priests of our age—the accountants and lawyers (including my own) who guide our prayers.

Once, many years after the making of *Cleopatra*, I was on a yacht in Monte Carlo with Elizabeth Taylor and Richard

Burton and after dinner we all sat down and watched *Carry On, Cleo,* one of the lowest-budget films ever made. They had brought it with them all the way from London—and in those days it wasn't a matter of tucking a DVD into your handbag or brief-case; films were all on reels, so they had gone to some real effort to get it there. We all roared with laughter at the silly jokes—there was one in particular I remember Elizabeth and Richard cracking up over. The two Caesars are arguing about whose gladiator is better, and one of them says, "My gladiator is the greatest," and the other one counters with, "My gladiator is invincible," and the first one comes back with, "Well, *my* gladiator is impregnable!" And the gladiator is standing there—he's a raddled old Cockney of about sixty—and he says, "It's not my fault, guv—my wife doesn't want any kids!"

Although they started in Hollywood, Universal Pictures moved out to a 250-acre lot in the San Fernando Valley in 1914. They were still there in 1966 when they gave my career two massive boosts. The first was when they bought and released *The Ipcress File* in America—the first time any of my movies had a general release there. No one told me they had done it. I was shopping in Bloomingdale's in New York during my pub-licity tour for *Alfie,* and I came out on the Third Avenue exit and there on the other side of the street was my name up in lights—it was a fantastic moment! It was Universal, too, that brought me to America to work with Shirley MacLaine on *Gambit.* That's another studio to which I owe a debt of gratitude.

Warner Bros. also started in Hollywood, on Sunset Boule-vard in 1923, and then followed Universal out to the San Fer-nando Valley in 1928 after their first great success, the first "talkie," *The Jazz Singer,* with Al Jolson. They have had a great eighty-year history there, and although I have contributed to a few of the blips along the way, including *The Swarm* and *Beyond the Poseidon Adventure,* I'm pleased to have made it up for them eventually with *Batman Begins*, *The Prestige*, *The Dark Knight* and *Inception*.

The third of the great studios in the San Fernando Valley is Disney. Walt Disney opened a small studio there in 1923 and it went on to become the biggest entertainment company in the world. Long ago, in what seems like another life, I actually met Walt Disney. I was working as a tea boy for the producer Jay Lewis, who was making *Morning Departure* with John Mills. I'd never been to a film studio before and one day he took me with him to Pinewood. While we were there we ran into Walt Disney. I stood there at Jay Lewis's elbow trying to merge with the wallpaper while they chatted and then he suddenly remembered I was there and told me to get Mr. Disney a coffee. "Milk and sugar?" was all I could manage to squeak to the great man—but I've never forgotten it. As a little boy I was a huge fan of Mickey Mouse, Donald Duck and Pluto and it gives me such pleasure now to watch the cartoons with the next generation of our family, my two-year-old grandson, Taylor. When I've been working in my study on this book, he'll come in, march over to me, climb on my lap and say, "Mickey Mouse!" until I give in. So, happily distracted, I enjoy it all over again.

As well as the enormous complexes owned by Universal, Warner Bros. and Disney, the San Fernando Valley is also home to NBC, the Getty Museum and the Hollywood Bowl. In spite of these high-prestige institutions, very few celebrities actually live in what's known as "The Valley," although of course most of them spend a lot of their time at the studios there. Bob Hope was one of the exceptions to this rule: he had an enormous mansion and estate there and even an airport named after him. The Valley is insanely hot for most of the year, and it is the porn movie capital of America. If you ever see an American porn film in which the participants are sweating before the action even starts, you'll know it was probably shot in the

Valley. In fact the Valley can be a great place to live, although people can be quite snobbish about it as an address. I once heard a Valley parent ask, "At what age do you tell your children they live in the Valley?"

The MGM studios are seven miles away from Hollywood, in Culver City, on the way to the airport. They were started in 1924 when a big cinema owner named Marcus Loew bought two production companies, the Metro Picture Corporation and Goldwyn Pictures. When these two were joined by Mayer Pictures, owned by Louis B. Mayer, the conglomerate was titled, with great imagination, Metro Goldwyn Mayer.

MGM once put out a movie with which I had the very slightest of connections. My friend Julie Christie had got a screen test for the lead role in *Dr. Zhivago*, which was being directed by the great David Lean. I offered to support Julie by playing the "back of the head" part opposite her in the screen test so she could play for the camera. David Lean liked the back of my head so much that he asked me if he could use it for all the screen tests, to which I agreed. I was just doing it as a favor, but it was obviously going quite well because one day David suggested that he actually test me for the main part. "Look," he said, "if we shoot it this way, and maybe comb your hair like this . . ." and we did, but when we saw the tests we both knew straightaway I wasn't right. "So what *do* you want?" I asked David. He thought a bit and then he said, "What I want is a man who's taken a long hard look at life and has decided there's absolutely nothing to be done." It came to me in a flash. I had just seen Omar Sharif in *Lawrence of Arabia* and I said, "Omar Sharif!" And David said, "Really?" He thought some more and then he said, "You know, you could be right—I'm going to test him." And he did—and Omar got the part—although I'm not sure I've ever told him how it came about. So there you are—if I hadn't failed the bloody screen test, like so many other things, I'd have been Dr. Zhivago. . . .

Next door to MGM there is another small studio, built by Thomas Ince, one of the first great silent-film producers. The front door is very posh, designed to look like the front door of George Washington's mansion, Mount Vernon. David O. Selznick, who was already a successful producer, bought the studio in 1935 for his own independent productions. One of these was *Gone With the Wind*—and the front door of the studio was used as the front door of Scarlett O'Hara's mansion, Tara. David O. Selznick was a great and also very frugal producer. When he needed to film the burning of Atlanta for *Gone With the Wind*, he did it here on the back lot and burned all the old sets from *King Kong*, *The Last of the Mohicans* and *Little Lord Fauntleroy*. Not only did he get free firewood, he created the space to build Tara itself out of plywood and papier-mâché. The set was eventually dismantled and is now for sale in 3 x 1-inch rectangles. As Selznick said at the time, "Like Hollywood, it was all a facade."

Facade or not, I am in awe of *Gone With the Wind*—it's one of my top ten all-time-favorite movies and Vivien Leigh is one of my all-time-favorite actors. I only met her once, while I was passing through London on my way to Louisiana to start the filming of *Hurry Sundown* with Otto Preminger in 1966. I was in a restaurant and John Gielgud came over and introduced himself and said that he and his companion—a tiny woman wearing sunglasses—had just been to see *Alfie* and had loved it. I thanked them and then the tiny woman whipped off her sunglasses and it was Vivien Leigh. I took a deep breath—even fresh from my first experiences in Hollywood I hadn't quite got used to rubbing shoulders with a screen legend—but I was determined not to miss this chance. I explained I was about to play a southern character in *Hurry Sundown* with Jane Fonda and I needed some help. "What's the basis of doing a southern accent?" I asked her. "It's easy," she said (and she was being very nice to an annoying young actor). "You say, 'Foah Doah Ford'—Four

Door Ford—all day long. That's all you do—'Foah Doah Ford'—
Michael, and it will come to you." And I did say it over and over
again, but I never quite sounded like Scarlett O'Hara.

After Selznick left, the studio became RKO Pictures and
Howard Hughes made some of his movies there, and after that
it became Desilu, Lucille Ball's studio. Now it is an independent
studio again. I did *Bewitched* there myself in 2005, though even
I would not claim it was in the same category as *Gone With the
Wind*, *Rebecca*, *Citizen Kane* or *King Kong*.

In their early years, Paramount, Warner Bros., Universal,
Disney and the other great movie studios were all run by the
moguls who had built them. By the time I arrived in Hollywood,
the studio system had moved from the hands-on personal domi-
nation of the great studio heads to the corporate structures they
remain today. And a new set of power players had emerged: the
actors themselves—and their agents. I always remember Henry
Fonda—who had been a huge star at the time—saying to me,
"You're so lucky to be a star now, because you'll make a lot of
money—we never did." The irony was that I had been devas-
tated when Joe Levine tore up my contract after *Zulu*: to me it
represented the security I had never had. But these contracts—
often for ten pictures or for five years—paid no heed to how big
a hit a movie was. They paid plenty of heed to failure, of
course—if an actor was seen as unsuccessful, there was nothing
to prevent the studio from ripping up his or her contract without
another thought. In other words, the studios couldn't lose.

Even as a newcomer making his way in Hollywood for the
first time, I was well aware that there were plenty of pitfalls.
Although there are no real holly woods, the name is actually
quite appropriate—a holly, after all, is a dark, impenetrable tree
festooned with bright attractive berries, surrounded by vicious
thorns. The berries are highly prized as decoration, but to get
to them, you have to find a path around the tree, choose the
correct gloves and then pick the berries with great care. You

need an experienced guide—and patience—to cut the right path through them and out into the sunlight.

If you can make it without getting hurt, then it's Christmas all the way.

In the holly woods, the path cutters are called agents—and over the years I am lucky to have had three of the best. Number one was, of course, Dennis Selinger, who was the first to inform me that there were any woods for an actor to make his way through. He guided me through the English woods and became my closest friend and mentor. He died in 1998, and I miss him still. Although he was based in London, Dennis taught me a lot about the holly woods and helped me on my long hazardous journey towards them.

If it was Shirley MacLaine who first parted the undergrowth to let me through, she left me at the edge of the woods in the capable hands of the greatest path cutter in the world, Sue Mengers. Sue was Hollywood's most powerful agent when I arrived in town, and I was her least known client. Fortunately for me, like Dennis, she became a close personal friend and although she's now retired, we keep in regular touch. Sue is a great getter-together of people and her dinners are legendary for the extraordinary group she'll gather. One time Shakira and I went and there were Barbra Streisand and Sting and Sheryl Crow and her boyfriend, a nice guy whose name was Lance Armstrong. "What do you do?" I asked him, being friendly. "I'm a cyclist," he replied. I hadn't got a clue. I thought he was going to ask me what I did.

Sue always says, "I want you all out of here by ten-thirty." But it's the company that makes the evening: you never know whom you'll meet there and there's always a bit of rivalry going on—"Were you at the Sue Mengers dinner?" I'd known Sue for a few years before I graduated to her dinners and when I finally went round, she introduced me to her husband. There was something about him I couldn't quite put my finger on and after a while I plucked up courage and said to him, "You know, it's very funny, but years ago I spent some time in Paris and I had this French friend and he looked just like you." And he said, "Michael—it *is* me!" And it was this guy Jean-Claude, whom I'd met on that trip to Paris my mum had funded all those years before.

Since Sue retired, I've been very fortunate to have the wonderful Toni Howard cutting my paths for the last fifteen years and I'm very lucky to have her on my side.

As you cut your way through the dark holly woods, the person you need to trim the tops of the trees to let the light in is called a press agent. I had acquired my first UK press agent with *The Ipcress File.* Theo Cowan was a big middle-aged man with no visible family life, very funny and my friends and I all loved him dearly. I always felt as if he had a sad romantic secret, an unrequited love, but he was one of the funniest men I've ever known. If you asked him what he was doing, he would always say, "Contrast." And if you asked him how he was, he'd say, "The hard ones first, eh?"

To help me see my way through the American holly woods I found Jerry Pam. Not only was he one of the best press agents in Hollywood, he turned out to be an Englishman and he went to the same school as I did, Hackney Downs. Jerry has recently retired, but while we worked together he lit my way through the woods and out the other side and kept the sun shining on me for over forty years.

The last hazards you may have to face in the woods are the stinging insects and the vermin that bite. For these you need to acquire an exterminator—or as they are known in the movie business, a lawyer. My lawyer, Barry Tyreman, is one of the nicest, gentlest, kindest men you could meet—unless of course you come under the vermin or insect category, in which case very quickly and *almost* painlessly, you are dead.

So these are the people who got me to the holly woods,

through them and then out of the other side. But of course that's just the start; it's still dangerous out there. Once you are out of the woods, you find yourself in the urban jungle and although the insects may have gone, some of the vermin are still lurking and sometimes they are bigger and more dangerous for being camouflaged. For these you need not only the combined forces of all of the above, but something extra—a business manager. I am lucky enough to have two: Stephen Marks in England and Nicholas Brown in America.

Hollywood is a rich and glamorous place, but without all these people on my side I'd have had a tough time. If you're poisoned it will be by champagne or caviar. If you are run over it will be by a Rolls-Royce. If you are strangled it will be with a string of perfectly matched pearls. But you'll still be dead.

In spite of the many traps it lays for the unwary, Hollywood is still a place that fosters and cherishes its own myths—and three of the industry's most significant places of pilgrimage are sited right in the center of town. The first is a cinema called Grauman's Chinese Theatre, now one of the great tourist sites in Hollywood. It was opened on Hollywood Boulevard in 1927 by Sid Grauman (well, that explains the "Grauman" element), who filled it with exotic Chinese art and topped it with a spectacular ninety-foot-high jade-green roof. The first shovel of dirt was dug by Norma Talmadge and the first rivet was inserted by Anna May Wong, both great stars of the time. In the forecourt, they installed a special exhibit where stars placed their hand- and footprints into the paving stones—a feature that has ensured the theater its place in Hollywood history. Grauman's has displayed the prints of just two hundred stars since 1927 and the first stars so honored were Mary Pickford and her husband, Douglas Fairbanks, who gave their hand- and footprints on April 30, 1927. One of the most recent actors honored is, I'm proud to say, me. I added my prints to the pavement on July 11, 2008.

The Hollywood Walk of Fame comes next. Stars each get a commemorative star-shaped plaque in the paving stones of Hollywood running west from Gower Street to La Brea Avenue, and south to north on both sides of Vine Street between Yucca Street and Sunset Boulevard, for three and a half miles. There are over two thousand stars in the pavement. The first recipient was Joanne Woodward on February 9, 1960. I haven't yet managed to go and receive mine yet, but I'm looking forward to it.

The last—but of course the one that has come to symbolize the film industry the world over—is the Hollywood sign itself that towers so proudly over the movie colony. The sign has nothing to do with the studios. It was constructed in 1923 by two real estate developers called Woodruff and Shoults to advertise their development HOLLYWOODLAND—which was what the original sign read. Over the years the sign deteriorated. The first "O" broke in half, leaving a "u" and then a second "O" fell off altogether, leaving a sign which read: "HuLLY-WODLAND." In 1932 an actress called Peg Entwhistle committed suicide by jumping off the letter "H" and in the 1940s the official caretaker, Albert Kothe, drove his car into the "H" while drunk and completely destroyed it. Since no one thought "uLLY-WODLAND" was much of an advertisement for one of America's most iconic exports, the Hollywood chamber of commerce took it over, replaced the missing letters, chopped off "LAND" and the legend was born. I've been delighted to call the place home on and off for more than forty years and its magic has never faded for me. I've just got much better at navigating through those wild woods.

CHAPTER EIGHT

THE FAST LANE

All that hard-won knowledge of the reality behind the dazzle of Hollywood was still years off when I returned to London after my first, almost overwhelmingly glamorous trip. I was still half-suspecting that all good things have to come to an end, and certainly those three months in Hollywood rushed by so fast that the first morning I woke up back in my flat in London, I thought that it had all been a dream. Had I really met John Wayne and Frank Sinatra and been round to Danny Kaye's for Chinese? Had Shirley MacLaine actually chosen me to play opposite her in *Gambit*? As I paced round my small flat and began to pick up the pieces of my London life, I felt very odd, almost as if I had been on another planet. I didn't have long to worry about it, though—before I knew it I was leaving London again, this time on my way to Berlin.

After the success of *The Ipcress File*, the studio was keen to keep going with Harry Palmer and decided to film *Funeral in*

Berlin, Len Deighton's third Harry Palmer novel. The last time I had occupied the city was during my national service days in 1951 and it had been a very different place. Now, the Wall dividing east and west was an ever-present reminder of the Cold War. The East German soldiers watched us through binoculars the whole time we were filming there. At one point they were obviously not happy with the way things were going and shone a mirror at our camera lenses until we had to give up and find another spot. The director, Guy Hamilton, had recently directed Sean Connery in *Goldfinger* and had himself been in British Intelligence during the war. I'm not sure in retrospect he was quite the right man to give Harry Palmer the gritty edge he needed to differentiate him from James Bond, but it was a great film to work on—and Berlin was a bit of a revelation, to say the least.

One of the scenes was shot in a transvestite club and it was quite an eye-opener. Waiting for the cameras to be set up, I was chatting to the receptionist, a beautiful girl, when a very burly, butch-looking man with heavy stubble and massive arms walked past. He was dressed as a schoolgirl and got up onstage to do his act, an unforgettable version of Shirley Temple's "On the Good Ship Lollipop." I leant over to my new friend and whispered confidentially, "He doesn't look very feminine." "Oh?" she said, with barely a flicker of interest. "That's my dad. He owns the place." Later on I spilled a drink and went into what I thought was an empty dressing room to clean it off. It was already occupied: an enormous transvestite was standing there in frilly knickers, black silk stockings, suspender belt and high-heeled shoes, but no bra. His hairy chest had been shaved to just below his nipples and when he saw me he screamed and covered them with his hands, as a woman might have done. I thought it was very strange, but, mind you, I was a lot younger then.

Just as we were finishing up in Berlin, I heard that *Alfie* was being entered for the Cannes Film Festival. I'd had such a ball there with John Lennon when I'd gone the previous year for *The Ipcress File* that I took a few days off filming and hopped on a plane for a bit of southern French sunshine. Unfortunately, *Alfie* didn't go down too well with the French, who couldn't believe that an Englishman could attract one woman, let alone ten of them, and although we won a prize, the director Lewis Gilbert found himself being pelted with tomatoes when he went up onstage. The trip wasn't entirely wasted, however. Paramount gave a grand lunch for *Alfie* at the Carlton Hotel and I found myself sitting next to an Austrian guy. Although I was partying hard every night, I made sure I was more or less sober during the day and this turned out to be just as well. "My name is Charles Blühdorn," he said in a thick accent. "I liked your movie and your performance very much." I thanked him and as we started eating I asked him what he did. He told me he was an industrialist and then he said, "But that is not interesting. You should ask me what I did yesterday." "And what did you do yesterday?" I asked dutifully. "I bought Paramount Studios!" he said. "So, if you ever have a script you want [he said 'vant'] to do, let me have a look at it." Well—nothing ventured . . . "As a matter of fact," I said, "there is something. . . ." And I told Mr. Blühdorn that my friend Troy Kennedy Martin (the creator of *Z Cars*) had written a script with a great part for me and a London producer called Michael Deeley had it. "What ['vot'] is it called?" Mr. Blühdorn asked. "*The Italian Job*," I replied. You never can know what a chance meeting might bring about, can you?

Since I had got into the festival habit, I went more or less straight from Cannes to Acapulco in southern Mexico. Not perhaps the best known of the international festivals, nor the most prestigious, but certainly one of the warmest and that seemed a good-enough reason to go there for *Alfie*. Along with Rita Tushingham, star of *A Taste of Honey* and a real sixties icon, and

Lynn Redgrave, star of *Georgy Girl*, we represented the cream of British talent. I had chosen to spend the day before the festival began on the beach and had got second-degree sunburn and a bright red peeling nose—and I had also picked up an appalling attack of diarrhea. Rita was tiny, pale and cute, but no sex bomb, and Lynn (pre–Weight Watchers) was just large and pale. The glamorous South American press was not impressed: after a few polite questions, they lost interest and went off in quest of some real movie stars.

Acapulco had its memorable incidents, most notable of which was attending a bullfight with Rita and Lynn. Witnessing the massacre of the poor bull from our prestige front-row seats was too much for Lynn who passed out as the blood spurted in front of our eyes. Carrying her out of the arena was almost too much for me and proved to be a more compelling spectacle than the fight itself for the thousands gathered in the bullring. When I finally struggled to the top of the long flight of steps leading to the exit with Lynn's considerable dead weight in my arms, and tiny Rita trailing behind with all our belongings, a great cry of *"Ole!"* rang out from the onlookers. What they didn't know was that the diarrhea that I thought I had well under control was not equal to the extra strain of my gallant mission. Thank God for dark trousers. . . .

Lynn Redgrave was one of the funniest actresses I've ever seen—I've never forgotten her performance in *Hay Fever* at the Old Vic, which was absolutely hilarious. We didn't see each other as much as I would have liked after she went to live in New York, and of course I knew she wasn't well, but I was very sad to hear of her death. Whenever we did meet we always had a laugh about Mexico.

In the next stage of my career, the legendary Otto Preminger, director of movies such as *Carmen Jones*, *The Man with the Golden Arm* and *Anatomy of a Murder*, offered me a part in his new movie, *Hurry Sundown*. I was so excited I barely bothered to read the script and headed off to the sun of the Deep South with only those few words from Vivien Leigh to help me. Otto was reputed to be a monster with a habit of screaming at actors and technical staff alike, but I decided up front that I was not going to let him scream at me. "You need to know something about me," I said to him on the first evening we met. "I'm very sensitive and I'll cry if you or anyone else shouts at me while I'm working." Preminger raised an eyebrow in surprise. I plunged on. "And if anyone does shout at me, I'll go straight to my dressing room and I won't work again that day." A long silence. Otto seemed puzzled. "But I would never shout at Alfie!" he said eventually—and he never did and in the end we became firm friends. Like many men—and perhaps this was one of the secrets of the film's success—Otto Preminger saw himself as Alfie and, again like many others, made the mistake of seeing me as Alfie, too.

Otto may have gone easy on me, but he made everyone else's life on the set a misery and was particularly tough on my young and beautiful costar Faye Dunaway, who was often in tears by the end of a day's shooting. Apparently he always chose a scapegoat, and poor Faye was in the firing line. From time to time our friendship meant that I was able to tell him to ease up on her. But I was warned that I wouldn't completely get away with telling Otto never to shout at me. And he had his revenge in a way that took no account at all of the feelings of Jane Fonda, also then a young actress, who was playing my estranged wife. We were due to shoot a scene in which I was supposed to rape her and, very nervous about how I should go about this, bearing in mind the U.S. censor and my costar's feelings, I asked Otto for some guidance. "Simple, Michael," he leered (Otto had an impressive leer. In his acting days he had been a remarkably realistic Nazi officer). "Just smash the door down, burst into the room and rape her. I'll call CUT when we've got what we need." So I did what he said. At one point, if began to feel there was a danger that things would get out of hand. "I'm stopping!" I shouted and sat up abruptly. Otto and the entire crew were sitting there with wolfish grins. They had long since switched off the camera. Jane, I'm relieved to say, just went along with it.

From the heat of Louisiana I went straight to Finland, for the third of the Harry Palmer movies, *Billion Dollar Brain*. I had never felt cold like that before—and I hope I never do again. But this was the first in a whole run of movies I was to make almost back-to-back, some of them memorable and some of them I'm only too happy to forget. Subconsciously I thought that my good fortune wouldn't last and that I should line up as many as I could while the going was good and make as much money as possible before I found myself back in the dole queue.

Aside from the cold, I was very pleased to be playing Harry Palmer again and I thought—and still think—that *Billion Dollar Brain* is a really atmospheric movie. It was way ahead of its time, too. I recently discovered that in *Billion Dollar Brain* I was the first person ever to use the Internet on-screen. At the time, I just assumed it was one more piece of technological spy wizardry and back then I certainly couldn't get the hang of it—so I did what all actors do, which is to ask the experts for some emergency coaching, to make me look as if I knew what I was doing.

A lot of the shooting was done out on the ice floes and, although the temperature never reached more than about three degrees, the ice was cracking under our feet and beginning to melt. Standing in three inches of water was a really miserable experience—and I got a sense of the potential danger we were in when our generator truck began sinking and had to be driven off the ice. It was followed by the catering lorry, which was a very serious business. Between handheld battery-powered lights and no lunch, we were thoroughly fed-up.

There were other problems with the extreme cold, too. I found close-ups very hard because my face had literally frozen.

So Harry Palmer's expression was not so much wooden as completely glacial. And in temperatures like this, the camera fogged up the minute we had to do an inside shot. Some of the scenes were filmed in the Helsinki botanical gardens, which were of course much warmer in order to preserve the plants, and there was a lot of hanging about waiting for the camera lenses to de-mist.

Inside, my head was warm, at least, but without my beautiful sable fur hat I wouldn't have survived. The first time I put it on, a Finnish journalist was standing nearby and said—with a completely straight face—"You know, you bear a remarkable resemblance to Anita Ekberg." Anita Ekberg—me? I stole a glance at myself every time I passed a mirror, but I couldn't quite see what she was getting at. Anita Ekberg or not, the hat looked pretty good on-screen and I became very fond of it and took it home afterwards to join all the hats from my other films that I had amassed in my bedroom. The only one missing from the collection then—the rest of it all disappeared long ago—was my pith helmet from *Zulu*. I'm sorry not to have kept that, but it was big and would have been a bit heavy to carry home from filming in South Africa.

I really enjoyed playing Harry Palmer in the three movies. In some ways I felt a certain affinity with the way his character develops during the course of them. In *The Ipcress File*, he was a complete innocent, just as I had been in the film business. By *Funeral in Berlin* we had both learned a lot more. And by the time we got to *Billion Dollar Brain* I felt that both Harry and I had become pretty hardened by our experiences. In many ways, playing Harry Palmer required a certain frame of mind, rather than straight-out dramatic acting. He's cool all right, but he has to be. Being a spy is a twenty-four-hour-a-day job and he can never afford to relax.

After *Billion Dollar Brain* I felt I could afford to relax, so after we left Finland to finish the movie in the distinctly milder climate of England, I shot off to Paris for a bit of fun. I had a bit part in Shirley MacLaine's new film, *Woman Times Seven*, and I was only too happy to do it in return for everything Shirley had done for me in Hollywood. Anita Ekberg was appearing with Shirley, so I also got a chance to look at her a bit more closely, which was nothing but a pleasure, although I still couldn't spot much resemblance.

Thoroughly defrosted by Paris, I then went off to Spain to do the first of a two-picture deal for Twentieth Century Fox. *Deadfall* was directed by my old friend Bryan Forbes and, although the movie didn't turn out as well as we'd hoped, it was a happy time. As soon as we'd finished filming in London I went straight back to Spain, this time for a Harry Salzman production, *Play Dirty*. I had signed to do this one not just because of Harry, but also because it was to be directed by the great French film director René Clément. Unfortunately as soon as I'd put my name on the dotted line, Clément walked out after a huge row with Harry—I should have taken it as an omen.

Play Dirty was being filmed in the southern Spanish town of Almería, which had become the center of the spaghetti Western industry after Sergio Leone made *The Good, the Bad and the Ugly* there and it was also a favorite location for wartime desert battle movies, which was why we were there. In fact there were only about four sand dunes and all the high crane shots also managed to include the local beaches, crowded with hordes of sun-loving tourists.

The "desert," such as it was, was rather overcrowded—there were two spaghetti Westerns being filmed at the same time as our movie, as well as a new British-produced Western, *Shalako*, starring my friend Sean Connery, and this made for some frustrating—if actually very funny—moments. One day we were shooting a scene in which Rommel's Afrika Korps were advancing their tanks across the desert sands, only to be confronted round one of the dunes by a horde of American

Indians in full battle-cry in pursuit of a nineteenth-century stagecoach. As soon as they saw the tanks, the horses reared up and threw their riders and we had to hang about while they were picked up and dusted off and all the horseshit and hoof marks eliminated.

Despite the overcrowding, it was still possible to get some peace and one afternoon my friend and stand-in Johnny Morris and I found a quiet spot to have a couple of beers. I was bemoaning the lack of beautiful girls around the place to my happily married companion, when he suddenly jabbed me in the ribs. "Michael!" he said urgently. I looked up and nearly fell off my chair. Standing before me was Brigitte Bardot. "'ello, Michael," she purred. "We meet at last. I 'ave been looking for you everywhere. . . ." She introduced herself and her two companions— two equally beautiful women: Gloria, her secretary, and Monique, her French stand-in. I leapt to my feet and promptly knocked the table and all the drinks on it flying. Not exactly the impression of *un homme du monde* I had hoped to make. Nonetheless, Johnny and I soon found ourselves whisked by white Rolls-Royce to the divine Miss Bardot's luxury suite. When I eventually found my voice I managed to ask how she knew I was in town. "My friend Sean tells me," said the screen goddess. Ah— Sean, again: BB was his costar in *Shalako*. Still, Sean was out in the desert somewhere and I was here in the suite. . . . Unfortunately it didn't quite work out the way I'd planned. It wasn't Brigitte who had had her eye on me, it was her assistant, Gloria. BB's own tastes ran to extremely young, very beautiful and very dark Spanish men and I didn't score highly in any of those categories.

Both Sean and I had been very busy and hadn't seen much of each other, but he did invite me to the end-of-filming dinner for *Shalako*. By now rather miffed at the way that BB had managed to resist my obvious attractions, I grabbed a table at the back with my friend the comedian Eric Sykes who was also in the cast. "Just watch," whispered Eric as Bardot swept into the restaurant, "she is completely crazy about me . . . just watch as she comes past. She'll pretend to ignore me completely. She's done it since the first day on set—but it's all an act." And indeed BB did walk straight past us without saying hello. "You see?" insisted Eric. By now I was so hysterical with laughter that I had to lay my head down on the table. I raised it just in time to get hit square on the nose with a hunk of stale Spanish bread and looked over to see the divine Miss Bardot smiling wickedly and rubbing bread crumbs off her hands. . . .

The Magus, my next film, was the second of my disastrous Twentieth Century Fox contract and one I'd rather forget, because I simply didn't have a clue what it was all about—and I still don't. It marked the end of a three-year stint of moviemaking and I was more than happy to find myself back home in London, in a new flat in Grosvenor Square with a grandstand view of the anti-Vietnam riots. It was a chance to pick up with friends and family again. My brother, Stanley, now happily working in Selfridge's department store, had been looking after my old flat and so I gave it to him, along with all its contents, and started afresh.

It wasn't long, though, before another picture came along and this one, I'm happy to say, was nothing but a pleasure from beginning to end—and a successful pleasure, too. I've always taken the view that you get paid as much for a bad film as you do for a good one, but I'm only too aware that you need to keep the proportion of good films to bad high enough to avoid the stink of failure and to maintain your credibility at the box office. *The Italian Job*—that script I had mentioned to Charles Blühdorn the day after he bought Paramount—satisfied on all fronts.

We started on location in London and one of the greatest pleasures of the film was working with Noël Coward. The director of the film, Peter Collinson, had grown up in an orphanage sponsored by Coward—he still called him "Master Coward," just like a schoolboy—and he had persuaded Coward to take on the role of the underworld boss who masterminds the entire heist from inside prison. It may have been an unlikely role, but Noël played it to perfection: he loved taking on the role of a gangster boss with all these tough guys under his command. He was gloriously unfussy and unstuffy about the whole thing and mucked in with everybody: it was a fantastic opportunity for me to learn from the master of comic timing. He was a generous, amusing and lovable man and every Wednesday while we were shooting in London we had dinner together at the Savoy Grill. Noël told me that he had been given a free room for life at the Savoy because he had played cabaret there during the war and had kept going, right through the Blitz. "Perfect for me," he confided, "a truly captive audience!" He was warm and witty and a wonderful dinner companion, although I relished his waspish side. On one occasion I was describing the anti-Vietnam demonstrations I could see from the window of my flat and how I had seen Vanessa Redgrave in the front line. Noël sniffed. "She will keep on demonstrating," he said. "But then she's a very tall girl and I suppose she's pleased to sit down."

From shooting in London we moved location to Turin where all the great car stunts took place. We spent days throwing little Mini Coopers off the top of Mont Blanc. We needed about sixteen altogether by the time we had assembled a team of crash cars, stunt cars, doubles and others on standby, so we went to the British Motor Corporation, as it was then, and asked if they would donate some in return for the publicity the Mini would receive. They were fantastically snooty about it and said they could only manage a token few. Fiat, on the other hand, completely got the idea and offered us as many cars as we wanted, including sports cars for the Mafia scene. No wonder the British car industry went down the toilet.

The Italian Job was a classic British comic caper—a real family film—and it did very well at the time in the UK. America was another story. I got off the plane in LA on the first leg of the U.S. publicity tour to be confronted by an ad in which a naked woman was perched in front of a gun-toting gangster—hardly family viewing. I more or less turned round on the spot and went back home. As a result, we never did the sequel and Charlie Croker and the boys are still in that bus hanging over the edge of the cliff.

I had no idea then of the cult status *The Italian Job* would achieve over the next nearly forty years: you can't be aware at the time that you're making an iconic movie. It's been voted the twenty-seventh favorite British film of all time, apparently, and my line, "You were only supposed to blow the bloody doors off!" was voted the favorite film one-liner ever. I don't know about that—there's plenty of competition—but I do know that it's a favorite of mine. We thought it was a funny line at the time. I remember we had to do several takes because we were laughing so much we ruined them, which pissed Peter Collinson off a bit because he just wanted us to get on with it, but we had no idea anyone would pick up on it. I've been a bit more aware of one-liners since, though. In *Get Carter*, the one-liner (two lines actually, but who's counting?) that everyone remembers is, "You're a big man, but you're out of shape. For me it's a full-time job." People are always quoting that at me. I wondered while we were making it if there was going to be an iconic line in *Harry Brown*, but it wasn't until I was watching it a while later that I suddenly spotted it. . . . It's the line where my character says to the drug dealer when his gun doesn't fire, "You failed to maintain your weapon." And I thought, the lads will use that. I can imagine a pub on a Saturday night and a guy comes in and says, "My girlfriend's left me," and they all turn to him and say in a chorus, "You failed to maintain your weapon!"

In *The Italian Job*, there's also the matter of the cliffhanger (literally) at the end. There's been a lot of speculation about this

My first publicity shot.
Me with my mother in
the only picture that
exists of me as a baby.

Bombardier
Micklewhite, of the
Royal Horse Artillery.
My father in 1925.

"Bubbles..." at the John Ruskin Infants School.
That wool shirt was the scratchiest I'd ever
worn until I joined the army.

My dad at his fish stall in Billingsgate Market. He's the third from left,
wearing a white coat and cap. Billingsgate is now a banqueting hall.

On the farm in Norfolk
with other evacuees
during the war

Back in London after the war at Clubland. I'm on
the right looking over my shoulder at the talent....

The Clubland trip to Guernsey. I'm on the far left, second row from the top.

A Hill in Korea. Manning my machine gun post. I'd nicked the helmet from the Americans—it was much lighter than the ones we were issued with.

A Hill in Korea—nothing like the real thing. My first ever appearance in a film: I only had eight lines and I managed to forget every one of them.

National Service Training, 1952. I'm in the back row, second from the right. I was lucky to make private.

Back on civvy street. My first job in the movies . . . in the mail room at Peak Films.

"You're nothing like your photograph, are you?" Application sent to Alwyn D. Fox. Name: Michael Scott Age: 21 yrs Height: 6' 1" Eyes: blue Hair: blond

My first major stage role, in Somerset Maugham's *The Letter*, with a sympathetic June Wyndham Davies, in 1953. Apparently I told her after the first performance that it had been more frightening than anything I'd done in Korea.

Ah—the magic of theater . . . On stage with Alwyn D. Fox in Horsham

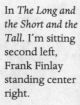

In *The Long and the Short and the Tall*. I'm sitting second left, Frank Finlay standing center right.

My first big break: playing in *The Compartment*, a two-handed TV thriller written by Johnny Speight. I played a psychopathic Cockney opposite Frank Finlay.

"Who told that silly bastard to pull his hat down over his f***ing eyes?" *Zulu*, 1963—the biggest piece of luck I ever had in show business.

Playing Horatio to Christopher Plummer's *Hamlet* in 1963. My one and only classical role.

Len Deighton teaching me to crack two eggs in one hand in *The Ipcress File*. In fact I never managed it— those are Len's hands you see in the movie.

At home with Mum and my brother Stanley, 1964

That's what it's all about, Alfie! On set with Lewis Gilbert in 1966.

Shelley Winters told me later that she hadn't understood a single thing I'd said....

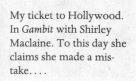

My ticket to Hollywood. In *Gambit* with Shirley Maclaine. To this day she claims she made a mistake....

Holding my Star of the Future Award from the National Association of Theatre Owners, New York, 1966. If you're an actor and live long enough you'll have an office full of these—from Star of the Future to Best Actor and finally to Lifetime Achievement....

With the "little Lancashire lad" Reverend Jimmy Butterworth, the genius behind Clubland, in 1969. I owe him so much.

Funeral in Berlin, 1966. The East German soldiers kept us under surveillance throughout filming.

On the set of *Hurry Sundown* with Otto Preminger and Jane Fonda. It's odd how many directors feel the need to offer hands-on advice during love scenes.

Keeping warm in my beautiful sable hat in *Billion Dollar Brain*, 1967

"Whatever you do, don't touch the Red Button!" Ready for take-off in *Battle of Britain*, 1969.

We didn't know it, but just around the corner a horde of American Indians was waiting in ambush.... Our overcrowded "desert" location in *Play Dirty*, 1968.

With Noël Coward on the set of *The Italian Job*, 1969

I should have suspected something . . . me on Fury, filming *The Last Valley*, 1970

We look as if we're lining up for a plate-spinning contest. Helping John Wayne celebrate his forty years in the movies. From left to right: Lee Marvin, Clint Eastwood, Rock Hudson, Fred McMurray, "Duke," James Stewart, Ernest Borgnine, me, Laurence Harvey.

Our wedding day, January 8, 1973, at the "Little Chapel on the Green" (really the "Little Chapel on the Astroturf"), Las Vegas. Jerry Pam is on the left, Dennis Selinger is on the right.

Sunday at the Mill House. From left to right: Jack Jones, Susan George, Dennis Selinger, Peter Sellers, Liza Minnelli, me, Shakira (pregnant with Natasha), Kay Thompson, Vincente Minnelli and Shakira's friend Jane Griffiths. A day after this happy picture was taken, Peter and Liza broke up.

With Shakira and Natasha, July 1975

With Nikki on our way to Los Angeles

Relaxing with Elizabeth Taylor on the set of *Zee & Co*, 1971. The director Brian Hutton is making us laugh.

With Sir Laurence Olivier and a small, hairy, black caterpillar in *Sleuth*, 1972

On the set of *Get Carter*, 1971

John Huston directing Shakira in *The Man Who Would Be King*. I never did manage to find out how he persuaded her to take it on.... You can see me in the background, cigar in hand, just before I was thrown off the set.

With Sean Connery in *The Man Who Would Be King*, 1975

With friend and fellow Mayfair Orphan, Doug Hayward

Love scenes are actually very hard to do—Glenda Jackson was in complete command in *The Romantic Englishwoman*, 1975.

With the magnificent Maggie Smith. She gave an Oscar-winning performance in *California Suite*, 1978.

A toast to *Educating Rita*, 1983. From left to right: Sean Connery, Jackie Collins, Julie Walters and me.

and in 2008 the Royal Society of Chemistry launched a competition for the most scientifically plausible solution to Croker's problem. The winner came up with an ingenious idea, but in fact what we had planned was that I would crawl up the bus, switch on the engine and wait until it ran out of petrol. That would rebalance the weight so we could all get out—but the bus (and the gold) would then drop over the edge of the cliff into the arms of the Mafia waiting below. The sequel would have been all about us getting it back—shame it was never made!

From Turin I went more or less straight on to my next project, which was a small part in Harry Saltzman's production, *The Battle of Britain*. Harry had had me under contract since *The Ipcress File*, but he was a fair man and as I became more and more successful he reflected this by upping my payment each year on my birthday. This birthday, my thirty-fifth, he gave me the usual envelope but, instead of the usual revised contract, it contained the original, ripped up. "You're on your own now," he said.

I only had a small part in *The Battle of Britain*, but it was a film I particularly wanted to be involved with. As a boy who had had to leave London because of the Blitz, as an evacuee who had grown up in Norfolk watching pilots taking off, some of whom never came back, I was well aware of the debt we owed to "the Few" and here was a chance to pay tribute to these brave young men. It was also a chance to get to know some of the pilots who had actually flown in the battle. Ginger Lacey and Bob Stanford Tuck were acting as technical advisers to the film—as was Adolf Galland, the Luftwaffe pilot who had led the German attack. What I couldn't quite get over was how young they had all been—until I remembered that I was only nineteen when I was in Korea.

Flying is way out of my league. I didn't learn to swim until I was twelve, and I've never learnt to ski or water-ski. I didn't drive a car until I was much, much older. These things just weren't available when I was growing up during and just after wartime, and they weren't available in the Elephant in peacetime, either. So I can't fly and I have no desire to learn: I like to leave that sort of thing to the professionals. But the director, Guy Hamilton, was very keen on absolute authenticity and wanted to film us in the open Spitfire cockpits speeding as if to take off. I squeezed myself into the pilot's seat and sat there waiting for "Action" to be called, almost as nervous as if I were really going into battle. "Whatever you do," yelled Ginger Lacey, who was coaching me, "don't touch the Red Button!" The Red Button? I looked down and there by my left knee was indeed a Red Button. "Why not?" I bawled back. "You'll take off!" he shouted cheerfully. "Action!" In a complete panic I shunted over to the far right as I hurtled down the runway, the only Spitfire pilot ever to get ready for takeoff with his legs crossed.

If Finland had been the coldest location I had ever worked on, then the Philippine jungle, where we shot *Too Late the Hero*, must be the hottest—and the most uncomfortable. *Too Late the Hero* is set in the Second World War and is the story of a British troop (plus an American soldier, played by Cliff Robertson) sent to knock out a Japanese radio transmitter on a Pacific island. The landscape we were working in was stunning, but the poverty of the local people and the food were anything but and so the director, Robert Aldrich, had us work in two-week stints, followed by five days R & R.

We endured the heat, the humidity and the mosquitoes and the often considerably greater risks attendant on our various R & R expeditions because we believed that the story behind *Too Late the Hero* deserved its authentic location. But when I finally got to see the finished picture, I can't say I thought the misery had been worthwhile. The jungle shots just looked like an anonymous mass of trees—it might as well have been filmed outside London.

After a brief respite in Hollywood, which I felt I thoroughly deserved, I set off for Innsbruck in Austria in autumn 1969 to film *The Last Valley*, which was set during the Thirty Years' War. Glorious Austrian location, delicious food, a costar like Omar Sharif—what could go wrong? Well, for a start, I couldn't get my hotel room cleaned. In the end, I had to complain to the hotel management who looked into it and came back to me a bit embarrassed. My room was on the same floor as Omar's but a bit further down the passage and it seemed that on Omar's days off, the maid somehow never made it past his room along to mine. . . . And then there was the fact that the film was set in the Middle Ages and I was playing the captain of a mercenary force: horses were involved again. My daughter Dominique— by now an expert horsewoman—had told me that I should make sure to ask for a docile mount and to stipulate that it had to be a mare. I duly followed her instructions and so was taken aback to find myself confronted with not only the biggest horse I had ever seen, but one that featured a pair of the biggest balls I had ever seen. The horse was as quiet as can be, I was assured, and had been chosen with me in mind. His name—I should have suspected something—was Fury.

My first few rides on Fury were uneventful and I began to relax. But on the first day of shooting, he seemed to switch personalities. I had changed into costume and had planned to start the day with a little trot. The trot began sedately enough but soon turned into a canter and then began to gather speed until it turned into a gallop I had no chance of controlling. We were eventually brought to a screaming halt (it was me doing the screaming) by a jeep from the unit, three miles from the set. I have rarely been angrier and let rip at the director, James Clavell, as soon as I was back. He sat calmly absorbing my anger and then got up, took me by the arm and led me to a quiet corner and gave me one of the best lessons of my life. "I was a prisoner of the Japanese during the war," he said. "And the reason I survived and others did not is that I never lost face. If you lose your temper in front of people you do not know, you lose their respect and it is almost impossible to win it back. You must keep control—if you cannot control yourself, then you have no chance of controlling others. The reason the horse ran away was that your sword was slapping against his side as you began to trot. He thought you were urging him on to go faster and faster." I have never forgotten his advice.

He may have been responsible for the fact that my room was never cleaned, but Omar Sharif was fantastic to work with. A great actor, he can maintain a poker face better than almost anyone else I know—I'm not surprised he's a champion bridge player—and he's a cool customer, too. We were once sitting in a bar when a group of tough Austrian lads came in. They had had a bit too much to drink and saw these two actors sitting there and started making loud comments about us and our sexuality—all in perfect English. We just sat there, ignoring them, nodding away and chatting. They ratcheted up the invective, but we hung in there and kept our cool, which seemed to rile them even more. Of course what they didn't know was that sitting all around us at the other tables was our entire stunt team, just waiting for us to give them the nod. After about ten minutes, the Austrians could take it no longer, pushed back their chairs and squared up to us. They wanted a fight. Omar and I stood up, too—they must have thought, blimey, these actors have got some guts—but then the stunt team stood up— and, well, I'm afraid there was a bit of a ruckus and some of those Austrians ended up being thrown out of windows that were firmly shut.

I'd taken on *The Last Valley* because I'd wanted to try my hand at something a bit more serious. Ever since *Alfie* I had been identified with his character as a bird-pulling Cockney bloke and I was determined to try to change that view. In *The Last Valley*, "The Captain" and his group of mercenaries wind up spending the winter in a peaceful valley. He was apparently a man of great brutality. I wanted to get behind that to show that in fact he was someone who had other qualities; that he was a man who had come to understand the futility of war. It is an understated performance—like most of my work—but it's one of the ones that I am most proud of, although I knew pretty well as soon as we finished filming that it wasn't going to work at the box office, despite the quality of the movie and the brilliant score by John Barry. It may have been timing again—we were in the middle of the Vietnam War and the Middle Ages seemed irrelevant—and it may have been the level of violence (the censors asked for some of the bloodier scenes to be cut), but I was right: the film was not regarded as a success when it was eventually released.

The 1960s ended for me on a bit of a depressing note. The decade had given me so much, but I was only too aware that all good things come to an end and that things—and people— were already moving on. Dennis Selinger and I flew off to spend Christmas with Harry Saltzman and his family in Acapulco and I took the chance to pause and decide what I wanted to do next. I had spent the past ten years going from film to film almost without a break. I had worked with some great producers, but I had also worked with some really bad ones. Now, I thought, I would do something I had always wanted to do: produce a film of my own. I made sure that my next project allowed me to do just that, alongside my friend, professional producer Michael Klinger.

There's a danger, when making films, of romanticizing violence. I know only too well what the other side of violence looks like and I wanted to show that other side in *Get Carter*, a film based on a novel called *Jack's Return Home* by Ted Lewis. In it, I play a tough London-based gangster who goes home to Newcastle to avenge the murder of his brother and deals ruthlessly with anyone who gets in his way. Mike Hodges, the director, came up with the idea of casting John Osborne as the gangster boss and I thought he'd be brilliant—which he was. We'd known each other well since before his *Look Back in Anger* days—we'd been out of work together—and we were old friends. He loved playing the tough guy and his performance is truly chilling.

Get Carter is the complete antithesis of films such as *The Italian Job*, with its larky criminals who get beaten up and appear in the next scene with barely a scratch on them. The only film I had ever seen (as a kid growing up in the Elephant) that seemed to me to give a halfway realistic portrait of gangland life was *Brighton Rock*, the Boulting Brothers' film of Graham Greene's novel, starring Richard Attenborough. Michael Klinger and I were determined to achieve at least as convincing a portrait as that.

Michael Klinger, Mike Hodges and I decided to shoot the film in Newcastle upon Tyne. Once a great shipbuilding town, it had long since fallen into decline and gave us exactly the dark and brooding atmosphere of urban decay we were looking for. Many people have taken *Get Carter* as a Western, and we were certainly aiming for that sense of a wild frontier. As for me, I wanted the challenge of creating a real villain. Up until *Get Carter* I'd more or less always played nice characters—even Alfie is nice in his way, a real charmer—but Jack Carter is a cold, cold man.

People often think that *Get Carter* is a film about vengeance, but it's not: it's about family honor. I understood all that, because there was a very strong code of honor where I came from. It was a bit like Sicily: you kissed a girl and the brothers came round and you had to get married the following Saturday or you would besmirch the family name—and you wouldn't get away with that. I was in a club somewhere in the West End just after *Get Carter* was released and the gangster I'd based Jack Carter on—not that he ever knew it—came up to me and said, "I saw that *Get Carter*, Michael." Uh-oh, I thought, but I kept a dead straight face and I said, "Did you?" and he went on, "Biggest load of crap I've ever seen." "Really?" I said, looking round for the exit. "What makes you think that?" And he said, "Michael, you weren't married, you didn't have any kids and you had no responsibilities. You don't understand why we do things. Me, with no special skills, I had to hold on to a wife and kids." And I thought—no special skills? He'd only killed about five people—not that he'd ever been charged with anything, but everyone knew . . . and I said, "Oh, blimey—you're right. That was a terrible mistake." I completely agreed with everything he said. You don't want to argue with someone like that.

Violence has consequences and you don't often see that in movies. It's a sort of pornography: people are struck time and time again and the next time they appear they just sport a small Band-Aid, not even a black eye or missing teeth. If you were a real victim of the violence you see in some films, you would be in hospital or dead. In *Get Carter* you see the effect of one whack, although we never cut to the gore.

CHAPTER NINE

FALLING IN LOVE

Get Carter was followed very swiftly by *Kidnapped*—a dud from the very start and the only film I've never been paid for. I couldn't wait to get back to London from location in Scotland, but when I finally got home, I was in a very poor way. I was drinking and smoking heavily and although I enjoyed living in my Grosvenor Square flat, I felt something was missing from my life. I had set up Stanley comfortably, and I had bought Mum a big house in Streatham, a suburb of south London, which I split up into flats so that various family members could move there with her. Everyone was happy with their new arrangements—but what about me? I was thirty-eight, unmarried, although not, you might say, without offers, and yet something in me felt unfulfilled. I looked back at my life and at the enormous journey I had traveled and I asked myself where I had really been happiest. Hollywood was a high, of course, and the last ten years had included some fantastic experiences, but it hadn't exactly been tranquil. And then I thought back to Norfolk. That's what I need to do, I decided. I need to become an evacuee again.

I wanted to be able to get to London quickly but I wanted to live in real countryside. Berkshire seemed to me to offer the best of both worlds; the Queen seemed to agree with me as she obviously enjoyed spending time at Windsor Castle. So I started to look for a place on the River Thames and I found what I wanted almost at once. The Mill House was two hundred years old and sat on a hundred yards of river frontage in five acres just outside the little village of Clewer, near Windsor. Both house and garden were in a bit of a state, but although this suited me, I decided to subject the place to the ultimate test and invited Mum and my old friend Paul Challen, from Youth Club days in the Elephant, along to view it. I'd read somewhere that you should only make an offer on a new home if, when you take your nearest and dearest along to see it, they sit down. When I got back from looking round the garden, I found them both sitting outside having tea with the owner's wife. I made an offer on the spot.

I've always loved gardens and gardening and over the course of my life I've created a few gardens from scratch. For me, working with your hands, designing and growing things, is the best form of therapy money can buy and tackling the Mill House garden was the beginning of a long slow climb back to health and happiness. In fact I had been given a timely helping hand on the health front from a surprising source. I was at a party in London one evening and chain-smoking as usual when I looked down just in time to see a hand snake into my jacket pocket, pull out my fag packet and hurl it on the fire. I opened my mouth to give the thief a bollocking and stopped. It was Tony Curtis. "That's the third cigarette you've had since you arrived," he said severely and proceeded to outline a very clinically detailed and convincing argument about the risks posed by smoking. I had been smoking for years—two packets of French Gauloises a day, which I considered very chic, but I did think about his warning and gave up cigarettes for a year, and then fell by the wayside and started smoking cigars. Many years later I was having dinner at Gregory Peck's house and when I went through to the drawing room to have a cigar I found myself sitting next to Yul Brynner. "I have lung cancer," he said to me quietly. I was absolutely stunned and, embarrassed, started to stub out my cigar, but he put his hand on my arm to stop me. "Don't bother," he said. "I'm already dying; your smoke can't harm me." He looked at me for a moment. "Do you know what I did yesterday?" "No," I said. "I made an anti-smoking commercial. To be played after my death." A few months later, Yul did die and the commercial was indeed shown. I took no notice. Yul smoked cigarettes, I reasoned; I smoked cigars and in any case, I didn't inhale (now where have I heard that before?). But one evening I was watching TV at home in Britain, cigar in hand, when the snooker player Alex "Hurricane" Higgins came on to do an anti-smoking commercial. I barely recognized him. He had lost a lot of weight and he looked terrible: he had throat cancer, he said. I sat there for a while, shocked, and then I put my cigar in the ash tray, got up and walked out of the room—and I have never smoked again.

But back in the seventies, although I had given up smoking cigarettes, I was still drinking very heavily. And I was bored. I had plenty of money, plenty of friends, plenty of work, but nothing seemed to satisfy me. I hadn't yet moved in permanently to Mill House so I was still spending a lot of time in London and although I would go out every night to all my old haunts, somehow my heart just didn't seem to be in it anymore. One evening I decided I was just too tired to hit the clubs and rang up Paul and asked him round for dinner. We'd watch television, I suggested, have an evening in. He seemed a bit surprised by this sudden onset of domesticity, but came round anyway and we settled down for the night.

What happened next is a story I'm often asked to tell. It sounds incredible but it's true and I often go cold when I think of all the things that could have gone wrong. I could have changed channels (although admittedly there were only two then—I was changing them, back in those pre-remote days, by means of a broom handle so I didn't have to leave my seat); I could have gone into the kitchen for a drink; we could have decided to go out after all. In the end, though, it's no use speculating on what might have happened, because what did happen is that during the commercial break, an ad for Maxwell House coffee came on and there, right in front of me, was the most beautiful woman I had ever seen. I threw the broomstick aside and crouched next to the screen, trying to get a closer look. "What on earth are you doing?" asked Paul. "You gone mad or something?" "That girl," I said hoarsely. "That girl is the most beautiful girl in the world. I have to meet her." "Now look, Michael," Paul said kindly. "That ad's been shot in Brazil. What are you going to do? Fly to Brazil?" "Yes," I said simply. He looked at me sympathetically, but I could tell he thought I'd really lost it.

I paced around the flat for a bit, desperate for time to pass so I could ring up Maxwell House headquarters the next morning and find out who had shot the commercial. Eventually I could bear it no longer and Paul and I grabbed our coats and headed down to a club called Tramp to find Johnny Gold, who could always be relied on for a sympathetic ear. Johnny pointed out beautiful girl after beautiful girl to me on the dance floor, but it was no good, I was in love. Eventually, emotionally wrung out, I decided to call it a night and just as I was leaving, I ran into Nigel Politzer, a guy I vaguely knew. "Going so soon?" he asked. "And alone?" "I'm in love!" I declared dramatically. "And it's hopeless. I saw this beautiful Brazilian girl on television tonight and I may never see her again." Nigel patted my shoulder. "Which show?" he asked. "It wasn't a show," I replied mournfully. "It was an ad for Maxwell House." He burst out laughing. "The girl with the maracas?" he asked. "Yes!" I howled. "How did you know?" "Because I work for the company that made the ad," he said. "Then you can help me!" I clawed at his jacket. "Paul and I are going to Brazil tomorrow to find her. Do you know how we can get in touch with her when we arrive?" Nigel roared with laughter again. "No need, mate! She's not in Brazil and she's not Brazilian. Her name is Shakira Baksh, she's Indian and she lives off the Fulham Road."

I spent the rest of the night alternating between bliss and despair. The Fulham Road—only a mile or so from my flat! So near—and, yet, what if she already had a boyfriend? What if she was married? Nigel had promised to give her a call the next morning and ask her if she would let me have her phone number. Eventually I dropped off into a fitful sleep only to be shaken awake by Paul at around noon. "Nigel's on the phone," he said. I grabbed the receiver. "She's agreed to give you her number," said Nigel. He sounded a long way away. Grabbing a pen, I took the number down in a shaking hand.

It took two vodkas and a cigar before I made the first call, only to be told by a flatmate (female, I noted with relief) that Shakira was in the shower and I should ring back in half an hour. It took another vodka and another cigar before I was ready to make the second call. This time she herself answered. Yes, she knew who I was. Yes, she had seen some of my films (no mention of whether or not she had liked them). But I should be aware that she didn't make a habit of giving her number to strangers. "Of course not!" I dithered and went on to make some silly point about us not being strangers because I had seen her on TV. I could almost hear her arching her exquisite eyebrow on the other end of the phone. Hastily I attempted to recover my position by asking if I could take her out to dinner. I could, it seemed, but not for ten days. *Ten days?* I agreed, of course, but those ten days were the slowest of my life and I counted the hours and minutes before I could call her again. The day before our date, two vodkas down, I called and suggested that I pick her up at eight the following evening. She wasn't having any of it. "No," she said firmly. "You give me *your* address and I'll pick *you* up." Not unreasonable—but by this stage I would have agreed to just about anything she asked.

I needed more vodkas to get through the following twenty-four hours, but by the time eight o'clock came around I had eliminated any sign of booze or cigars in the flat and had gargled with so much mouthwash my mouth was on fire. I don't think I have ever been as nervous as I was that evening, waiting for the doorbell.

At last it went: a long assertive ring. Trying my best to remain cool, I walked calmly to the door, opened it and fell in love. Shakira was even more beautiful in the flesh than she had been on-screen. I couldn't speak. She held out her hand for me to shake and I took it but then just held it because I never wanted to let it go again. Eventually I came to my senses and ushered her into my flat—and she walked into my flat and into my life, and she has been at the very center of it ever since. We did, of course, eventually make it out to dinner. And I discovered that she was from a Kashmiri family that had immigrated to Guyana, which was where she was born, and that as Miss Guyana, she had come to England to compete in the Miss World competition. "Where did you come in?" I blurted out gauchely. "Third," she said sternly.

I can't remember everything we talked about now, but I will never forget the intensity of our first meeting. We spent the next few weeks constantly in each other's company, until she had to leave for a modeling job in Mexico and I had to go to Malta to make *Pulp*, the second film Michael Klinger and I produced together. This would be a good test, we decided. Our affair had become so intense so quickly that I think we were both frightened by the strength of our feelings and a week apart seemed like a good idea. In fact it was a terrible idea; we missed each other desperately and phoning Mexico from Malta in 1972 was an almost impossible task. As soon as Shakira's shoot was over, she flew to join me in Malta and we have been together ever since.

What first drew me to Shakira was, of course, her beauty—and she is one of the most beautiful women I have ever seen. But it was not just that—after all, I was in the movie business and I worked with beautiful women every day. She has a far more important quality, which I sensed the moment she walked into my flat: she is a completely good person. I have met very few people in my life with no bad side, but she is one of them—she doesn't have a nasty bone in her body. Of course, like most women, she has a steel wire running right through her should you choose to find it, but although she is a very strong person she is also incredibly sensitive to everything and everyone. There is absolutely no wickedness or unkindness in her anywhere—as I always say, I have enough of those for the two of us—and on that very first evening with her I could see that straightaway.

When we got back to England, Shakira moved first into my Grosvenor Square flat and then, when the lease expired, we decided to make the Mill House our permanent base. This, I realized, was what had been missing from my life: the chance to make a country home—and a garden—with the woman I loved. When Shakira pointed out what no one else had dared to, that I was drinking at a really quite dangerous level, I made an immediate decision to cut back drastically and then—as now—rarely drink anything besides wine with my meals.

So healthier, happier and certainly thinner and fitter from all the exercise I was getting from gardening, I felt in top form. Professionally I was facing one of my greatest ever challenges—playing opposite Laurence Olivier in the film version of Anthony

Shaffer's stage play, *Sleuth*, which involved fourteen long, tough weeks on set, but I was going back to the Mill House and to Shakira every evening and so I felt more than equal to the task. Summer slipped into autumn and I thought nothing could disturb our idyll together until, one day, I was passing our bedroom and heard the sound of Shakira sobbing. "What is it?" I asked, coming over to sit next to her on the bed. I had never seen her cry before and I was worried. She looked up at me. "I'm pregnant," she said. "But that's wonderful!" I could hardly believe it: we were going to have a baby! "But I thought you wouldn't want a child," she said, smiling through her tears. "You never said anything about wanting one." There was something else I had never said anything about either. "Will you marry me?" I asked. "It's not just because I'm pregnant?" she asked suspiciously. "No," I said. And it wasn't. I could not imagine a future without Shakira and as far as I was concerned we were already committed to each other—so much so that, I admit, the fact that we had not actually gone through the formalities had simply passed me by.

We were so in love that it had not really occurred to me to wonder what my mother's reaction to the news of our marriage might be. I have always loathed racism whenever I encountered it. My memories of the way the white bosses treated the black workers in South Africa when we were filming *Zulu* and the appalling prejudice I encountered in Louisiana when we were on location for *Hurry Sundown* still make me shudder. I'll never forget the way the Ku Klux Klan, who had dubbed us "the nigger picture" because black and white actors were working together, targeted us: peppering our dressing caravans full of bullet holes during the night and even blowing up the hotel swimming pool because we had all swum in it together. I had traveled widely and had many friends of different color but I did wonder what my mother would think about the fact that I was marrying an Indian woman—or rather, I was marrying a woman who happened to be Indian. In fact she made no comment at all except in passing one weekend when she was staying with us at the Mill House. "Where's Sharika?" she asked. She never did manage to get her name right. It was eleven o'clock in the morning, and I told her that Shakira was still in bed. "They do sleep a lot, Indians, don't they?" said Ma and it was her only racial comment ever. In fact Shakira was just tired from being in the early stages of her pregnancy, but I let that pass.

The only racism we ever encountered in the English countryside occurred a few years later. We were relaxing at the Mill House one evening, when the doorbell rang and Shakira went to answer it. "I need to see Mr. Caine," the man standing outside insisted and, handing his hat and coat to Shakira, walked straight past her. I came out of the living room to see what all this was about. "Mr. Caine?" the man said, holding his hand outstretched. "Good to meet you. I wonder"—he turned round and looked at Shakira—"could we have a word *in private*?" I took him into my office. "How can I help?" I asked warily. He lowered his voice. "Are you aware that the house for sale further down the street is going to be bought by *Indians*?" He paused for full effect. "Once you get them in you never get them out again!" "It is a problem," I agreed, ushering him out. "And it's one I fully understand." I steered him past the living room where Shakira was curled up on the sofa watching TV. "This is my wife," I said. The man's jaw dropped. "Once you get them in," I said, "you never get them out again." The man grabbed his hat and coat and fled and never came back.

We got married in Las Vegas on January 8, 1973. The agent Dennis Selinger flew out with us to give Shakira away and we were joined there by Jerry Pam, my Hollywood press agent. I had to be in LA anyway for the publicity tour of a picture, so we managed to keep the whole thing a secret. The ceremony took place in the "Little Chapel on the Green"—so named because it was surrounded by a strip of AstroTurf rather than for any resemblance to an English village parish church—and it was a glorious mixture of style and commerce. The basic wedding cost a bargain $75, but there were some optional extras . . . flowers for the bride, buttonholes for the gentlemen, photographs of the vows, an audiotape—we paid (or rather Dennis paid) for the lot. The only hitch occurred just before the actual ceremony when, sitting rather nervously in the waiting room, I glanced up at all the pictures of the happy couples who had passed through the Little Chapel on the Green on their way to wedded bliss. They included more than a few Hollywood reprobates and I knew for a fact that the marriages so triumphantly displayed were all long since finished.

The ceremony was over very quickly and Shakira and I emerged onto the main strip of Las Vegas as man and wife. A quick dinner, and then it was back to the airport and a plane back to LA. As we strolled back into the Beverly Wilshire, as if nothing had happened, we congratulated ourselves on having got away with the whole thing but somehow word had got out and we found ourselves moved to one of the bridal suites. And not just any one—perhaps to honor Shakira, they had put us in the Indian one. It was beautiful, but in an (in my view) unnecessary nod to tradition, not only was the bed suspended from the ceiling, but each of the bedposts featured a bell, which tinkled gaily every time the bed moved. I didn't feel inclined to provide the other hotel guests or staff with any evidence of our amorous inclinations and was determined to get the bells off. I struggled for a bit without success, and was about to give up when I had a bright idea. Room Service obliged. And with the buns from four hamburgers stuffed inside the bells, we passed a silent night.

I had vowed never to get married again—until I met Shakira.

And then it wasn't about getting married: it was about marrying Shakira. To me, the wedding ceremony is the least important thing about getting married. I always worry a bit about massive weddings and whether people have them because they are trying to convince themselves they are doing the right thing—as if they think that spending a huge amount of money will make up for up a lack of confidence in their choice of husband or wife. That said, I gave both my daughters grand weddings when the time came, because it was what they wanted and because they wanted to do it "properly"—and I loved doing it. As for wedding anniversaries, we don't make a song and dance about ours—in fact I have been known to forget it completely. And when I do remember, it's most likely to be a bottle of champagne and some flowers. But for me, what's really important is the way we live every day; because we are so much in love with each other, every day is a celebration of our love and the specific date doesn't matter. But the fortieth is on its way—and after that, the fiftieth—and that really will be some party, I can tell you!

While I continued on the publicity tour—a grueling twenty-two-city schedule—Shakira went to New York to visit her mother, Swabera, known to all of us as Saab, who was now living in Queens. Saab had spent Christmas with us and had got on like a house on fire with everyone, including my mother, but Shakira was still nervous about telling her that not only had we got married, but that she was three months pregnant. In the end she took her mother out to lunch and confessed everything. "She just smiled, Michael!" Shakira told me on the phone the next day. "She said she'd read all about it in the *New York Post* a month ago!"

I couldn't wait to get home and be with Shakira again and we spent an idyllic spring and early summer at the Mill House getting ready for the baby, due in July. I was determined to play my part and prided myself on the way I had thoroughly prepared mentally for what was to come. Even so I was taken aback when I arrived at the clinic with Shakira in early labor to be handed not only a set of scrubs, but also a pair of white rubber waders. Waders? There would be so much blood I might need *waders*?

The labor lasted twelve hours. In the end, although I dutifully donned the waders, I stayed up near Shakira's head, pushing when she did, so enthusiastically that I thought I might give myself a hernia. We heaved together on cue until the obstetrician gave a sudden cry—"the head!"—picked up some scissors, which he waved menacingly in the air, and then plunged them into Shakira's nether regions. At this point I was nearly sick—on my waders, this time, rather than my shoes—but then I saw his triumphant expression and the lock of black hair he held up between his fingers. "Nearly there!" he said encouragingly and with a few more heaves, our daughter was born.

While Natasha was taken away to be weighed and measured, I knelt by Shakira's bed, covering her with kisses. When a nurse brought her back again, we held her between us, marveling at how perfect she was. Eventually I was sent home so that my wife and daughter could rest—but I was on such a high I went straight round to Dennis's place to tell him the news. One glass of wine led to another, and I was just beginning to relax when the phone rang. Dennis picked it up. "It's for you, Michael," he said. My heart started pounding. The only person who knew where I was going was Shakira. I took the receiver. "I'm afraid there's a bit of a problem," said Dr. Bourne. "We've had to move the baby to the intensive care unit at King's College Hospital. I think you should come here right away."

I have no recollection of how I got to the hospital, but I will always remember walking into that intensive care unit. There must have been about thirty incubators, each with its own tiny inhabitant. "I don't understand," I said to Dr. Bourne, trying to keep the fear out of my voice. "She wasn't premature—and she was six pounds twelve ounces." It wasn't her size, he explained. A sharp-eyed night nurse had been doing her rounds and noticed that our daughter was struggling to breathe; she had called Dr. Bourne and he saw at once that her lungs had collapsed. She had cried lustily at birth, so there had been no reason to suspect this might happen and there was, he assured me, a 70 percent chance of survival. Those seem like good enough odds in a bar-room brawl, but to a new father standing by an incubator, gazing at all the tubes and wires attached to his tiny daughter's body and watching the monitor bleep with each beat of her heart, they seemed very frightening indeed.

Perhaps the worst thing of all was being able to do nothing. The doctors and nurses—who were wonderful—flitted from incubator to incubator, calmly reading gauges, taking temperatures, adjusting drips. I just stood there, helplessly. Eventually a kind nurse showed me how to wash my hands with antiseptic soap and then pointed out a little hole in the side of our baby's incubator. My hands were too big to fit, but I did manage to slip a finger through and touch the little hand nearest to me. To my astonishment, the baby uncurled her hand and slowly curled it again round my finger. Her grip was so powerful that I felt sure that this was a life force that could not be extinguished. I sat there, holding her hand and listening to the soft steady bleeps of the monitor that told me her heart was still beating, until I was told to go home.

The following two weeks were two of the longest of my whole life but thankfully our daughter recovered and I was able to take both Shakira and the baby back to the safe haven of the Mill House. We had given our child two names, the Christian one of Natasha and Shakira's choice, the Moslem one of Halima, which means wisdom. She could, we thought, decide for herself when she was older which religion—if any—she wanted: she would have a name for both. Over the rest of the summer and into the autumn, as Natasha put on weight and passed all her developmental milestones with ease, Shakira and I started to relax into the pleasures of parenthood. What we had been through had, if anything, strengthened our love for each other even more; now, with our daughter, we were bonded forever as a family.

But I am aware that it could all have been very different and the strain of it all came back to me when Natasha herself was due to give birth to her first child. I was probably as anxious as her husband, Michael, when she went into labor and I remember pacing up and down the sitting room during the long wait for news. Of course these days the anxiety is really more about the mother than the child. We'd seen pictures of the baby in the womb and so we knew he/she was fine, but I couldn't help thinking back to Natasha and how tiny and vulnerable she had been in that incubator, and how tightly she had gripped my finger. It has all turned out well—not only once, but three times!—and Natasha is an incredible mother, which is something she has learnt from Shakira. We are lucky, indeed.

CHAPTER TEN

THE BEST OF THE BEST

Despite the fact that I had felt instantly at home in Beverly Hills and love Hollywood life, what matters to me is not and has never been the trappings of stardom. I've never existed in what I've always thought of as the "Hollywood bubble"—the way some of the really massive stars do. For people like Frank Sinatra, for instance, even though he became a great friend of mine, everything was on his terms. When you went with him, you went into his world. Frank, of course, was a law unto himself; with Frank there was no equal partnership. Wherever he went he was surrounded by a retinue to smooth his way. I remember one of his guys whispering to me when I turned up one time, "Frank's in a great mood today!" (You very definitely did not want to see him in a bad mood.) I said, "And what about me? What about my bad mood?" And the guy said, "Who gives a shit? No one cares how you feel." Frank was always the Guv'nor.

But stardom comes in many guises and although Holly-wood has its fair share of egos and Guv'nors, one of the most challenging and remarkable superstars I ever worked with was Laurence Olivier. *Sleuth* is inextricably bound up with that first magical summer Shakira and I got together and it almost seemed as if I needed the time and the space that our life in the Mill House offered in such abundance to prepare myself psy-chologically for playing opposite the most celebrated actor in the world at that time. It proved to be an extraordinary experi-ence.

I was nervous enough about the acting, but I was also ner-vous about something else, which sounds a bit ridiculous now: how to address Larry. It may seem a quaint and particularly English problem, but he was "Lord Olivier" and I didn't know whether or not I should use his title. *Sleuth* is a two-hander and it seemed absurd to have to address the only other actor on set as "My Lord," but on the other hand I didn't want to get off on the wrong foot. I needn't have worried. Larry had enough imagination and grace to anticipate my concerns. He sent me a charming letter a few weeks before we began shooting. "It would be a great idea if you called me Larry."

Once that immediate problem had been dealt with I was able to focus my worries on the thing that really mattered: the work. The first rehearsal was taking place at Pinewood and we were going to use the actual sets. As I sat in the car on the way to the studio I made a pact with myself: Larry Olivier may have been one of the greatest actors of all time, but I was not going to let myself be intimidated by him or his reputation. When I arrived I made my usual preparations. I didn't want to over-familiarize myself with the set because in my first scene my character would be entering it as a stranger; on the other hand I didn't want to go blundering about either. I took myself off quietly and just walked it through. Joe Mankiewicz, who was directing, watched me go through the motions and when I had finished he came over. "Don't worry, Michael," he said. "I'll take care of you." They were just the words I needed to hear.

At precisely ten o'clock, the great man arrived. Smaller— it's true, they almost always are—than I expected, he made straight for me, hand outstretched. "Michael," he said. "We meet at last." He could not have been friendlier, but I felt far from at ease. After all, my costar was not only a great stage actor: he was a great movie actor and had been a screen idol in the thirties and forties. I looked over at Joe and wondered how he was feeling. Larry was not only a great stage director: he was a great movie director, too. . . . I wasn't the only one who would need nerves of steel over the next few weeks.

The first thing I noticed about Larry was that he treated the first rehearsal—and every subsequent one—as if it were a performance. He was incredibly intense that first day and it was all I could do to stand up to the onslaught. But there was something bothering him and he left in a rush at the end, clearly frustrated. Joe and I were just packing up and chatting when Larry burst back in. "I've worked it out!" he announced. We waited for more, but he knew the value of suspense all right. "You'll just have to wait until tomorrow," he said airily and left.

Next morning he turned up and, with a triumphant and extravagant theatrical flourish, produced what looked like a small, hairy, black caterpillar from behind his back. He held it to his upper lip. Joe and I looked at each other. "Well," he said, "what do you think?" "If you really think that's necessary . . ." began Joe warily. "I do!" Larry insisted. "I really do!" He leant forward as if to take us into his confidence. "I've discovered something." He paused for dramatic effect and took a deep breath. "I can't act with my own face," he suddenly yelled. "I have to be disguised!"

It seemed to work. From then on rehearsals ran smoothly except for something very strange: Larry couldn't remember his lines. It didn't matter how short the scene was, or how few lines he had, he simply couldn't do it. And this was a man whose last job had been onstage for three and a half hours every night in a Eugene O'Neill play. All became clear a few days later. Larry, the builder, the founder and the main driving force behind the establishment of the National Theatre, had been forced out of the project, just before the official opening. The side effects from the pills he had been taking to combat stress included memory loss.

Once Larry was off the tranquilizers, he was back to his old self—and it was a formidable self, a real force to be reckoned with. He was used to being the star of every show he was in and had no hesitation in placing himself center stage in every scene, which meant that I had to find a way to act around him. And whenever I had a line that cut across a move he wanted to do, he rather grandly ordered Joe to cut it. After this had gone on for a while I went to Joe to complain. "Don't worry, Michael," he said. "I promised you I would look after you. This is a film, not the theater and we have skilled camera operators and an editing suite. Trust me."

I did—and got my confidence back, which was just as well, as we were working up to the most difficult scene in the whole movie: Larry's character puts a gun to my head and says he is going to shoot me and I have to break down and beg for mercy. In the end, it went well and as we were walking back to the dressing rooms, Larry came up and put his arm round me. "When we started this film," he said confidentially, "I thought of you as a talented assistant." He gave another one of his dramatic pauses. "But now I see you as a partner." I don't think I have ever received a compliment that has meant more. On the last day of filming, he gave me a cherry tree for my garden. It came with a plaque that read, "To one right-thinking deceitful man from the other." I think it sums up Larry's attitude to the craft of acting—the putting on of the mask of character—perfectly.

Larry died in July 1989. His memorial service was held the following October in Westminster Abbey where his ashes were interred alongside those of the only other actor in the Abbey, Edmund Kean. With the sort of theatrical gesture that could almost have been devised by the man himself, actors who had been particularly associated with Olivier over the course of his life were asked to carry certain items that had meant something to him, to be buried with the urn. I was very honored to be part of a roll call of some of the greatest actors of our times, including Peter O'Toole and Paul Scofield, and to be given the script Olivier had used for *Henry V* to carry. It was an extraordinary national occasion and one I will never forget—although I've often wondered if I shouldn't also have slipped that little hairy black caterpillar of a mustache in among the pages.

———

Perhaps we are only now able to appreciate the incredible stream of acting talent that emerged from Britain during the middle years of the twentieth century. Some of these theatrical giants, like Olivier, moved from stage to screen (and back again); others began in the time-honored American way, as child stars. And of those, very few indeed survived such early exposure to become truly great.

Elizabeth Taylor is one of those few. To me, she epitomizes the glamour of a Hollywood star. I once worked with her in *Zee and Co.* in 1970, after I had moved into the Mill House but before I met Shakira. It was filmed at Shepperton Studios in England, and I very quickly got a sense of the awe with which she was regarded. Unlike the rest of us, who were expected to be on set at 8:30 in the morning, her contract stipulated that she didn't have to show up until 10:00—and we were given a running commentary on her journey: "She's just left the hotel . . . the car's pulling up outside . . . she's in makeup . . . she's in hair . . . she's *on her way!*" By the time she actually arrived on set, preceded by an army of minions, I was a bag of nerves. In fact I shouldn't have worried—she was delightful, utterly professional and the only actor I've ever been on set with never to mess up a line.

Of course, because Elizabeth Taylor had been a star ever since she was a child, she was used to the star treatment, but she had a great sense of humor about it all—although I wouldn't have dared tease her. Brian Hutton, the director of the film, had no such qualms. He'd heard from the older MGM staff, he told her, that unlike most child stars she was never a pain in the arse. Elizabeth graciously inclined her head to accept the compliment as was her due and said, "Thank you, Brian," in her most charming way. "So what I want to know," Brian went on, "is when did you become one?" The set went very quiet while we waited for the explosion—but when it came it was an explosion of laughter. And after only a minute or two, we all joined in.

Many years ago, Richard Burton bought Elizabeth Taylor a diamond necklace for—at that time (well, at any time, really) an extraordinary sum. Several years later I ran into her at a party and she was wearing it. She looked stunning and I was just telling her how beautiful I thought it was, when she suddenly pulled me towards her and whispered in my ear, "It's not the real one—it's paste!" "Why don't you wear the real one?" I asked. "It's too dangerous," she said, looking around her. I followed her gaze: all I could see was multimillionaires. "Surely you're safe here?" I said, pointing at the two enormous bodyguards standing behind her chair trying to pretend they were part of the furniture. "Oh—them," she said. "They're always here when I'm wearing this." I thought for a moment. "But surely you don't need them if the necklace is paste?" She looked at me pityingly. "If I didn't have the guards, Michael," she explained as if to a small child, "everyone would know it was paste."

Of course some of the truly great stars are very happy to remain discreetly behind their on-screen roles. Once I was waiting outside the Beverly Hills Hotel with Cary Grant. We had bumped into each other and were just chatting when a woman tourist suddenly noticed us and came over. She seemed very excited. "Michael Caine?" she said breathlessly. "Is it really you? I've been in Hollywood two weeks and you're the first movie star I've seen! I'm just leaving for the airport—this is my final day—and at *last* I see a real movie star!" And she looked over at Cary Grant and she said to him, "You just never see stars in Hollywood, do you?" And Cary Grant said, "No, ma'am, you don't."

As far as I'm concerned, one of the greatest stars I have worked with—one of the greatest stars I think the movie business has ever known—is Sidney Poitier. I had taken a part in *The Marseilles Contract* in the winter of 1973–74 mainly because it was being filmed in the south of France and I was keen to get Shakira and Natasha to a warmer climate. I managed that all right, but the film was not a success and when the opportunity to play opposite Sidney in the antiapartheid movie *The Wilby Conspiracy* came up, I leapt at the chance. My experiences on the set of *Zulu* had made me an implacable opponent of the apartheid system and I was pleased to be able to make a contribution to highlighting its cruelty. And of course Sidney was, and still is, one of my closest friends. He was one of the first people I met when I arrived in LA. In fact he was there at the *Gambit* party Shirley MacLaine threw for me. We got on from the very start— but our friendship was cemented and deepened by our work together on *The Wilby Conspiracy*.

In the mid-1970s, apartheid in South Africa was in full force so for obvious reasons we had to shoot in Kenya. Sidney was already a massive star in Hollywood but in Kenya he was treated like a god, whereas absolutely no one seemed to know or care who I was.

Sidney remained as cool as ever—although he did get very excited when he was invited to meet the president of Kenya,

Jomo Kenyatta. This was a great honor and Sidney was very proud of it. I was disappointed that no one had asked me to come along, but I pretended I didn't care. He was flown to Nairobi for the great meeting and I waited around for him to come back from the visit. When he turned up, I asked casually, "How did it go?" He looked at me for a minute and then he said, "The first question Jomo Kenyatta asked me was, 'And what do you do, Mr. Poitier?'"

Jomo Kenyatta may not have known who Sidney Poitier was but the staff at the Kenya Safari Club were well aware of the identity of their guest. I went there with Sidney a couple of times for dinner and I noticed that he always got much better food than the rest of us, no matter what we ordered. So I'm going to claim credit for one of the best lines in a comic movie ever, because at every dinner I had with Sidney, when the waiter said to me, "And what would you like, sir?" I'd say—just like the customer in the diner when Meg Ryan is faking an orgasm in *When Harry Met Sally*—"I'll have what he's having!"

Sidney is, of course, a mold-breaker. Always an actor first, this hugely talented man has had a great impact on the advancement of black people without ever making a big deal of it. But he can be funny with it. One evening, about ten years ago, we were both at the house of a mutual friend, Arnie Kopelson, the producer of, among other films, *Platoon*. As is usually the case when you go round to people's houses in Beverly Hills, Arnie was showing a film, a comedy with an all-black cast, in his home cinema. We finished this film without a single laugh: it was dreadful. And we all turned to Sidney, who was the only black person in the room, and he said with a completely straight face, "This movie has put African Americans back exactly eleven months."

Not only is Sidney a great friend and someone I see whenever I'm in LA, there are also a few big things in my life that he's answerable for. One of them is golf. Sidney Poitier is one of two reasons that I don't play golf. He's the kindest, gentlest person you'd ever wish to meet, but when he tried to teach me the game, I was so bad he *nearly* lost his temper with me—and I decided I'd better give up trying to learn for his sake.

After *The Wilby Conspiracy* I was keen to settle down in England for a while so I took on a so-called art movie, *The Romantic Englishwoman*. This gave me exposure to the politically active kind of star—in this case, Glenda Jackson. The whole movie turned out to be rather a serious business compared with *The Wilby Conspiracy*, which had been *about* a serious business, but still managed to be fun at the same time. Joseph Losey, the director of *The Romantic Englishwoman*, was not a bundle of laughs, for a start. He had a very grim face and didn't crack a smile from the first day of shooting to the last. I pride myself on being able to make people laugh and bet one of the crew $10 that I'd get one from Joe by the end of the film. I lost hands down.

In *The Romantic Englishwoman* I was playing a wimpy husband who lets his wife (Glenda) get up to all sorts with her insatiable lover, who was played by Helmut Berger. Glenda and I got on fine, and Helmut and I got on fine, but Glenda and Helmut didn't get on at all well and I found myself in a whole new role as I shuttled between them. Their love scenes in particular lacked conviction and I was determined to do better when it came to my turn. Love scenes are actually very hard to do in movies. For a start they are rarely romantic—both partners are usually wearing a sort of padded codpiece to prevent anything untoward and it's hard not to get a bit embarrassed. Glenda, however, seemed in complete command—although she managed to unnerve me completely. We were all set up in bed and ready to go when she held up her hand to stop proceedings and rummaged under a pillow. She'd hidden a little screw of toilet paper there and, unwrapping it, she revealed a tiny false tooth, which she popped into her mouth to fill a gap.

Somehow I just couldn't summon the same passionate zeal after that. . . .

In the autumn of 1974, Shakira and I were on a mini-honeymoon staying at the Hotel George Cinq. We'd had a wonderful long weekend and were just sitting up in bed with our first cup of coffee of the morning discussing how we'd spend the day when the phone rang. "Michael Caine?" The voice seemed unmistakable, but even so I couldn't quite believe it. Was it one of my friends? "Yes?" I said cautiously. "It's John Huston here." I nearly dropped the phone. He was very easy to imitate—I always thought if you ever heard God talk he would sound just like John Huston—but this really *was John Huston*! I shook myself. "Michael? Are you still there? I'm in the bar next door—can you spare me a few minutes?" It took me just eight to get shaved, washed and dressed and round the corner to meet the director above all directors I most admired, the man who had directed my hero Humphrey Bogart in six of his greatest films, the man I regarded as the greatest all-round movie talent of our time.

The greatest all-round movie talent of our time was sitting at the bar nursing a large vodka when I walked in. When my own drink arrived I downed a large slug of it without flinching and he nodded approvingly. "For twenty years," he began, "I've been trying to make a movie based on a short story by Rudyard Kipling called 'The Man Who Would Be King.' I had it all set up. In fact"—he paused and looked me in the eye—"the two stars I had lined up were sitting right where you are now." It would have been cooler to say nothing but I couldn't help myself. "Who were they?" I asked. "Gable and Bogart," said John Huston. I drew in my breath. There was a dramatic pause. "And then they both went and died on me." There was another long pause while he looked down mistily into his glass and I tried to work out what all this meant. At last he looked up again. "But I've got the backing now and I want you to play

Peachy Carnehan." I hardly dared to ask, but went ahead anyway. "Which part was Bogart going to play?" I blurted out. "Peachy," said John. "I'll do it," I said. "Without reading the script?" he asked, raising one of those bushy eyebrows. I had to admit it looked a bit eager. I tried to calm down and be sensible. "And the Gable character?" I asked. "He's called Daniel Dravot," said John, "and he's Peachy's best friend." I sincerely hoped it would be someone that could be *my* best friend. This time it was my turn to raise an eyebrow. "Sean Connery," he said. There was nothing more to be said.

Peachy and Danny were two sergeants with the British Army in India who go AWOL in an attempt to become kings of the ancient—and fabulously rich—kingdom of Kafiristan. We were shooting the movie on location in Morocco and *our* ancient and fabulously rich kingdom was the Mamounia, a magnificent old hotel in Marrakesh. It was a wonderful place to base ourselves and although we had to get used to the rather slow pace of service in North Africa in those days, it was a haven for our team. I have very happy memories of the shoot. As well as Sean, I was working with Christopher Plummer to whose Hamlet I had played Horatio in my one and only venture into Shakespeare just before *Zulu* came out, and the camera crew, sound technicians and one of the assistant directors were also old friends. In John Foreman as producer, too, we had a man who shared John Huston's vision for the movie—which is not always the case—and so the team was a joy to work with from top down.

For me, as ever, one of the great pleasures was having Shakira along on the shoot. In fact it turned out that it was just as well she had joined me. On the night before we began, John Huston told us the news that the girl due to play the part of Roxanne, the beautiful Indian princess, had dropped out at the last minute. He seemed to be casting his eyes around the room rather helplessly looking for inspiration, but I couldn't help noticing that his gaze kept returning to my beautiful wife. Shakira had noticed it, too. "No," she said firmly. "Absolutely not." John shrugged and smiled enigmatically. "Of course not, honey," he said smoothly.

I spent most of the night trying to persuade Shakira to have a go, but she was adamant and eventually I gave up. I didn't blame her—it was not what she had signed up for and I could understand her reluctance. She turned up loyally on set, though, to watch us start shooting and I saw John go over to where she was standing, during a break. After just a moment she started smiling, after a few more minutes she was actually laughing and just before we began shooting again John announced that Shakira had agreed to play the part of Princess Roxanne. I've never managed to find out what he said, but I'd like to know!

Shakira was very nervous about stepping into the role at such short notice and with so little experience, but John was a brilliant director who inspired confidence in all of us. I was probably more nervous than Shakira was herself and John eventually told me to make myself scarce during her scenes unless I was actually in them, because I was not helping matters. In the end she played her part magnificently—including a very difficult scene in which she had to go into a strange sort of fit or trance, something which would have been hard enough for a very experienced actress let along a beginner.

In *The Man Who Would Be King*, John Huston lived up to every inch of his reputation as a great director. Throughout the making of the movie he addressed Sean and me as "Danny" and "Peachy," even off set, and he was somehow able to convey with the minimum of fuss or explanation exactly what he was looking for in a character. He didn't tell you much, he just watched you very closely and you knew you were doing it right just by looking at him. He held the view—rare among directors—that good actors know what they are doing and should be left alone to do it if at all possible. I said to him once, "You don't really tell us much, do you?" And he said, "Two things, Michael. The art of good direction is casting. If you cast it right you don't have to tell the actors what to do. Also," he went on, "you're being paid a lot of money to do this, Michael. You should be able to get it right on your own—you don't need me to tell you what to do!" He only ever stopped me once mid-take, when I had to tell Christopher Plummer (who was playing Rudyard Kipling) what Danny and I were up to. Kipling warns us that what we were planning was very dangerous and Peachy replies, "We are not little men." I put the emphasis on the word "not," but John held up his hand. "We are not *little* men," he said. I shrugged and did it his way and when we finished the take I saw he was smiling. He was right. We were not little men—under Huston's direction we became giants.

Working with Sean was another great pleasure. He is one of the most generous and unselfish actors I have ever worked with and because we trusted each other—and because John trusted both of us—it meant that we could risk some improvisation and experiment, which I think paid off in the finished film. Off the set, Sean and I were not seeing as much of each other as you might have thought. He was a fanatical golfer— he'd had to learn the game for the James Bond movie *Goldfinger* where there's a scene in which James Bond and the arch-villain Goldfinger have to play golf with each other—and he was spending most of his spare time on the links. Trying to take an interest in my friend's all-consuming hobby, I asked him what playing golf on a Moroccan golf course was like and he told me that if you lost your ball in the lake you couldn't get it back because of the crocodiles. I was a bit puzzled as to why he seemed *quite* so obsessed with the game but after a while I found out why. He had met a beautiful French woman on the course, someone who shared his passion for the game. . . . Michelene went on to become his second wife.

Sean lives full-time in Nassau these days, but we stay in

touch regularly. The last time we met we had dinner in London and had a great time reminiscing about the old days. I reminded him about how tough he'd been. There was one time in the early 1960s, when we were in a London club together and it was amateur night and people were standing up to sing. They weren't very good, but they were only kids trying their best. There was a group of drunks behind us and they started taking the piss out of the kids and Sean spoke to them a couple of times politely, asking, "Will you give the kids a chance? They're trying to make their way in life." Finally Sean had had enough and he got up, said, "Shut the fuck up!" and knocked all four of them out. I didn't even leave the chair. You wouldn't mess with Sean unless you were very silly.

The relationship that developed between John Houston, John Foreman, Chris Plummer, Sean and me made for a very special atmosphere on set. This was just as well, because *The Man Who Would Be King* was a hard picture to make. I had picked up terrible diarrhea and had to play most of my scenes with half an eye on the location of the portable toilets—not that they offered much of a refuge. I remember rushing over to them once, desperate, and being knocked back by the unbelievable stench and the cloud of flies. The attendant, who was reading the paper, apparently oblivious, had forgotten the disinfectant. I bawled him out for this, but he just shrugged. "Come back at lunchtime," he suggested. "The flies will have moved on to the kitchen by then." You couldn't fault his logic.

Chronic diarrhea and—for me—a mild but frightening typhoid attack from breathing in filthy dust and dried camel dung were unpleasant enough, but neither Sean nor I was ever in real physical danger. The closest Sean got to it was shooting the last scene of the film, where his character is executed by being forced to stand on a rope bridge above a ravine before the ropes are cut and he plunges to his death. The bridge was built specially, but it seemed to both of us to be swaying in the breeze in a rather too convincing manner. I couldn't manage more than a few steps, but Sean had to go right out into the middle. "It's leaning to the right," he said to John Huston. "It wasn't doing that yesterday." "Ah—that's because yesterday you didn't have to walk on it and today you do," said John. "You're looking at it from a different point of view." I could see Sean weighing this up, but there was no way he wouldn't accept the challenge and he turned round and walked straight out to the middle of the bridge. His character has to sing as the ropes are cut and Sean sang at the top of his voice, with not a wobble in it, as the fake ropes were cut—but there was no mistaking his relief when he got back to solid ground.

The real hero then took his place. Joe Powell was an experienced stuntman and the bottom of the ravine had been filled with foam and mattresses, but it was a genuine heart-in-the-mouth moment when the axes fell on the real ropes and then he leapt off the bridge. It was windy and I've never forgotten looking down at those mattresses, which seemed to present a very small landing target all those hundreds of feet below. Joe fell so skillfully, twisting and turning on the way down to avoid all the sharp rocks, countering the pull of the wind as he went, and at the very last minute straightening himself out so that he hit the mattresses dead center. There was a gasp of relief all round and then cheers as he got up uninjured, and John Huston turned to me and said, "That's the darnedest stunt I've ever seen."

I adored John Huston. He was like a father figure to me, a director who was very gentle with actors because he loved being one himself. Men like John have an aura about them that you can sense from a mile away. You could call it charisma or you could call it star quality, but whatever it is, it commands attention and respect. In a very different and rather less reassuring way, one of the other Hollywood greats whom I got to know well and who had this in spades was, of course, Frank Sinatra. We first met at the *Gambit* party, but we got to know each other better when I started dating his daughter Nancy, shortly afterwards, and he took us on a memorable weekend trip to hear him sing with Count Basie in Las Vegas.

Nancy and I flew to Las Vegas with Frank in his private plane and I sat next to him on the flight, quite unable to believe that I was there next to my idol. He noticed that I seemed a bit on edge and asked me what was wrong and I told him and he laughed. When he first came to Hollywood, he said, he was equally struck dumb when he found himself sitting next to Ronald Colman. "Relax!" Frank said to me. "We're all the same. We live, love and die." And then he told me his motto, which was: "Live every day as though it's your last—because one day it will be."

When we got to our hotel, however, I realized that Frank wasn't quite the easygoing guy he sometimes seemed. The Sands Hotel consisted of a squat square block with a tall tower next to it and I was booked into a suite in the square block. As I was going along the corridor I bumped into Frank. "Where's Nancy's room?" I asked, without thinking. He smiled and led me to a window. "Up there," he said, pointing to the very top of the tower. He then opened the door of the suite next to mine and said, "And you're down here with me."

My intentions were entirely honorable as far as Nancy was concerned, in fact, but I was a bit worried. When I first arrived in Hollywood, Frank had just charged his friend the scriptwriter Harry Kurnitz with keeping an eye on Mia Farrow (Frank and Mia were about to get married). Harry became one of my mates and he, Mia and I all went out together in a gang with Steve Brandt. We were very effective at keeping Mia away from trouble until one evening we went to a film premiere together and the four of us were photographed in a row holding hands and smiling. Innocent stuff—until I opened the papers the next day and saw the same picture, but with Harry and Steve cut off the end and the caption, *"Mia with new beau Michael*

Caine." It was a nasty moment: I was only too aware that it wasn't a good idea to get on the wrong side of Frank. Luckily Harry was there to put in a good word for me and disaster was avoided.

Over the years I became good friends with Frank and, later, Shakira and I would enjoy spending time with him and his wife, Barbara. I've often wondered why Frank liked me, but I think it was because he thought I was funny—and he liked to laugh. He also liked my accent and he used to say to the people around him, "Did you hear that? *Good morning?* Did you hear the way he said that?" And he always said I made too many movies. Every time we met he'd say, "How many movies you make today?" and I'd say, "Only one, Frank, only one." I think Frank also found me a bit unusual. He didn't suffer fools and I think he respected the fact that I didn't defer to him. He was very generous about my acting, too. He loved *Alfie,* in particular. It wasn't surprising, I guess—he *was* Alfie and then some! I think there was also a connection between us because of our backgrounds: he was a slum kid and I was a slum kid. He liked the fact that I wasn't a toffee-nosed Englishman. And then there was his affection for London. He told me about the time his career was in the doldrums and how he'd just finished *From Here to Eternity* and they asked him to go to the Columbia offices in Wardour Street to see the finished movie. "And from the moment I saw it," he said, "I knew that there I was, in London, and I was on my way back. And, Michael, I always remember it was in London."

I was in England when Frank died in 1998. Of course the surprise wasn't that he'd died, but that he lived so long. He smoked like a chimney, which was unusual for a singer, and he was a heavy drinker. One of the last occasions we met was at a dinner he gave in Palm Springs. I was standing near the bar about to place an order when Frank came over. He put his hand on my elbow. "You're not going to order a Perrier, are you,

Michael?" he said with only the faintest hint of menace. "No, Frank," I said, hastily changing my mind. "Vodka and tonic."

It seems to me that the stars of today are not the big characters I used to know and work with in Hollywood. I've just watched the Academy Awards and all the people nominated seemed to be very small young men who had just been in a vampire film. They were all dark-looking and a bit pale—as I guess you would be—and I'm not sure that among them I can identify the new De Niro, Pacino or Hoffman. There's the physical thing, too: they really do seem to be getting smaller. Sean Connery, Peter O'Toole and I are all over six foot: Tom Cruise is short and so is Jude Law. Bogart was small, but then he made it work for him by getting all the parts George Raft didn't want to do.

I suspect one of the reasons the old star system worked was because there was no TV at the time and when those big stars were up there on the huge screen they seemed much more remote than they are now when they are beamed directly into our sitting rooms. These days there's complete fluidity between movies and television and it's possible to switch between the two seamlessly. Alec Baldwin, for instance, who almost became a great film star and then suddenly he made a success of *30 Rock* and his movie career took off again. Tina Fey—to me, she's the funniest girl in the business and she makes me laugh just to look at her—began in TV and has now moved into movies. Of course, it can work the other way round—Lucille Ball started off as a movie star but the peak of her career was in television.

Stars of the magnitude of Elizabeth Taylor and Vivien Leigh—and male stars like Cary Grant, Robert Redford, Paul Newman and Clint Eastwood—have always been careful about the roles they chose. I took a different view. Between *Gambit* in the late sixties and what I thought was going to be my retirement from the movie business in 1992, I was in well over seventy films. I always took a pragmatic view: if a movie came along and I liked the look of it and I needed the work, I did it. I had no concerns about letting down my fans by playing a particular role. I am an actor and I work for a living. And I think it's why, when the time came to morph from movie star to leading actor that—once I'd got used to the idea—I was able to do so. I have always kept the example of Sir John Gielgud in my mind, too—a wonderfully gifted actor who kept working right until the end of his life. His agent told me that even aged ninety-two, Gielgud was still ringing to ask, "Are there any scripts this week? Is there any work?" And he famously sacked an agent when he was ninety-six for not getting him a part in the TV adaptation of *David Copperfield*. We worked together on one of my more obscure works, *The Whistle Blower*, which was released in 1987, and I always found him eccentric, charming and very funny.

Stars from the so-called Golden Age of Hollywood were much more remote than today's stars. There is much more of a movie community now, and actors are no longer stuck in ivory towers. Early Hollywood was rather like a closed order, and the contract system meant that the studios had complete control over their players' public image, whereas the actors control that for themselves now.

CHAPTER ELEVEN

AN ENGLISHMAN IN LA

After *The Man Who Would Be King*, I think any movie would have been a bit of a comedown, but it was 1976, the summer was glorious, we were enjoying living at the Mill House and I was filming *The Eagle Has Landed* only fifteen minutes further up the Thames. Life was good and the film could have been brilliant—the cast included Donald Sutherland, Robert Duvall, Donald Pleasence and Anthony Quayle, as well as Jenny Agutter—but despite the book, which I love, the film was never more than mediocre. I think the director, the Hollywood veteran John Sturges—who had a great reputation—had by this stage in his career rather lost interest in the movie business. He openly admitted to me one day that he only took on a picture when he needed to fund his very expensive hobby of deep-sea fishing and as soon as the filming was done, and he'd been paid, he took off. I can't pretend I haven't taken on the occasional movie for the money, but much of the real work for directors comes in the editing and postproduction work, and although it was perfectly well handled, without his input it could never have reached its potential.

The Mill House was the center of our social world in the mid-seventies and we welcomed our friends there most weekends. Sunday lunches had become quite a tradition although not all of them were as memorable as the one to which we invited Peter Sellers and his girlfriend Liza Minnelli; Liza's father, Vincent, and his companion Kay Thompson, the Broadway star; and the singer Jack Jones, with his then fiancée Susan George. Liza and Peter were so in love and I took a wonderful Polaroid photograph (then a relatively new invention) of them, as well as a group photo, to mark the occasion. Sunday lunch was just the warm-up to Liza's birthday party, which was due to be held on the following Tuesday at Rex Harrison's flat, but when I got there, I found Liza in floods of tears. She and Peter had broken up the previous day. "Look!" she said, handing me the photograph I had taken of her and Peter two days before. "Turn it over." It said, *"Thanks for the memory, Peter."*

I didn't know what to say. I was a friend of Peter's and I had had no inkling that this was about to happen. I was shocked, and sad for Liza. Unable to think of anything that would be of much comfort, I grabbed a plate of food and took an empty chair at a table beside an elderly woman I recognized vaguely. I smiled at her and then did a double take: it was Marlene Dietrich. "Michael Caine?" she demanded sharply. "Yes," I said, rather taken aback by her tone. "You are a friend of Peter Sellers?" "Yes," I said, rather more cautiously. "Well, you may tell him from me that he's a bastard to treat Liza in this way! Why are you friends with a man like him?" Her blue, blue eyes were fixed on me in a way that made me very uncomfortable. I muttered something to the effect that Peter had always been nice to me, but it didn't wash. "Liza is my goddaughter," Marlene Dietrich said coldly. By now I was gobbling down my food so I could escape. As I rose to leave the table as politely as I could, she suddenly burst out, "And you should dress better when you go out! You look like a bum!" An encounter I'll never forget!

I loved being able to host our friends at the Mill House, so I was in for a bit of a shock when my accountant summoned me to a meeting to let me know that with taxes at the unprecedented levels they were back in the seventies, we were living just too lavishly for our income. I was outraged—I had worked hard to make a life for my family and myself and I was not going to be bullied into cutting back now. There seemed only one option, and although I knew that there was much I would miss about my life in England, it was one I felt ready to take: we would move to Hollywood.

The movie producer Irwin Allen was just one of a number of friends encouraging us to leave England and move to Los Angeles—but he was the only one who also offered an inducement to do so. My mum was happy in her new home in Streatham and Dominique's career as a show-jumper was going from strength to strength, so I felt happy about making the move from that point of view, but I had a real problem. Even taking into account selling the Mill House (which I eventually did to Jimmy Page of Led Zeppelin), I couldn't afford the incredible house prices in Beverly Hills, and this is where Irwin stepped in with an offer of the lead role in a picture called *The Swarm*, to help pay for my move.

Irwin was the producer of *The Towering Inferno* and *The Poseidon Adventure*, so I reasoned that he knew a thing or two about disaster movies, and I was intrigued at the idea of working on a film with spectacular special effects. What I hadn't quite thought about was that a burning skyscraper and a huge upside-down ship are high-stakes visual drama, whereas a swarm of bees is—well, let's just say it's not in the same league. In fact, making our movie was in reality probably a great deal more dangerous than either of the other two, which merely involved plywood sets, some flames and a big water tank. *The Swarm* required us to spend much of the time filming inside big glass cages along with millions of real bees, none of which had been told they were only acting. They were all supposed to have been de-stung, but it was an inexact science and every so often there would be a yelp and the cry "Hot one!" would go up and we'd all take cover. One of my costars on the movie was Henry Fonda and it was an enormous privilege to work alongside a screen legend like him, as well as Olivia de Havilland, another movie great. Hank actually kept bees and was always handing out small pots with the modest legend "Hank's Honey" written on the sides. Unfortunately, his expert knowledge didn't extend to the lavatorial habits of bees, and he was as surprised as Fred MacMurray and I were (we were all playing scientists) when the bees were released from their boxes and took their revenge on us by immediately crapping all over our white coats. I should have taken it as an omen: when it was eventually released, the critics followed suit.

With the money from *The Swarm* and the proceeds from the Mill House we finally made the big move in autumn 1977. We had a wonderful welcome from our friends when we arrived in LA. We spent the first week moving into our lovely new home and sorting out furniture and so on. The only thing missing— unusual for Beverly Hills—was a phone, but I managed to persuade the phone company to come out on a Saturday morning and install it for us and so we were all set. That evening the composer Leslie Bricusse and his wife, Evie, close friends of ours from London way back, gave us a party and it was great to see everyone we knew there. Shakira—who loves Hollywood and thrives there—was in great form, but about halfway through the evening her leather belt suddenly snapped. She's always been very slim and so there were lots of jokes about how much she might have eaten and whether there was a baby on the way, but we thought nothing of it and eventually went home, exhausted but happy at the beginning of our new life.

In the middle of the night I was woken by a fist crashing into my nose. Shakira had turned over and hit me in her sleep. "Hey!" I protested, and rolled over, but just as I did so, she hit me again, this time on the ear. She'd never done this before, but I tucked her hand back under the cover and turned over once more. This time she hit me in the mouth. I sat up and put the light on—and froze in horror. Shakira's face was a terrible gray color, her eyes had rolled up into her head and she was on the verge of passing out. She had been trying to get me to wake up before she lost consciousness. With my heart beating wildly I grabbed the phone—thank God I had insisted on getting it put in—and dialed 911.

I desperately felt for a pulse—and couldn't find one, although her eyes flickered for just a moment. My Shakira was cold, almost dead cold, and I held her in my arms, trying to warm her, while Joan, my secretary, gathered some things together to take to the hospital. At last the paramedics arrived and—in consultation with a doctor at the UCLA hospital—within minutes had rigged up the life-support system that would keep her alive while she was taken to the emergency room. She had a burst appendix, which is incredibly dangerous.

As soon as we got there, Shakira was wheeled into the operating theater and—this being America—I was pointed in the direction of the cashier. "That will be five thousand dollars, please," he said. Five thousand dollars? It was seven o'clock on a Sunday morning—where was I supposed to find that sort of money? Not for the first time it made me grateful for the NHS. "No money—no operation," said the cashier. Just as I was about to become completely apoplectic with rage and worry, he suddenly asked, "Aren't you an actor?" I had reached boiling point. Did he want my autograph while my wife was dying? Luckily for him he went on, "If you're a member of the Screen Actors Guild, you'll be covered." I was; we were. I signed the form in a shaking hand and went back out to the waiting room. As I paced up and down, a man on a gurney beckoned me over. He had an oxygen mask over his face and was struggling to breathe. He seemed to be trying to say something. As I leant close, he took a couple of extra gulps, let the mask fall and gasped, "I loved you in *The Man Who Would Be King!*" and then collapsed. I grabbed the mask and shoved it back over his mouth; no fan of mine deserved to die!

At last the doctors came out of the operating theater to tell me that Shakira was out of danger. Although I felt enormous relief, I couldn't help thinking about all the "what ifs." What if we hadn't got the phone installed in time? What if the ambulance hadn't been able to find the house? What if I hadn't woken up? What if we'd still been in England where the ambulance men were on strike? What if I'd never joined the Screen Actors Guild and was uninsured? These questions rolled round and round in my mind over the next few days and weeks as, gradually, Shakira began to get better. And they roll round in my mind still, when I look at my wife and at Natasha. I know that I owe my family and the happiness they bring to me to the medical profession—and I'm very grateful.

Once Shakira was on the mend we began to be able to enjoy our new surroundings and to get to know the neighbors. Films, TV series, gossip magazines always seem to make out that LA society is full of ruthless, bitchy, mean men and women— but we met nothing but kindness from friends old and new. This was partly due to the brilliance of Irving Lazar, who took us in hand and introduced us to all *his* friends—and Irving had an address book like no one else's on the planet—but mostly it was because of Shakira; she won everyone over. People—women as well as men—warmed to her, because unlike some women in Hollywood, she was uncompetitive. Other women like her because she isn't after their husbands or boyfriends. She's very cool and she never flirts, so while people may have liked me, or found me funny—everyone *loved* Shakira. In fact I once told her that if we ever divorced I'd sue her for loss of status. We were lucky, too—and perhaps it was because we were British—we were invited everywhere. Hollywood society divides itself quite sharply into the executives and the stars, but we found ourselves able to mix freely with both groups and to be accepted by all.

Real life couldn't have been better for us at this point but my celluloid life was in the doldrums. I'd had a run of disasters—*The Swarm, Ashanti* (no, you won't have heard of it and I hope you never see it), *Beyond the Poseidon Adventure* and *The Island* (which, as it was written and produced by the team who made *Jaws, ought* to have been good, but very definitely wasn't . . .)—and even the good reviews I had picked up for *California Suite* with Maggie Smith couldn't disguise the fact that I badly needed a success.

Who would have thought that the role that would rescue my career at that point would be that of a transvestite psychiatrist turned murderer? You couldn't make it up . . . but *Dressed to Kill* became a huge box-office success. It was an opportunity for me, too, to show the versatility of my acting skills, not to mention a first outing for me in women's clothing. It had to be the most uncomfortable costume I ever wore. I hated the tights, couldn't walk in the high heels, found that the lipstick got all over my cigars and stubbornly insisted on wearing my own underpants. Apart from my experiences in Berlin during the filming of *Funeral in Berlin*, the only other encounter I had had with cross-dressing was secondhand. I was friendly, in her later years, with the great swimming star of the 1940s, Esther Williams, who told me a story about Jeff Chandler, a very handsome second-string actor, with whom she was romantically linked for a time. One day she found him wearing a woman's dress. She told me this quite matter-of-factly, although it must have been a bit of a shock. "What did you say?" I asked, fascinated. She said, "I told him, 'Jeff, you are six foot four. You cannot wear polka dots.'"

In the end, many of the long shots in the film were actually played by a double—a real woman—who was as tall as me, but needed a bit of padding out. It was she who played the most notorious scene in the film when my character slashes Angie Dickinson's character to death with a razor. It is a horrifying scene—one that I only saw later on—and it caused a lot of trouble at the time. Brian De Palma—who is one of the most technically proficient directors I've ever worked with—was insistent that it was the right thing to do. It was the only death in the entire movie and he wanted maximum impact: he got it, all right.

In fact Brian De Palma's approach to directing reminded me very much of Alfred Hitchcock's—not that I ever worked with Hitchcock, but I did get to know him very well. Neither of them were exactly Mr. Warmth, but both of them were brilliant technically and went for a very cool approach, which is probably right for scary movies, where the editing has to be spot on because it's less about the actors making connections with their audience and more about the atmosphere.

I'm pretty sure my mother never got to see my performance in *Dressed to Kill* (just as well—it might have triggered memories of my father's worst fears about my chosen career), but she did come out to visit us in Los Angeles at about this time. She was now eighty-one and almost everything about the trip and our life there was a completely new experience for her. She wasn't going to let it faze her, though—rather like the mother of another British working-class lad made good and Hollywood neighbor of ours, David Hockney. When Mrs. Hockney came over for afternoon tea with us and I asked her what she thought of Beverly Hills, she said, "It's lovely, dear—but it's a terrible waste." "Waste of what?" I asked. "All that sunshine," she said, "and no one's got the washing out!" My own mother hit the nail right on the head without meaning to, in her usual guise as Mrs. Malaprop. "Oooh," she said, pointing out of the car window at the lush flowers and plants on the way in to Beverly Hills from the airport, "look at all that hysteria climbing up the walls." She'd summed up Hollywood, in a nutshell.

When Dominique flew over to join us, the whole family was reunited and I took her and Mum to Las Vegas as a special treat. My mother was in her element and stayed up every night until three o'clock in the morning, partying as I suppose she'd never had the chance to as a young woman. Eventually she would agree that it was time to go to bed, although she wasn't happy with the décor of her bedroom at Caesars Palace. "That mirror over the bed," she said. "What's that for? Complete waste of money." I had to think on my feet: Mum still undressed in the dark. "It's so women can put on their makeup before they get up," I offered. Mum sniffed. "Lazy cows," she said. Indeed.

After Mum went back to England (she was keen to catch up with her favorite soap opera *EastEnders*), and we had taken a short holiday there, too, I went off to Hungary to work with John Huston again. This time it was on a film called *Escape to Victory* set during the Second World War and telling the story of a group of prisoners of war who play a game of soccer against a German team. Not only was John directing it, but Sylvester Stallone—who had just made the smash hits *Rocky One* and *Two*—was playing the goalkeeper. Sly was great to work with, if a bit exhausting: he never stopped exercising. If there was a five-minute break he would do push-ups, if there was a ten-minute break he would do push-ups and sit-ups. I lost weight just watching him. On the whole he was great fun—except for one piece of Hollywood "star" behavior he had picked up from somewhere. He was in the middle of writing *Rocky Three* (but then again it might have been *Four*, or *Five*) and insisted on only being called to the set if his scenes were about to be filmed. He had much better things to be getting on with than hanging around waiting. One morning he was called to shoot a scene and the weather changed and he was kept waiting for three hours while another scene was shot. He would, he informed us, make us all wait three hours the next day to make up for this. And so the following day we all had to sit around so he could make his point. Everyone was waiting for me to explode—and I was pissed off—but I had had a better idea. When Sly eventually deigned to appear, I asked him if I could have a private word. "I just want to say thanks," I said. "I was at a party last night and hadn't learnt my lines—those extra three hours saved my bacon." He looked a bit nonplussed and I went on. "And I've got another party tonight, and more dialogue tomorrow—so could you be three hours late again so I don't get into trouble?"

Although I was happy to be living in the warmth of LA and we had a regular flow of British friends passing through, all of them in despair about the state of the British film industry, I was aware that I was beginning to miss my own country. I even found myself re-creating our Mill House Sunday lunches with the traditional roast beef and Yorkshire pudding, which was bizarre in one-hundred-degree heat. I've always enjoyed cooking, and although after Shakira and I got together I expanded my repertoire from the classic English dishes I'd loved as a kid to include some healthier options, the roast Sunday lunch has always been a family favorite. And here in California it seemed a way of connecting with a piece of England I have always loved.

My father, of course, believed that cooking was women's work and real men didn't go near it. He was always a bit dubious about the acting profession for the same reason. He would have been horrified enough if he had lived to see *California Suite* (in which I played a gay man) and *Dressed to Kill*, but what he would have thought of *Deathtrap*, my next film, doesn't bear thinking about. In this film I achieved what no other male actor has ever managed before or since: I kissed Superman. My costar was Christopher Reeve, already an international star through *Superman*, and a good friend of mine, which was perhaps just as well: Christopher and I were playing closet gays who murder my "wife." We were filming in New York, which was great for me as I could hang out at Elaine's and spend time with friends like Elaine herself, Bobby Zarem, my press agent, his brother Danny, who was in the menswear business, and the producer Marty Bregman and his wife, Cornelia. The director of *Deathtrap*—which was an adaptation of Ira Levin's brilliant play of the same name—was Sidney Lumet. I had wanted to work with him and I was delighted to have a chance to work together.

With a great script and a costar like Christopher Reeve, who had been keen to take on the role to avoid the almost inevitable typecasting that he feared would come with a role like Superman, the filming was going really well. But eventually we got to the point where there was no avoiding the big moment. Although we had had several dry runs, as it were, where we just mimed the kiss, we both knew what was coming. Christopher and I had been drinking brandy to get up courage steadily over the course of the afternoon and by the time we got to the real thing, we'd had so much to drink we couldn't remember the dialogue and Sidney Lumet got very pissed off. I really don't remember much about the actual kiss itself, but I do remember saying to Christopher just as we were getting into position and before Sidney Lumet called "Action," "Whatever you do, *don't open your mouth!*" It must be the longest closed-mouth kiss in cinema history. . . . I was in a café quite recently and bursting for a pee and there were only two cubicles, one for men and one for women. The Men's was occupied but Ladies' was free, so having checked no one was around, I dived into it. While I was in there, the doorknob rattled; unfortunately a real lady had turned up. When I'd finished, I opened the door and said to the woman waiting, "It's OK, I'm a lesbian." And she said, quick as a flash, "No you're not. I saw you kiss Superman in *Death-trap. . . .*"

After *Deathtrap*, I went back to Beverly Hills for some time off. Shakira was loving the Hollywood life and with Natasha happy at a wonderful school we were delighted to take a break and just enjoy ourselves. I became a sort of unpaid social ambassador and, among other events, hosted a dinner for Princess Michael of Kent at Morton's, the newest, hottest restaurant in LA, as well as being roped in whenever other visiting royalty came to town. My agent, Sue Mengers—who was besotted by the British royal family—was chosen to give a dinner for Princess Margaret and invited me as a "safe" dinner party guest. Sue, truly one of Hollywood's toughest dealmakers, was so overcome by the proximity of royalty that she nearly collapsed with nerves on the night, but she needn't have worried. The stars all turned out—for Sue, as much as for Princess Margaret—including Clint Eastwood, Jack Nicholson, Barbra Streisand and (apparently by special request) Barry Manilow. The evening was a huge success.

When the Queen visited Los Angles, there was a very grand affair, held at the Twentieth Century Fox studios, with the British Hollywood contingent lined up on a dais either side of the Queen and the rest of Hollywood at tables below. The evening had been financed by a multimillionaire car dealer who, as a reward, got to sit on one side of the Queen, while the director, ex-husband of Vanessa Redgrave and father of Natasha and Joely Richardson, Tony Richardson, sat on the other. The Queen seemed happy enough chatting with Tony, who always had a great fund of stories, but she was obviously finding it harder going with the car dealer. I was sitting on his other side and I sympathized. . . . It was not long before I heard an unmistakable voice. "Mr. Caine!" There, peeping round the side of the tongue-tied car dealer, was the Queen. "Mr. Caine!" she said again. "Yes, Your Majesty," I replied, hoping that was the right way to address a sovereign. "Do you know any good jokes?" she asked. "I do, ma'am," I said, "but I'm not sure they would be suitable . . ." "Well, why not have a go?" she suggested with a twinkle. "And then I'll tell you one." Not sure whether or not I was risking extradition and a spell in the Tower of London, I embarked on a story about a four-legged chicken, which seemed to go down very well—and we spent the rest of the evening swapping jokes.

While I might have been enjoying a reputation as a bit of a comedian offscreen in Hollywood, most of the films I had starred in over the previous few years were not at all funny. By the time we'd finished *Deathtrap* I was beginning to long for a really good comedy—and when it came, it was worth the wait.

CHAPTER TWELVE

OSCAR NIGHTS

I am often asked which of my films has come closest to my own ideal of performance and I always answer, *Educating Rita*. To me, *Educating Rita* is the most perfect performance I could give of a character who was as far away from me as you could possibly get and of all the films I have ever been in, I think it may be the one I am most proud of.

I'm proud of it, too, because taking the part wasn't immediately the most obvious thing for me to do—for a start it involved turning down a film costarring Sally Field, who had just won an Oscar for *Norma Rae*, in favor of playing opposite Julie Walters, who had never appeared in a film at all. But the director was Lewis Gilbert, director of *Alfie*, and the screenplay was by Willy Russell, who had adapted it from his own novel and play and he had opened the play out so that the backstory of the two characters is played out on-screen. The story was also very close to my heart, because although it was a comedy, it was the story of the late flowering of a woman who has had few opportunities in life, and it carries a strong message about class and education. It's rare, too, to find something in cinema that is deeply written enough for the characters to change each other the way Frank Bryant and Rita do: they have a profound effect on each other. And when I look back at my own films, the ones that stand out for me in terms of character development like this are all films that began in the theater: *Alfie, Sleuth, California Suite* and *Deathtrap.*

While I could appreciate the strengths of the script, taking on the character of an overweight, alcoholic professor was a real challenge for me. To help get into the role, I grew a shaggy beard and put on about thirty pounds and called on every nuance of alcoholic behavior I could recall. It would have been easy to play the part the way Rex Harrison played Professor Higgins in *My Fair Lady*—but I saw Dr. Frank Bryant as far less attractive and more vulnerable than that and went back to Emil Jannings's performance as the ugly professor who nurses an unrequited love for Marlene Dietrich in *The Blue Angel* for inspiration. I became so immersed in the part and what I imagined to be the "type" that I felt as if I had known academics all my life.

Julie Walters was brilliant. Of course she had already done a lot of television and had played Rita in the West End stage play, but it was her first ever movie, although you would never have known it—she was a completely instinctive film actress. Like John Huston, Lewis Gilbert was a hands-off director and believed in letting the actors get on with it. A measured man, he was nevertheless obviously pleased at the way the filming was going and one day he said to me—just as he had fifteen years before with *Alfie*, that he thought both Julie and I would be nominated for an Academy Award for our roles in the movie. And just as he had been fifteen years previously with *Alfie*, he was right.

For *Alfie*, I had had the misfortune to be up against my friend the great actor Paul Scofield who had been nominated in the Best Actor category for his role as Sir Thomas More in *A Man for All Seasons*. I had seen his performance and thought it was brilliant and realized I had no chance of winning with *Alfie* so I didn't turn up. The next time I was nominated was for *Sleuth* in 1973, again for Best Actor, but my costar Laurence Olivier was also nominated for his role in *Sleuth,* so we had cut our own chances in half from the start. On that occasion I decided to go to the ceremony anyway because I had never been and I thought it might be fun. Big mistake. For a start, in a moment of madness I'd agreed to host a quarter of the ceremony, with Carol Burnett, Charlton Heston and Rock Hudson doing the other three quarters.

Presenting the Oscars was the most nerve-racking job I have ever done in show business. It's very much a live show: they have comedy writers waiting in the wings and as you come off between presentations they hand you an appropriate gag to tell. As if that wasn't bad enough, it was destined to get even more stressful when it got to the Best Actor nominations. Marlon Brando won it for *The Godfather,* but—as we all knew he would—he refused to accept it and sent a Native American girl called Sacheen Littlefeather on his behalf, to read a fifteen-page speech protesting the treatment of Native Americans by the film and television industry. The producer of the show had told her beforehand that she would be slung off if she spoke for more than forty-five seconds so she restricted herself to a short speech—which got quite a few boos—and read Brando's letter to the press afterwards. I think that any gesture in a good cause is admirable, but it turned out that the young lady's name was in fact Marie Cruz, that she was an actress whose mother was Caucasian, and that three months after the Oscar ceremony she posed for *Playboy* magazine. Of course it doesn't invalidate the cause, and Sacheen Littlefeather continues to work as an activist today, but it does show you, yet again, that Hollywood is never quite what you think it is!

Littlefeather's performance that night certainly caused consternation backstage. I was standing there with everyone else while it was going on, waiting for the finale, which was to be John Wayne leading the entire cast in singing "You Oughta Be in Pictures." By the time we got on, everything was a bit chaotic: no one knew the words and John Wayne couldn't sing in tune anyway. I was so embarrassed that I started to edge towards the back of the stage. I had been talking to Clint Eastwood, who had just been presenting an award, and he felt the same so he edged back with me. The problem is that we both edged back so far we fell off. It wasn't far, and neither of us was hurt, but we both became hysterical with laughter and couldn't finish the song.

As Lewis Gilbert had predicted, I was nominated for Best Actor in *Educating Rita* in 1983—as was Julie for Best Actress—but once again the odds were stacked against me, this time because, of the five nominees in my category, four were British: Tom Courtenay and Albert Finney in *The Dresser,* Tom Conti in *Reuben, Reuben* and of course me. The only American in the running was Robert Duvall in *Tender Mercies*—he was brilliant as a burned-out country singer, but I suspect he would still have won even if he hadn't been.

And I was in for an agonizingly long wait to find out. The Academy Awards ceremony is a tense and very long evening. It starts very early, at around five o'clock in the afternoon, so that it makes prime-time TV on the East Coast, which means that you have to set off for the venue at about three-thirty because of the appalling traffic. It seems incongruous to have to put on evening dress in the middle of the day and of course you know you're going to have to wait until nearly midnight for any food, so although it may all look glamorous, the reality is different. And as soon as you get inside the theater you know what the likelihood of winning is: if you are seated on the aisle or near the front, then it's clear you are in with a chance. If you are on the inside of a row, the chances are you're not. I had already decided that I wasn't going to win for *Educating Rita*, but as soon as I was shown to my seat, halfway back, and looked over to see Robert Duvall sitting bang in the front row, I started practicing my gallant loser's smile. I could see that Shirley MacLaine was in pole position for *Terms of Endearment*, too, so it wasn't a wild guess to make that Julie Walters had also been unlucky for Best Actress.

Tedious though all the hanging about might be, the annual Academy Awards is the most important fixture in the Hollywood calendar and has been since it started. Perhaps the most iconic event in the Hollywood *social* calendar—and certainly the aspect of the whole Academy Award business I enjoyed the most—was for years Swifty Lazar's Oscar party. Along with the other two top parties, media mogul Barry Diller's lunch and the late Hollywood agent Ed Limato's dinner, Swifty's party ranked as the place to be and to be seen. Swifty's Oscar parties were real high-octane affairs held first of all at the Bistro restaurant and then at Wolfgang Puck's Spago. Swifty's party may have been the hot ticket, but you could find yourself seated at the back of the restaurant in "Siberia" if he didn't like you or think you mattered—and he had a very keen sense of priority. He once invited me to dinner and I had to turn him down because I was already having dinner with someone else. When I told him who it was he looked at me, rather disappointed. "He's not a dinner, Michael," he said, "he's a lunch!" So sitting at the front of Spago at Swifty's Oscar parties were the "dinners"—the "lunches" were at the back. . . .

After Swifty's death, the mantle passed to Graydon Carter, the editor of *Vanity Fair*, who started the very small and very exclusive Oscar party at Morton's, which very quickly became the massive—but funnily enough still very exclusive—*Vanity*

Fair party at Morton's. I discovered just how exclusive the *Vanity Fair* party was when one year Shakira and I were invited and we found ourselves seated right by the kitchen. This would definitely have been classed as "Siberia" and a real social stigma, but so many stars were seated round us that it was very clearly not. In addition, it had two great advantages: we were served first and the food was piping hot! But it wasn't until I went to the Gents that I realized quite what an exclusive crowd it was. There were three urinals. Left and right were occupied so I went for the middle one. All three of us finished round about the same time and we went to wash our hands and I found myself in the company of Rupert Murdoch and George Lucas. Back at our table, I found myself sitting next to an old friend, Arianna Stassinopoulos Huffington. She had a BlackBerry with her and every now and then would pick it up either to speak on it or to fiddle with it. As the awards show played on the giant television screens placed around the restaurant, we all started to give our uninhibited opinions—both negative and positive—of each award. During a commercial break I asked Arianna what she was doing on the phone. "I'm texting my blog," she said. I had never heard of a blog at the time and she had to explain to me that she was texting what was happening to her right now, live on the Internet, to all the readers of her very popular Huffington Post. I panicked. "You haven't put out what I've just been saying about some of the winners for millions of people to read, have you?" I couldn't keep the note of fear out of my voice: I had not been discreet. . . . "No!" She laughed. "I wouldn't do that—I've just told my readers that I'm here sitting next to you, that's all." Phew!

Morton's restaurant isn't big, so when the dinner and the Oscars show are over, they open up a door and you go into an enormous pavilion and wait for the people who went to the actual ceremony to come to join the party. It doesn't take long before the first ones come in, usually slightly pissed off and demanding a drink. These are the losers and the presenters who don't have to stay at the Oscars for the Governor's Ball. The winners do, and eventually turn up much later, brandishing their trophies. I remember bumping into Jack Nicholson, who was smoking. I started to give him the lecture I'd first had from Tony Curtis about the dangers of smoking, but he interrupted me. "Michael," he said, with that wolfish Nicholson grin, "it has been proved that people who are left-handed die earlier than smokers. I am right-handed, so I am ahead of the game."

Even Hollywood and the Oscars have been affected by the credit crunch. Morton's has now closed down and been turned into another successful restaurant, and the *Vanity Fair* party is now a much smaller affair, held at the Sunset Towers restaurant on Sunset Boulevard—a trip down memory lane for me as I lived in that building on my first stay in Hollywood while I was making *Gambit*.

There are hosts of other wonderful and much larger parties, of course—Elton John's annual AIDS Foundation party, for instance, which is now a regular fixture in the Hollywood calendar and combines high glamour with fund-raising for a worthy cause—but for me part of the pleasure has always been about finding the smaller, more intimate occasions in the midst of all the glitz.

Being one of the six thousand industry members of the Academy of Motion Picture Arts and Sciences who vote for the awards involves being sent the most fantastic Christmas present any film buff could ever want: the "screeners." These are the DVDs of the eligible films made over the previous year, sent to us by their producers, all of whom are hoping to get nominations. The screeners arrive at the beginning of November and my family and I hibernate into the cinema and live on those screeners.

Although British winters were one of the many reasons Shakira and I had decided to relocate to LA, by 1983 I had found myself becoming increasingly homesick. I had given the performance of my life in *Educating Rita* and we decided that, much as we loved Hollywood, if I didn't win the Oscar, there was no professional reason to stay on and we would move back to England. I didn't win, but in my mind I *had* won—because I was going home, and so my delight at Robert Duvall's Oscar was genuine. That was the year of Swifty's first Oscar party and I was completely unprepared for what awaited me there: as I came into the restaurant I was greeted by a standing ovation from all the brightest and best in the movie business. As I stood there with tears streaming down my face, Cary Grant came up to me and gave me a hug. "You're a winner here, Michael," he whispered. I was overcome—how could I leave people like this? But I knew I had made the right decision—and I knew, too, that we would be back and that the friends we had made would be friends for life.

After a trip to Brazil for *Blame It on Rio*, an adaptation of a French comedy in which a middle-aged man (me) is seduced by his best friend's daughter (unfortunately the charm of the original was lost in translation and it got panned by the critics), we went back to England to look for a house. The summer of 1984 was just gorgeous and the perfect time to house-hunt: the countryside was looking its absolute best. We wanted to find a house on the river, like the Mill House but further away from London in the deep country and, above all, in a village that had no through road. Property prices were booming in southern England at the time and with this and our list of stipulations it was very difficult to find the right place. We had just been gazumped (a nasty English practice in which someone jumps in with a higher offer after a seller has accepted yours) on a house that met all our criteria and were feeling very grumpy when the estate agent told us an offer on another house in the same village had fallen through that day. As we drove up through the gates marked "Rectory Farmhouse" Shakira leant over to me and whispered, "We've got to have it!" "We haven't even bloody seen it," I grumbled—but I should have known better. Shakira has an uncanny ability to *know* things—and in this instance she was absolutely right. The house was gorgeous— about two hundred years old, with gabled windows and beautiful oak beams—and it was surrounded by what had once been a magnificent garden with—I could hardly believe our luck— two hundred yards of river frontage. We bought it on the spot— and what's more, we arranged with the owner to rent it from her for the summer until the purchase went through.

So from all the glamour and organized luxury of Hollywood we moved into a house that needed just about everything, but that we knew, from the moment we stepped inside it, would be the family home we were looking for. It proved the perfect project: Shakira got on with plans for the old house, I began designing the new part we wanted to build and the garden, and Natasha made friends with Catherine, the daughter of a farming family just up the road and spent the entire summer on their farm. We indulged ourselves with all the most English summer pastimes we could find—the Derby, Wimbledon, evening dinners at Thameside restaurants—and gave the first of several annual July 4 parties, bringing American and English friends together.

It was hard to tear myself away from such an idyllic summer, but I had to pay for it all somehow (and the builders were coming in) and so I headed off for ten weeks in Germany to film *The Holcroft Covenant*. It turned out to be yet another bad film, although it was good fun at the time, and as soon as it was done I headed to LA to join Shakira and Natasha where we were still living while Rectory Farm was being renovated. In LA, the autumn is party season and I had always looked forward to it, but this year Hollywood had a really special surprise for me: a private party at the Beverly Wilshire thrown by my friend the producer Irwin Allen just for Shakira and me—and all of Hollywood's best comedians and their wives. It was a roast and I was guest of honor. I couldn't have asked for anything better. I've always been a bit of a comedian myself and I've often thought that if I was young today I might have been a stand-up comic, so an evening in the company of such comic greats as George Burns, Milton Berle, Bob Newhart, Steve Allen and Red Buttons to name just some of the lineup, was my idea of heaven.

The movies I worked on in 1984 were taken on more with the new conservatory at Rectory Farmhouse in mind than their critical reception, but in November I went to New York for a film that would come to mean a great deal to me. Woody Allen was a director I had long admired and never worked with so I was very excited to be starting on the filming of *Hannah and Her Sisters*.

There are many myths about Woody Allen, most of which are untrue. I'd always heard that he never gives actors the script until the day of shooting—and even then he only gives you your part. I got the script of the whole thing weeks before we began with the only proviso being that I didn't reveal it to anyone, which seemed fair enough. And it was a great script, I could tell that straightaway. Woody works on the dialogue for months before a shoot and yet his films always have a very natural atmosphere, almost as if the actors were ad-libbing, which is absolutely not the case. And as an actor himself, Woody brings something very different to the role of director—and he notices everything. Once, he stopped a take and asked me why I had not moved my hand the way I had done in the rehearsal a few minutes before. I had no idea I had even moved my hand at all, let alone in what way, but he had spotted it, liked it and we repeated the take to get it in.

It takes a great deal of skill to achieve the levels of naturalism that Woody does. In *Hannah and Her Sisters*, Mia Farrow plays my wife (she was Woody's partner at the time) and we shot the film in her apartment. It really was a family affair: some of Mia's large brood of children played our children in the film, and when she was not required on "set" (her own flat!), Mia could be found in the kitchen doling out food to the others. Being directed by Woody and doing a love scene with Mia in her own bedroom gave an added piquancy to the whole business, too—especially when I made the mistake of looking up at one point only to see Mia's ex-husband André Previn watching the proceedings. . . . As well as having her partner, children and ex-husband around, Mia's real mother, Maureen O'Sullivan, was playing her screen mother and we were also occasionally visited by a little old man who used to wander in and try to sell us watches, who turned out to be none other than Woody's dad. It was a bizarre and unforgettable experience!

My nomination for an Academy Award for Best Supporting Actor for *Hannah and Her Sisters* came in 1986. It was a surprise on two counts: first, I'd never been nominated in this category before, and second, Woody Allen was very publicly anti-Oscar. In fact he was so opposed to the whole idea of the Awards that he was always publicized playing his clarinet with his group in New York during the broadcast of the show, even when he got nominated himself. The film had also been released in February the previous year, eleven months before the nominations, so I had assumed it had been long forgotten by then.

In fact, I was so sure I would not be nominated, I hadn't even bothered to put the date of the Oscars in my diary and the irony was that I had signed to do a small ten-day part in the Caribbean in *Jaws 4* (not a film that was ever likely to feature on the Academy nomination list, at least in any of the acting categories), which coincided with the show. By the time the nomination came through it was too late to do anything about it and so when, finally, I won an Oscar, I wasn't even there to collect it and it was Shakira and Natasha who rang me from one of Swifty's Oscar parties to give me the good news. I was reminded of the time during the filming of *Too Late the Hero* when my costar Cliff Robertson heard he'd won an Oscar as Best Actor for a film called *Charlie*. As we were stuck in the Philippine jungle he couldn't go and pick it up, but he was determined not to lose a PR opportunity and got a local woodcarver to make him an exact replica of the statuette so he could be filmed carrying it when we eventually got home. It seemed like a good plan and indeed there was a huge press pack waiting for us when we got off the plane, Cliff clutching his replica Oscar, but there was a surprise in store: Gregory Peck, the president of the Academy, had turned up to make a presentation of the real Oscar. As the crowds parted and Greg came forward, Cliff reacted with lightning speed and chucked his fake Oscar over his shoulder so he could reach out and accept the real one. It hit me square on the forehead. So there is Cliff, triumphant with Oscar aloft, and me behind, clutching my head and pouring blood. . . . In the end, I learnt my lesson—and the next two times I was nominated I made sure I was there in person (though I've never made the mistake of hosting the ceremony again!).

After *Hannah*, I took on a number of movies, again with Rectory Farm in mind, and we began to prepare for our imminent relocation back to England. Renovations on the house were going well but slowly and it wasn't until the summer of 1987 that we made the final move, after eight and a half years in Hollywood. It was good to be home and to be able to spend more time with my mother. She was eighty-seven now, and although she was still pretty lively, she didn't always cotton on to what was going on. We invited her to Natasha's fourteenth birthday party to show her the new house. We still didn't have any curtains in the living room and she told me that she thought the place looked bloody awful. "You'd think," she said, gesturing round at all the guests, "that if they're doing this sort of business they'd be able to afford curtains, wouldn't you?" I realized she thought our house was a pub. "And have you run short of money?" she demanded. "No, Ma," I said. "Why do you think that?" "Well, look at Shakira!" Ma said. Shakira was pouring out drinks and refilling glasses. "Why's she working as a barmaid?" I gave up. "It's only a part-time job, Ma," I said. It was a sad moment but I was just glad to be back in the UK so that we could make the most of the time we had left.

There are no part-time jobs in the movie business, and at this point in the late eighties, the British film industry was on its knees. As I didn't want to leave Shakira and Natasha behind to do a film abroad, I went back to television for the first time in twenty-five years. When I last worked for the BBC I got paid in guineas—and very few of them at that; this time, with an American TV company attached to the deal, the fee was as much as I'd have got from a film. It was a drama called *Jack the Ripper* based on a new theory of the identity of the killer. We shot it in London, which suited me perfectly—although the TV shooting schedule was a bit of a revelation after the slower pace of movies. Still, I kept up, and we were rewarded by the most incredible ratings for the show—I think only the wedding of Charles and Diana had ever achieved a higher rating.

I was feeling pretty pleased with myself about this, but I was even more excited when the next project came along. *Dirty Rotten Scoundrels* appealed from the very start. My costar was to be Steve Martin, and the director was Frank Oz, who is only slightly better known as Miss Piggy from the Muppets. I asked them both down to Rectory Farm for a lunch party to discuss the film, and was surprised to find that Steve was actually very shy. There were about thirty of us gathered there that day, but because the sitting room was huge, it was far from crowded. "I'd love to have a place like this," Steve said rather wistfully, looking round. "Well you could!" I said, surprised by his comment: I knew how successful Steve was. "Yes . . ." he said, "but I wouldn't have the friends to fill it." It's strange how often actors who are able to come across as the most gregarious of people on-screen can actually be quite inhibited in real life.

Inhibition is not one of my problems and eventually, at the end of the lunch, I broached the subject of location with Frank. The story for *Scoundrels* is set—according to the script—in the south of France in summer, but I was all too aware of the costs that would be involved in taking a crew there at the height of the season. "So where are we actually shooting, then, Frank?" I asked, prepared for some decaying Eastern European resort. "It's set in the south of France," Frank replied, "so we shoot in the south of France." Those words were music to my ears.

The south of France is one of my favorite places in the world. I first went there when Peter Ustinov lent my friend Terence Stamp his yacht and house in the hills behind Cannes as a present for starring in Peter's movie *Billy Budd* and Terry took me along for the ride.

Although I went back to Cannes several times for the film festival, it was always so crowded that it was impossible to leave the hotel without being pursued and it wasn't until I was invited by Peter Sellers, who was filming *There's a Girl in My Soup* with Goldie Hawn there, that I got to know the south of France better.

While Peter and Goldie were working, I explored St. Tropez. It was right in the middle of the boom that Brigitte Bardot had created after she and Roger Vadim made the movie *And God Created Woman* there in the late 1950s. The beaches were incredible, the restaurants were unforgettable and the whole place was full of the most beautiful people I had ever seen. I fell in love with the place and have spent the rest of my life looking for excuses to head back there.

I couldn't have had a better excuse than *Dirty Rotten Scoundrels*.

We rented a villa close to Roger and Luisa Moore's and our friends Leslie and Evie Bricusse, and as it was the school holidays Natasha came out to join us with two friends. The movie was nothing but a pleasure from start to finish—although I had a moment early on when I suddenly remembered why the script had seemed familiar. I had seen it years before when it was released under the title *Bedtime Story* starring Marlon Brando and David Niven, and it had been a complete flop. "Why," I asked Frank and Steve, "are we remaking a movie that flopped first time round?" "Because," Frank said very reasonably, "there would be no point remaking a film that had been a success." I tried to think of a good counterargument, but this was Hollywood logic and I gave up.

Hollywood logic or not, Frank was a fantastic director—and comedy takes some real directing. In the film, Steve and I play con men who make their living off middle-aged ladies; any time it looked like one of our marks was becoming a bit too serious about me, Steve would appear disguised as one of a series of eccentric relatives to put them off. He was so off the wall in his characterization that it was actually quite difficult to play opposite him. In the end, though, the solution was simple: I played my part completely straight and let the laughs take care of themselves.

Dirty Rotten Scoundrels is one of my favorite films—for me it's the funniest movie I ever made. I think its appeal lies in the fact that my character and Steve Martin's are rogues who only ever hurt the pompous and the rich—and they always get away with it. It looks fabulous, too; it's stylish, it's wicked and people love it. Whenever it comes on television, I always stop and watch a bit of it and it still makes me laugh. There's one scene in particular I just can't resist, where I'm pretending to be an eminent psychiatrist, Dr. Emil Schaffhausen, who is lashing the legs of Steve Martin, who's posing as a psychosomatically crippled soldier, to prove they don't work. I had to intersperse each of my words with a lash of the whip: "My name is—" *lash*, "Dr.—" *lash*, "Emil—" *lash*, "Schaffhausen," *lash*. On the second—and final—take I added an ad-lib. After "Schaffhausen—" *lash*, I added, "the Third—" and a final *lash*, to give him one more. I just wanted to have the last lash. . . .

CHAPTER THIRTEEN

FAMILY SECRETS

After that glorious summer in the south of France, I plunged straight back into work and by the end of 1988 I was pretty exhausted. I did a small-budget thriller, *Shock to the System*, set in New York, and then went back to England to follow up the success of the Jack the Ripper mini-series with *Dr. Jekyll and Mr. Hyde*, which was five weeks on location in London, so easy to manage from that point of view, but a lot of my time was spent in makeup being turned into the hideous Mr. Hyde. Never again! I have no idea how John Hurt managed to get through *The Elephant Man*. . . .

The end of the year looked like running its normal course and we were just planning our usual over-the-top Christmas, when we got the phone call I had, of course, been half expecting for some time. On December 12, 1989, my brother Stanley's birthday, my mother died. Ma had been living in a nursing home for many years, where she was looked after beautifully. As was typical of many women of her generation and background, she viewed all doctors with great suspicion and the only way her thoughtful nurse, Gemma, managed to get her to see one at all was by finding an Indian doctor and telling her he was Shakira's brother! If it was family, you see, that was all right. . . . Ma wouldn't have wanted to hear the message that a doctor would have given her, either. For the last twenty years of her life she had been smoking over eighty cigarettes and drinking a bottle of white wine a day, on top of her favorite English fried foods, not to mention the cups of tea with full-fat milk and spoonfuls of white sugar. Still, at the age of eighty-nine there was no point in arguing.

Gemma called on December 11 to say that Ma had a bad cold and I rushed over to see her, knowing how frail she was and how the slightest setback can escalate into something more serious with vulnerable old people. We had a great old time and she was very perky and I left feeling relieved that she seemed to be fine, but the next morning Gemma called to say that she had died in her sleep. Apparently she had eaten well, drunk well, as usual, smoked her fags and gone to bed very happy—and they hadn't been able to wake her the next morning.

When I went in to see her, she looked so peaceful and almost as if she was smiling. I held it together as I kissed her for the last time, but first Gemma—who had been very fond of my mother—burst into tears and then I did, too. Gemma and I held on to each other and sobbed our hearts out before I managed to get a grip and we went outside to see the rest of the staff, who were waiting with the usual British solution in times of grief—a cup of tea.

Ma's funeral took place on a cold, wet London winter's day. Stanley was ill with pneumonia and couldn't come, so Shakira and I were the only family members there. I was very conscious—I think anyone losing a parent is, no matter at what age it happens—of her passing as the end of an era, of the loss of the last link to the previous generation, a chapter closed.

But the past wasn't quite ready to let me go. In the spring of 1991 I was filming *Noises Off* in Los Angeles. The year 1990 had been a grim one in the aftermath of the stock market crash in 1989 and the hurricane that had swept across Britain. Then 1991 had started even more grimly with the first Gulf War. Although we couldn't escape the news, it was a relief to escape the cold weather in Britain and we were delighted to find ourselves back in the Californian sunshine. We were even more thrilled to hear that Natasha had been given a place at Manchester University—it felt as if a new chapter was opening for the whole family.

One Friday afternoon, just as I'd got in from a day's filming, the phone rang. I picked it up without a thought—and in an instant the story I thought I knew about my family changed forever. The guy on the other end was a reporter from the English tabloid newspaper *The People* and he was calling to say that they had discovered the existence of my half brother.

My mother's first child, a son called David, was born illegitimate and with epilepsy in a Salvation Army hospital in 1924. In those days there was little treatment available for epilepsy and as a result of the fits he had as a child, during which he would bang his head repeatedly on the stone floors of the workhouse, he became brain-damaged and would remain in an institution for the rest of his life.

It was a terrible shock to me and to Stanley. I'd had absolutely no idea of David's existence—and neither had my father or any of our large extended family. My mother had kept him a secret for sixty-seven years, and yet she had visited him every Monday, except when we were in Norfolk during the war. Shock soon turned to admiration when I found out how loyal

she had been to him. And I started to think back to our childhood and to wonder how she had managed to keep this secret
for so long.

I was never aware of her absence on Mondays, as a little
boy—when we were babies she probably took us with her, but I
have no memories of that. And then when I was six and Stanley
was three and a half, we were evacuated. When we got back to
London—and David had been moved by then and I think she
had to trace him all over again—we didn't think anything of
the trips she took on a Monday to see Aunt Lil in Dagenham.
Dagenham was a long way from the Elephant so she'd be gone
all day, but we were at school and there was no reason to question it at all.

What is extraordinary is that it took so long for the secret to
emerge. Apparently my mother always carried a Bible in her
handbag and would get any new members of staff, first in the
asylum and then in the nursing home, to swear to keep the fact
that David was my half brother a secret—and no one ever spilt
the beans. But as I've thought more and more about it over the
years, some little things begin to make sense—little oddities
that had never been enough to arouse any suspicions on their
own, but that all came together with this incredible revelation.
Whenever we were in the UK, Ma used to visit Shakira and me
in the country every Sunday and she would be driven back to
London the next day. One day, the driver mentioned that she
always insisted on getting out at the bus stop on Streatham High
Road, rather than being taken back to her house. The penny
never dropped, of course, but she must have been going straight
off to the asylum to visit David. And then there was Ma's incredible consumption of sweets, biscuits and chocolates. She always
used to leave us on Monday morning piled up with packets and
boxes and yet when I'd go there and see her on a Wednesday
for a cup of tea and ask for a biscuit, she'd always insist that

she'd eaten them all. And I'd think, bloody hell, she gets through all these chocolates and biscuits very quickly—but of course she was saving them to take to David.

The People had got hold of the story completely by accident. They had sent a reporter to do a piece on conditions in the old lunatic asylums—by now they were all shut down and the former inmates had been transferred to more humane nursing homes—and he was interviewing a group of people, amongst whom was David's girlfriend, who was more lucid than the others and who could also speak distinctly. "Do you see that man over there?" she said to the reporter. "Do you know Michael Caine, the actor?" "Yes . . ." said the reporter, obviously not quite sure what was coming. "Well, he's his brother." And of course the reporter went—"Wait a minute. . . . I've got a scoop here!" I was very impressed by the way the paper handled it all. They rang me straightaway and they didn't try to make anything salacious out of it at all. In fact what they went with was the story that really matters: the story of my mother and her incredible loyalty to her son.

My first reaction was to jump on a plane straight back to England to visit David, but *Noises Off* was way behind schedule and I couldn't get there for a couple of weeks, although Stanley went in the meantime. According to the matron of the nursing home, David knew all about us; he had seen *Zulu* on television and my mother had given him a picture of her with me so he knew I was his half brother. When I eventually got home from LA—Shakira insisted on coming with me because she could see how shaken I was by the news—I went straight to the nursing home. Although the nurses had warned me that David was very handicapped, it was still a terrible shock to meet him. I went into his room and there he was: a very small man, with dark, slightly graying hair, in a wheelchair. No one knew who his father was—and he certainly bore very little physical resemblance to Stanley or me. Most upsetting of all was that when I held my hand out to shake his, I realized that he couldn't speak—or at least not in a way that I could understand. The nurses hadn't mentioned this, but I realized it was because they *could* understand him—it wasn't that he couldn't speak, it was that I was incapable of hearing what he had to say.

By the time I met David, there was very little I could do for him except make him comfortable. I got him a bigger room and his own television and the nurses said he was just happy to know that he had a family who cared for him. He died in 1992, and his ashes are buried alongside our mother's, together at last in the way they were never able to be during their lives.

Now, of course, the birth of a child outside wedlock is nothing to be ashamed of; when my mother was a young woman, it was a terrible shame. The tragedy is that, had David's epilepsy been properly treated, he might well have gone on to live a fulfilled and normal life; he might have had the chances that I did. But out of the tragedy emerged something else—the story of a courageous woman. My mother kept David a secret initially because of society's condemnation of her "sin" and later because she was convinced that the existence of a half brother in an asylum and not right in the head would ruin my career, and she was determined to protect me at all costs. As I've said before, there was nothing Ma wouldn't do for her boys—but perhaps that was also because there was one boy she hadn't been able to do much for.

CHAPTER FOURTEEN

KITCHEN SINK DRAMAS

The death of my mother, the discovery of David and the publication of *What's It All About* were all watershed moments in my life. And when these were coupled with what looked as if it might become a permanent gap in my movie schedule, I was forced to take stock and consider the future. The book had gone brilliantly, and I had loved writing it, so I decided that writing might be one way to go. Then there was my restaurant business. It had been part of my life for thirty years, but it had definitely played second fiddle to my movie career. I could, I decided, perhaps take this chance to move it more center stage.

The London I grew up in after the war was a bit of a culinary desert, to put it mildly. Restaurants were the province of the rich and the dress code of suit and tie was meant to keep the likes of me out. But gradually things began to change and when two Italians, Mario Cassandro and Franco Lagattolla, opened their Italian restaurant La Trattoria Terrazza on Romilly

Street in 1959, it had no dress code at all. Not only that, it stayed open until the last customer had left and it was open all day Sunday. The waiters were all friendly and helpful—unlike many of the English waiters who used to start looking at their watches and sighing before you were even halfway through your meal—and the whole atmosphere was fun and relaxed. As the sixties got into full swing and London began to be the cosmopolitan city it is today, eating out started to be part of our culture.

As the London restaurant scene began to liven up, an idea began forming in the back of my mind: I wanted to open a big brasserie, a bit like La Coupole in Paris. This might have remained a fantasy if it hadn't been for Sidney Poitier. He and I were in London together, working at Pinewood putting the final touches to *The Wilby Conspiracy* in 1974, and he and his wife, Joanna, and Shakira and I would eat out together a few evenings each week. When it was Sidney's turn to take us, he always chose Odin's, a great restaurant just off Marylebone High Street. On this particular evening, we had just been seated at our table when a short fat man reeled towards us, rather the worse for wear. He seemed to know Sidney. "Hello!" he said and stood there, clutching the back of a chair for support. Sidney, who is a very polite man, immediately introduced us. "This is Peter Langan, the owner of Odin's." Peter stood there swaying for a bit, frowning. He appeared to be trying to retrieve some long-lost piece of information. Eventually light dawned. "Michael Caine!" he said triumphantly. "Sidney tells me you want to open a restaurant!" "Well—yes . . ." I said, rather reluctantly. He bent over me and I nearly passed out from the fumes. "When you do, kid," he said, "give me a call. I'd like to be your partner." And with that he hauled himself upright and tottered away. "Is he always like that?" I asked Sidney. "I don't know," said Sidney, carefully. "But I have never seen him when he wasn't." "Well, if I ever do open a restaurant," I said, "he'd be the last partner I'd choose."

I didn't bump into Peter again until some time later—and when I did, he was completely sober. I almost didn't recognize him: he was off the booze, he explained, because someone had bet him he couldn't stay away from it for a whole month. He asked me whether I'd had any more thoughts about opening a restaurant and I was about to say no, when something stopped me. Sober, Peter was very impressive—and his track record in the restaurant business was very good. "Yes . . ." I said cautiously. He beamed. "I'll be in touch as soon as I've found some premises," he said. "Do we have a deal?" We shook hands and as we parted I shouted after him, "When's the month up?" "Tomorrow!" he yelled back.

We next met in the lobby of the Ritz. He had found premises, he said, and went on to outline a business plan that would give me a third of the profits in return for an investment of £25,000. "Was I in?" he asked. I looked over at this scruffy Irishman—the last person you would ever think of as a trustworthy and reliable person to go into business with—and I thought of what my father would have said, and I said, "Yes." There was no reply: Peter had fallen asleep.

When I'd woken him up, we went across the road to look at the premises he'd found in Stratton Street. It didn't look very enticing, but I trusted Peter to get it right and he did. He stripped out all the interior walls to leave a big open room, which he painted a faded orange color that looked as if it had always been there. He covered the walls with pictures that were hung randomly to give an informal look and lit the place so that although you could see what you were eating, you would never be blinded by looking at a lightbulb. We hired a chef from Alsace to re-create good bistro food and opened very quietly on a Monday lunch. The word got round very quickly: our Alsace chef was used to feeding French manual laborers and the portions were enormous. On the second night we were full, and by the third there was a queue round the block so long we actually ran out of food.

And so Langan's was up and running. Peter's antics—he would occasionally get so drunk he would insult the customers and one time actually got under the table and bit a woman's leg—ensured us constant coverage in the gossip columns, but our long-term success was really established when the chef Richard Shepherd joined us to give us the stability we needed.

As Langan's thrived, Peter's alcoholism worsened. By the time Shakira and I had moved to Los Angeles in 1979 he was really out of control. He had taken to sleeping under a table at the restaurant overnight and would often still be there at lunchtime the next day. But he seemed completely oblivious to the havoc he caused and I was rather alarmed to hear that he was planning to come out and see me in LA to discuss opening a restaurant there. The English find drunks quite amusing, but it's not like that in health-conscious Beverly Hills so I was dreading his visit. I was right to do so. He'd asked me to get together some investors to discuss the project; with a certain amount of dread, I did. Peter was half an hour late for the meeting and when he arrived he collapsed in a drunken heap on the floor. There was a long silence and the potential investors looked appalled. Eventually one of them said, "So—if we invest, who would be in charge?" I pointed to the crumpled, snoring heap on the floor. They got up and left without another word.

I should have learnt my lesson, but ever hopeful, I invited Peter to lunch at Ma Maison, at that time *the* star-studded restaurant in LA. We sat outside and he was surprisingly well behaved during the meal, in spite of his prodigious intake of cocktails and champagne. I wasn't taking any chances, though, and when he decided he needed a pee, I went with him into the restaurant to make sure he found the toilet. Unfortunately, he put on a turn of speed and before I could stop him he had lurched over to a table where Orson Welles was sitting. "Orson Welles?" he asked politely. Orson said yes. Peter stood up straight and with all the misplaced dignity of the very drunk announced, "You are an arrogant fat arsehole." All hell broke loose. Patrick Terrall, the owner, came over and barred Peter from the restaurant for life and told me off for bringing him in the first place. I stayed behind to apologize to Orson while Patrick escorted Peter off the premises. As I dashed out after them, I heard a scream and emerged to find Peter peeing in the flowerpots lined up by the entrance. Peter left LA the next day.

Over the following years Peter's behavior got more and more out of hand. He was on a path of self-destruction and neither Richard Shepherd nor I had the slightest chance of persuading him off it. There was no chance of getting him to Alcoholics Anonymous, so I tried at least to get him to a doctor, but he refused, with the inevitable and tragic result that one night, in the middle of his customary drunken stupor, and in a set of very bizzare circumstances, he set fire to himself. He lived on, in agony, in an intensive care unit, for five terrible weeks before finally succumbing to the oblivion he had been looking for. I owe him a great deal—a career in the restaurant business, friendship, those good times, when we were buzzing with the delight that running a successful convivial restaurant brings— but eventually the demons took him over completely. I miss him still.

My partnership with Peter was the first of a number of such ventures. At one time I owned seven restaurants, including The Canteen in Chelsea Harbor, which we opened in 1993 with Marco Pierre White as chef. I had always sworn I wouldn't work with another temperamental partner after Peter, but Marco was so talented that I made an exception. The sous-chef under Marco at The Canteen was Gordon Ramsay. One of the invisible costs involved with this sort of talent was the installation of extra doors between the kitchen and the restaurant so the customers couldn't hear the language.

After three very successful years at The Canteen, we had to close it down. I also got an offer from my partner in the Langan's Group of restaurants, Richard Shepherd, to buy me out and I decided to call it a day. I have absolutely no regrets about getting involved in the restaurant business, but it is a relief to be out of it now. It isn't only the challenges of dealing with brilliant chefs, it's the customers, too. I was minding my own business on a British Airways flight the other day, when a woman came up to me and said, "I had a steak in Langan's the day before yesterday, and I asked for it to be medium and it was well done." I was very glad to be able to say to her, "Madam, I no longer own any restaurants, so it's not my fault."

CHAPTER FIFTEEN

HIGHS AND LOWS
IN MIAMI BEACH

In 1992, I had a bit of a surprise. As part of the American publicity tour for my first autobiography—*What's It All About?*—I went to the Miami Book Fair. I wasn't expecting much: the first time I'd been to Miami was in 1979 for a horror/thriller movie called *The Island* and I didn't have very happy memories of that. The film should have been a success: producers Richard Zanuck and David Brown and author Peter Benchley had all been involved in the blockbuster *Jaws* and consequently the budget was huge. The Caribbean location was a plus, too, but somewhere along the line the film just wasn't scary. And in the end, the only sharks frightening enough to pose a real threat turned out to be the critics. Nonetheless, Shakira and I enjoyed our stay on the luxury Turnberry Isle just outside Miami itself and were looking forward to exploring the area.

It started off very promising. We headed for Miami Beach and were driven there across MacArthur Causeway, which runs for a fabulous three miles. We discovered that Miami Beach is a completely separate city from Miami itself, forming a barrier island between the Atlantic and Miami proper, with a beautiful fifteen-mile sandy beach. That was fine, but South Beach, which starts at the end of the causeway, was a shock. It was a dumping ground—not just for litter, but for people, too. Human waste and wasted humans were everywhere; bums and junkies were holed up under every bridge and in every doorway of the many closed shops. Driving through in the daytime, it seemed as if everything was shut for business—but after darkness fell we soon found out that business picked up, as all the drug dealers came out of the woodwork.

There was a feeling of death everywhere: the old baking to death under the sun, the young drug addicts dying for pleasure at any time and the dealers killing for territory after dark. South Beach was two miles of the most beautiful Art Deco buildings, beaches and weather in the world and it was a rubbish dump. In those days it was known as "God's Waiting Room" because of the number of old people there. Looking at it on that first trip, I couldn't see that God had anything to do with it: this was a man-made hellhole and we vowed never to come back.

What we didn't know was that things were about to get a whole lot worse. In 1980, President Castro of Cuba graciously allowed any Cuban citizen who wanted to immigrate to the United States to leave—and 125,000 people took up the offer and headed to Miami. Among them must have been a criminal element, because the city nearly went under in a new and even more vicious crime wave. Sometimes situations need to get desperate before solutions emerge—and this is what happened. As the inhabitants of God's Waiting Room fled and the hotels emptied of the dying, it was not the demolishers who moved in, but the preservers. Under the leadership of entrepreneurs like Tony Goldman, Barbara Capitman and Chris Blackwell, the "Art Deco District" was born, the place chilled out, livened up and the world's Glamorati began to sit up and take notice. From 1984, which was the year *Miami Vice* was first shown on TV, to the Miami Book Fair in 1992, the place began to grow and prosper. International photographers, models and designers came, lured by the winter sun, and international hotels, clubs and restaurants sprang up to cater for their every need. The Glamorati glowed, the Glitterati glittered—and South Beach was reborn.

When I turned up for the Miami Book Fair, I barely recognized the place. Granted, as we came over the causeway and onto Ocean Drive there were still some bums and druggies and pushers around, but they were skulking out of sight rather than strutting their stuff in the bright daylight. The violence had gone, to be replaced by a fantastic young scene: I loved it immediately. "I want a holiday here!" I said to someone. South Beach was up and running and I felt like running with it.

I couldn't get South Beach out of my mind. In 1993, during the considerable lull that had suddenly developed in my moviemaking schedule, Shakira and I were in New York visiting Shakira's mother. While they spent time together, I spent a great deal of time not only with my best New York friend, restaurateur Elaine Kaufman, but also with Danny Zarem, the brother of Bobby, the press agent who had had to get me out of bed for the *Today* show on my first U.S. publicity tour. Danny had been the vice president and head of design for Bonwit Teller, one of the best clothing stores anywhere, and he is still the most stylish man I know. We always lunch at the Russian Tea Room, which is one of my favorite restaurants in New York—not just for the food, but because when it opened and they put up their first Christmas decorations, they liked them so much they just left them. It's always fun going in there on a boiling hot day and finding the Christmas decorations up.

During one of our many lunches amid the baubles, I told

Danny all about South Beach. Of course it turned out he was already in the know and the two of us took off there for a long weekend and stayed with Danny's friend the restaurateur Ray Schnitzer. Ray lived in the South Pointe Tower, at twenty-eight stories then the tallest building in South Beach. It was amazing to sit in Danny's apartment and watch the huge boats pass by his window as they sailed into Miami Harbor.

In the year since I'd last been in Miami, things had got even more exciting: Jack Nicholson was now spending a lot of time in South Beach. Jack, of course, knew where all the fun was to be had (and if he couldn't find it, either it sort of found him or he'd make it himself) and I tagged along for the ride. And then I was delighted to discover that Oliver Stone, the director of the 1981 film *The Hand*—a movie that did not reflect great credit on either of us—was also there. I had taken on *The Hand* in the first place partly because I had never done a horror movie before, but mainly because I'd wanted to work with Oliver. I made two discoveries during the course of filming: first, that I hated making horror movies, and second, that Oliver Stone was a genius. It turned out that he, like me, was an ex-infantryman and we spent a lot of our time together on set talking about our time in the army. He was not surprised to hear that I had never seen a film that remotely captured the atmosphere and reality of Korea: he had never seen one that reflected his experiences in Vietnam, he said, and one day he would put that right. . . . I've often reflected on the irony of having had the chance of working with a director like Oliver Stone—who would go on to direct *Platoon* and *JFK*—on a picture in which the real star of the show is my hand, which, severed in a car crash, takes on a murderous life of its own. . . . As my mother used to say: be careful what you wish for. In spite of our mauling by the critics, Oliver and I had remained good friends and once I knew that he, Jack and another Hollywood friend, Sylvester Stallone, had invested in South Beach, the attractions of the place proved hard to resist.

I flew back to New York to pick up Shakira and persuaded her to give Miami a try again. Although she was prepared to admit that things had improved, she wasn't quite as enthusiastic as I was. But in the new dawn of what I thought was going to be my retirement dual career of writing and restaurant owning, I was very excited by the possibilities and eventually decided to extend the restaurant empire from London to Miami. Ray Schnitzer and I went into partnership and I bought an old church on the burgeoning—although still quite risky—Lincoln Road and we opened the South Beach Brasserie. It was a great success; I managed to win Shakira over and we rented a flat in South Pointe Tower and for several years we went back every winter, eventually buying a flat there, which we still own.

South Beach was booming. New restaurants and clubs seemed to open every day—and close with equal rapidity. The South Beach crowd were fun, but they were also flaky and fickle; I often thought that South Beach was like a lamp burning extra bright and then blowing its bulb every year or so. The night when the bulb finally blew beyond repair was a very bright one indeed. Chris Paciello and Ingrid Casares, two people we all knew and liked, had opened a club called Liquid, which was the biggest thing so far in the new South Beach and the Glamorati and Glitterati, including Madonna, all turned out for the launch on Thanksgiving weekend 1995, which was a party to celebrate Madonna's brother Christopher Ciccione's birthday. We arrived after dinner at about 11:00 p.m. and were surprised to find that we were almost the first people there. Almost, but not quite. As Chris greeted us, I noticed six portly older gentlemen with very thick necks sitting in the darkest corner of the bar. "Who are they?" I asked. "Oh—just some of my investors," Chris answered vaguely. He seemed to be a bit nervous but I'd had a few drinks and thought nothing of it. After all, an invitation to this party was highly prized and had been extended to only the favored few. Gradually the club began to fill up. Madonna and her entourage arrived and were very friendly and then the "Favorati" began to crowd in in such numbers that the roped-off VIP area ended up with more guests crammed in shoulder to shoulder than the rest of the club. We left quite early—I love parties and clubs, but even I had had enough—and as I left I looked around and for some reason I thought of the last ball on the *Titanic*.

My instincts—so hopeless at picking up the signs of doom in my own movie career—that South Beach was changing were absolutely right. Shortly afterwards, Chris Paciello was arrested, convicted of being an accessory to murder and imprisoned. It turned out that he had been a career criminal for years, long before he came to South Beach, and that the empire he founded in Miami was based on his Mafia connections. An era was beginning to come to an end.

While it lasted, however, Miami was the perfect place to sit back and contemplate the new life I thought I was going to be leading. At the time of the Miami Book Fair in 1992, when my love affair with the place began, I knew that if I wasn't going to be a movie star any longer, I didn't need the oxygen of LA; if I was going to be a restaurant owner and a writer, then I could do that for most of the year from England with winters spent in Miami.

But the movie business still had one last surprise for me. Over the years I had watched as all my friends had appeared on *The Muppet Show* and I tried not to mind that I was never invited—but of course in the end I got the big part. I played Scrooge in *The Muppet Christmas Carol* and I had a wonderful time doing it, although I found it a very long process because the continuity is a nightmare. I loved working with the Muppeteers who are all very gentle souls and really do inhabit their characters and I found that I didn't have to change my style as an actor at all: working with the Muppets was just like working with real people. Apart from anything else, it gave me the chance to work again with the director of *Dirty Rotten Scoundrels*, Miss Piggy herself, better known as Frank Oz. Whenever anyone asks me whether I have been in a movie directed by a woman, I always reply, "Yeah—Miss Piggy!" People also always assume that working with the Muppets would be nonstop fun. Well it was, but in fact comedy is a very serious business; you can get far more laughs on a horror film. I once asked Anthony Hopkins—an actor who, like me, at one point thought his career was over—what it was like working on *Silence of the Lambs* and he said, "We had a lot of laughs on that." He would know—he's a very funny man and one of the best impressionists I've ever met. I've got an audiotape he once gave me of him impersonating Sir Laurence Olivier standing on Waterloo Bridge at the time he was founding the National Theatre and asking passing actors to come and do Hamlet—and I think it is one of the funniest things I have ever heard.

The Muppet Christmas Carol was a success—but it was the last I was going to have for quite some time. The scripts started to dry up completely—even the bad ones—and if there is one thing worse than being offered bad scripts it's being offered none at all. It wasn't all terrible, though—I had a wonderful, joint sixtieth birthday party back in Hollywood with my old friend Quincy Jones, who is my "celestial twin." We've worked out that, taking into account time differences, we were born at exactly the same time, on the same day and in the same year—me in London, and him in Chicago. We took over a club on Beverly Drive and had a fantastic celebration. With his friends and mine, it was quite a star-studded affair and it was wonderful to see so many people from both our pasts and presents all gathered together—from John Barry and Sidney Furie from my *Ipcress File* days, to Barbra Streisand, Oprah Winfrey and Jack

Nicholson. There were many highlights of that night, but I'll never forget rapping with Ice-T—I actually surprised myself; I wasn't bad—and perhaps most memorably of all, having Stevie Wonder himself singing "Happy Birthday" to Quincy and me. What a night.

The birthday party was a high spot in an otherwise low year. The wait for a decent movie can make you desperate, and in the end I got desperate to the point that I accepted a picture in Alaska with Steven Seagal, the martial arts expert. The movie was called *On Deadly Ground* and the title was to prove very apt. Although Stephen and the rest of the team were great to work with, I had broken one of the cardinal rules of bad movies: if you're going to do a bad movie, at least do it in a great location. Here I was, doing a movie where the work was freezing my brain and the weather was freezing my arse. I vowed never to work in a tough location again. The litmus test for this, I decided, would be my wife. If Shakira refuses to come, I ain't going. That was going to be my motto from now on.

I've been lucky over my career; like most people, I've screwed up a couple of times and got away with it. The thing I was about to do sounded really attractive. What I was about to do almost finished me off. The thing is, it sounded really attractive— reprise the role of the spy Harry Palmer in two back-to-back sequels to the 1965 film *The Ipcress File: Bullet to Beijing* and *Midnight in St. Petersburg*. It turned out to be my worst professional experience ever. Of course like all bad experiences, there were some good things—Jason Connery, Sean's son, whom I'd met as a small boy and was pleased to meet again, and Marsha, the assistant and interpreter who guided Shakira and me around St. Petersburg. (Yes, in my defense, Shakira had agreed to come with me on location.) Marsha was intelligent and melancholic in equal measure, in a very Russian way. She came to work one day with eyes all red from crying. "What's wrong?" Shakira asked, very concerned. "I've been crying all night," she replied. "What for?" Shakira persisted. She just shrugged her shoulders. "We all do," she said.

Eighteen years ago and in the immediate aftermath of the fall of Communism, St. Petersburg was a very different place from the way it is today. It was beyond chaos—and the Mafia had jumped into the vacuum and taken over. The first lunch-time on the set just before we started filming, we were all given personal Geiger counters to test the food for radiation. The first thing we all did was buy new batteries. Radioactive or not, the food was terrible and Shakira would go back and forth to London, returning to St. Petersburg with Marks and Spencer's steak and kidney pudding and other goodies to keep us all going.

Our hotel turned out to be the center for the local Mafia. Oddly enough, they didn't hang out in the dimly lit bar or the disco, but in the central café that only served tea and cakes and played genteel light music. It was a very ladylike place and it was very strange watching some of the toughest men on earth plotting mayhem over afternoon tea and scones.

One afternoon, we were sitting peacefully in the tearoom when out of the blue, with no shouting or warning, a dozen men in black overalls and black masks came tearing across the café—not on the floor, but leaping straight across the room, crashing on top of the tables and hurling themselves straight at their tar-get. It was all over in a second, but we were in complete shock. It turned out that what we initially thought was a hit squad of rival gangsters was the OMON, an elite force of the Russian police—they wore masks so the Mafia could not recognize them and retaliate against their families.

I was eventually assigned a few bodyguards, two guys with Kalashnikovs who followed me everywhere in the street in a jeep and another one with a pistol who apparently was watch-ing over me when I was inside. I never found out who he was, but I took the production manager's word that he existed and I hung on to those guards right up to the last passenger barrier at the airport.

A couple of days before I left, I was sitting in my usual corner of the café (now with the damage repaired) when one of the Mafia guys came over and asked if he could join me. As if I could possibly say no. "Why do you have these stupid bodyguards?" he asked. I replied to him all innocently, as if I had no idea of his occupation, "They say that there's Mafia here in St. Petersburg and I'm worried about our safety." He let out a great laugh and slapped his enormous thigh. "You work for—" and he gave the name of a Russian movie company I didn't quite catch. Did I? He stood up and said, "We own that. There's no need to worry—you're the safest man in the whole of St. Petersburg," and walked away.

The city architecture of St. Petersburg, and the Hermitage in particular, was fabulous. Shakira and I spent hours wandering around the museum. But the filming itself was a joke. The final blow came when we were shooting in the Lenfilm studio itself. I wanted to go for a pee and they directed me to the toilet. I could smell it fifty yards away and when I got there I found the filthiest toilet I have ever seen in my life. I went outside and peed up against the soundstage, which I noticed several other men had done before. So this is where my career has ended, I thought to myself: in the toilet. I'm done.

It was winter. I picked myself up and took the family off to our place in Miami straight after Christmas. The sun was shining, everyone was happy, the book was still selling, my restaurants were doing well. Fine, I thought, life was different—but that was life.

And this is when Jack Nicholson changed everything. He'd moved on from Miami—but he suddenly turned up there again with the director Bob Rafaelson and a script called *Blood and Wine* that they were going to shoot there. The combination of the three was very seductive and I decided to have one last shot at being a movie actor. It was the best decision I ever made.

Jack's a tremendous actor who takes life easy and I owe him for restoring my faith in the business. It was a joy working with him and a great bunch of professionals again. Jack's attitude to work was summed up for me one day when we were hurrying to get a shot before the sun went down. I started to run towards the set. "Don't run, Michael!" hissed Jack. "They'll know it's us who are late!" So we kept strolling—and I still do.

Jack has a deservedly great reputation for the ladies, but he had me fooled one day. We broke for lunch and I saw Jack go into his motor home with one particularly pretty but very young girl. After lunch I tried to broach the subject diplomatically. "That was a very pretty girl I saw you with at lunchtime," I said, trying to keep a disapproving note out of my voice. He looked at me for a moment and then the wolfish Nicholson smile gradually spread across his features as he read my evil thoughts. "That was my daughter, Michael," he said, pretending to look puzzled. "By Miss Denmark," he added with a careless flourish. I dropped the subject immediately.

Allthough *Blood and Wine* was never a big hit with the public, it was a big hit with me. Filming was suddenly fun again and there were a whole new bunch of talented young actors to get to know—Jennifer Lopez, Heath Ledger, Sandra Bullock, Christian Bale, Charlize Theron, Scarlett Johansson to name but a few. It was the beginning of an exciting new phase of my life—slower to take off than I'd have liked, but I was definitely on my way back!

CHAPTER SIXTEEN

BACK IN THE GAME

Back in England, the weather was terrible and I found myself further away from London than before. It had taken us fifty minutes to get from London when we first moved there, but now the traffic was so bad it was taking me an hour and a half. I was starting a new professional life—maybe, I thought, it was also time to start a new home life? And so I began looking for a new house and a new movie at the same time.

The movie came quite quickly. I had sifted through the pile of post when I got home to find the usual bundle of crap scripts with fingerprints and coffee stains all over them from the other actors who had turned them down—but among them was a small gem. It wasn't a big movie—it wasn't even really a movie as I would have defined one—it was a made-for-TV film called *The Mandela Story*, which told the story of the collapse of apartheid in South Africa and the election of Mandela as president. And my old friend Sidney Poitier was, as they say in Hollywood, already "attached" to play Nelson Mandela. I read the script with great excitement. I would be playing South Africa's last president under the apartheid system, President de Klerk. It would be a challenge—it always is playing a real person—but I felt it would be a worthwhile one and we packed our bag for Cape Town.

I encountered a problem with my South African accent. I'd listened to and learnt the way white South Africans spoke on the set of *Zulu*, all those years ago, so I felt very confident when my language coach asked if I could do a South African accent and proudly showed her that I could. She listened for a moment and then looked at me. "That's an *English* South African accent," she said. "De Klerk is a Boer." I struggled for weeks trying to identify the tiny differences between the two.

I had dinner with de Klerk one evening at his home, which was a very grand official residence. I asked him where President Mandela lived and he said that he lived round the corner in a smaller house. "But he's the president," I said. "I know," de Klerk said, "but he didn't want to live here because of its connections to apartheid and so I stayed on." I asked de Klerk how he got on with Mandela and his reply was a guarded one. They got on fine, he said, except for one moment at the ceremony in Sweden when they were jointly awarded the Nobel Peace Prize. De Klerk told me that he was surprised and upset when, during his acceptance speech, Mandela made a personal attack on him. He looked at me in a rather sad and disillusioned way. "After all," he said, "I was the reason he was there in the first place." De Klerk reminded me a little of President Gorbachev of Russia: both were key players in the dismantling of ruthless and terrifying regimes and yet both were eventually sidelined by the onward march of the progress they had helped initiate.

It was to take another year for something else to attract my attention, but I spent the time happily involved in my restaurant business, working on the first draft of a novel (still not finished . . .), spending time with the family, cooking and gardening. Life was slower than it had been, but it was great—and I was biding my time. My patience paid off in the end and although it seemed that I still wasn't flavor of the month in the movie business, eventually an interesting script did come along. It was another made-for-TV film, a remake of Jules Verne's *Twenty Thousand Leagues Under the Sea*. I was to play Captain Nemo and what really appealed about it was that the sea it was going to be twenty thousand leagues under was off the Gold Coast of Australia.

My whirlwind tour of Australia for *What's It All About?* had really whetted my appetite for the country and this was a fantastic opportunity to go back and see what all the fuss was about. I wasn't disappointed. The crew on the film, the people I met and the landscape were all wonderful and we had a great time shooting the movie.

We had a great place to stay, too; we rented a house right on the beach. I've lived in hot climates and I've lived by the sea and so I thought, lovely though it was, that I'd seen it all before. And I was right: the weather was amazing, the sea was as blue as any I've ever seen, but the people swimming in it were very different. Long before those of us who live in the Northern Hemisphere realized the danger of the sun's rays, the Australians were being careful. The first time Shakira and I went for a stroll on the beach we stopped and stared in amazement: it was like a seaside painting from Victorian England. Everybody had covered as much of themselves as they possibly could and still walk and swim. And what little exposed flesh there was left was slathered in gallons of suntan lotion. We did spot several bright red sunbathers in bikinis and Speedos, but of course these turned out to be recent British immigrants who weren't having any truck with this nonsense about global warming and skin cancer. Even after my own experiences with sunburn in the army on the trip out to Korea, I was a bit skeptical about such extreme measures. I would be learning a lesson about that in due course.

On another walk, we were confronted by an even more unexpected sight: a Japanese wedding party with the men in full morning dress—tails and top hats—and the bride and brides-maids in all their regalia, being photographed on the beach. It looked most incongruous, but it was only the first of many as one wedding party after another posed on the sands. A local told me later that the reason so many Japanese come to Austra-lia to get married is so that they can escape the huge expense of a full ceremony at home to which they would need to invite everyone in the community to avoid losing face.

I was beginning to enjoy the straightforward attitude of the Australians I met. I'd decided to stop drinking for a few weeks—something I do occasionally—and went into a liquor store, or "grog shop" as it was described on a sign outside. "Can I have some alcohol-free beer?" I asked the assistant inside. He looked at me rather puzzled. "What for?" he asked. A perfectly reasonable question, I thought, so I said, "I'm on the wagon." "OK, mate," he said helpfully. "What you need to do is go next door to the supermarket and look under 'lemonade.'" Very sensible advice: I did, and there it was.

This straightforward attitude carries over to food. We had some fantastic meals out while we were there, and I particu-larly enjoyed the Morton Bay Bugs—a delicious shellfish. I asked the waiter why something as good as that had such a basic name and—like my friend in the grog shop—he looked a bit puzzled for a minute and then said, "It's because that's what they are and that's where they come from." Fair enough—you can't argue with that! In fact, I was surprised by the quality and variety of Australian cuisine (I think I had been expecting some sort of old-fashioned duff English food), and I mentioned it to an Aussie restaurant owner I got talking to. "You Pommie bastards are all the same," he said, "you always underestimate us!" I agreed

Is this me or my double?
Dressed to Kill, 1980. I hated the
tights, couldn't walk in the high
heels, got lipstick all over my cigars
and stubbornly insisted on wearing
my own underpants.... Who would
have thought the role that would
rescue my career at that point would
be of a transvestite psychiatrist turned
murderer?

With Sly Stallone,
Pelé and John Huston
on the set of *Escape to
Victory*, 1980. No
one could beat us!

Just before my kiss
with Superman in
Deathtrap, 1982.
Christopher Reeve
and I had been
drinking steadily
throughout the
afternoon to get our
courage up. All I
could smell was the
brandy.

Promoting *Mona Lisa* with
Bob Hoskins in Raymond's
Revue Bar, 1985. Every single girl
in the dressing room had a picture
of Marilyn Monroe pinned to her
mirror.

Steve Martin and me in *Dirty
Rotten Scoundrels*, 1988. One
of my favorite films and
probably my all time favorite
location—the South of France.

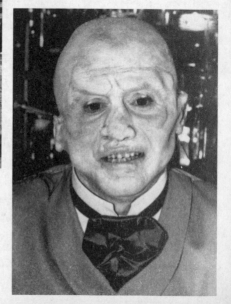

Undergoing my transformation from Dr.
Jekyll to Mr. Hyde, 1990. I have no idea
how John Hurt managed to get through
The Elephant Man.

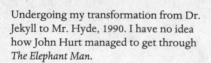

With Swifty Lazar at his legendary Oscar party at Spago in 1989. His size was the only small thing about him.

Re-creating an English Sunday lunch with the traditional roast beef and Yorkshire pudding at our home in California

The surprise farewell party Irwin Allen threw me with all the comedians. Guests included George Burns, Red Buttons, Bob Newhart, Larry Gelbart, Milton Berle, Steve Allen and Sid Caesar.

Collecting my CBE from the Palace with Shakira, 1992. One of the few bright moments of "the twilight years."

Comedy is a very serious business. . . . At last I got to work with the Muppets in *The Muppet Christmas Carol*, 1992.

With the first person to tell me I will be a star

1993: a sixtieth birthday party to remember—shared with my "celestial twin,"
Quincy Jones, on the left. Keeping us apart is the legendary Ray Charles.

With Jack Nicholson in *Blood and Wine*, 1996. I owe Jack for making the movie business fun again.

Sidney and me posing with each other's election posters in *The Mandela Story*, 1996

With the man I was playing: ex-President de Klerk of South Africa

Outside the South
Beach Brasserie in
Miami in 1996 with
Nikki, Shakira and
Natasha

The photograph taken while we posed for David Hockney's drawing for the
Langan's menu. Peter Langan is on the left, Richard Shepherd is on the right.

With my fellow stars in *Little Voice*, 1998. From left to right: me, Brenda Blethyn, Jane Horrocks and Ewan McGregor.

Miss Congeniality, 2000. As we emerged from the aircraft hangar after I had "transformed" Sandra Bullock from a dowdy FBI agent into a beauty queen there was a collective gasp and I heard one of the crew say: "Who the f**k is that?" They hadn't recognized her...

Dancing with the Rockettes—and Charles Bronson—at Radio City Music Hall

Holding the 2000 Oscar for Best Supporting
Actor for my role in *The Cider House Rules*

At Buckingham Palace with Natasha, Shakira and Nikki after receiving my
knighthood in 2000

With Brendan Fraser on the set of *The Quiet American* in Ho Chi Minh City, 2001

With Natasha, Shakira and Nikki at the 2003 Academy Awards, where I was nominated for Best Actor for *The Quiet American*. I knew in my heart of hearts I didn't stand a chance that year. . . .

At home in
Chelsea with
Shakira

Unveiling a blue plaque outside the place I
was born, St. Olave's Hospital, Rotherhithe.
The man from the council said to me: "You
know you're supposed to be dead to get one
of these?" "Well, I don't feel too good this
morning," I replied.

With two of my closest friends.
Sean Connery and me celebrating
with Roger Moore after he was
knighted in 2003.

With Shakira on the "Diana bench" at the Taj Mahal

With Shakira on top of the Sydney Harbour Bridge. The apartment we were staying in is just behind my shoulder.

Shakira, Jackie Collins and Scarlett Johansson at my birthday party in 2006. Scarlett had just sung "Happy Birthday" in my ear like Marilyn Monroe did to JFK....

A gathering of most of the Mayfair Orphans. From left to right: Philip Kingsley, Doug Hayward, Terry O'Neill, me, Johnny Gold and Mickey Most.

At the premiere of *Batman Begins*, 2005. From left to right: Gary Oldman, me, Christian Bale, Katie Holmes, Morgan Freeman and Liam Neeson.

Actors, writer and director of *Sleuth*. Clockwise from top left: Kenneth Branagh, Jude Law, Harold Pinter and me.

With David Cameron launching his National Citizens' Service initiative just before the general election, 2010

In front of the mural depicting me and Charlie Chaplin at The Elephant

Shakira and me with Natasha and her husband. Michael, and all the grandchildren, in our garden August 2010

My perfect weekend. Collecting the potatoes with Taylor, aged eighteen months.

My hand and footprints at Grauman's Chinese Theatre. A lasting impression of Hollywood!

with him and in return he assured me that "Pommie bastard" was an affectionate description of the English (hmmm . . .). I told him I quite understood and we parted on excellent terms.

For years after making *Twenty Thousand Leagues* I was puzzled as to why the young American actor who played the romantic lead—who was wonderful and very talented—hadn't made it big. I was sure he would become a star as soon as the film was out, but nothing happened. I had forgotten all about him until I was in America a couple of years ago and suddenly he was everywhere: *Gray's Anatomy* had become one of the most popular shows on TV and Patrick Dempsey one of its biggest stars. It proves again just how fluid the worlds of film and TV are—and I like to think it proves I know a star when I see one!

After my travels to South Africa for the Mandela film and our trip to Australia for *Twenty Thousand Leagues*, plus a couple of trips to Miami, it was quite a relief to be back in England for a while. But I knew I needed a great part in a real movie, not a made-for-TV movie, and I needed it to be set in England because I was fed up with traveling. Actually, from where I was standing, it looked as if what I really needed was a miracle—and to my astonishment I got one.

The bringer of my miracle was the American producer Harvey Weinstein who with his brother Bob ran the film company Miramax—charmingly named after their parents, Miriam and Max. Among other great films they had put together were *Pulp Fiction* and *Shakespeare in Love*, so I was very excited when Harvey sent me the script for a movie called *Little Voice*.

The star of *Little Voice* was a brilliant young actress called Jane Horrocks, who had had great success in the theater with the same role. Not only was she a great actress, but like the character she was playing, Jane could do incredible singing impersonations of stars like Edith Piaf, Marilyn Monroe, Shirley Bassey and Judy Garland—very much my era of music—which is all the more incredible because she is a tiny, slender woman whom you wouldn't think would have the power. The playwright Jim Cartwright heard her doing these impressions as a warm-up before she went onstage in his play *Road* and then wrote a play around her talent, which he called *The Rise and Fall of Little Voice*. It was directed by Sam Mendes and it was such a hit in the West End that Harvey bought the movie rights. The story is about a talented but shy "little voice" who is forced to perform by a sleazy agent (me), with disastrous consequences. I was very pleased to join a talented cast that included Brenda Blethyn, Jim Broadbent and Ewan McGregor, all of whom were excellent actors. It was a very different experience from the blockbusting *Twenty Thousand Leagues* and I sensed we were on to something good from the start.

Off we went to Scarborough to film. A seaside town, in the north of England, in the winter—I know I'd said I wanted a film in England, but this was pushing things a bit far. But the work and the people were so great I put on an extra sweater or two and settled back into the pleasure of making a really good movie and found myself happier than I had been for some time.

I was a bit taken aback by some of the nightlife in Scarborough, though. I have never thought of myself as someone who is easily shocked, but every Saturday night I was there, I saw hordes of young women drunk out of their minds, stumbling about and spewing up. I wasn't used to drunken girls. In my day we used to try to ply girls with alcohol so we could have our wicked way with them; here they were doing it for themselves. But as far as I could see none of the men were able to take unfair advantage of the situation: they were so drunk themselves that they wouldn't have been capable of having their wicked way with anything. I thought it was very sad and very unromantic. I was also astonished at the way, despite it being midwinter and absolutely freezing, none of the girls—drunk or sober—wore a coat. I asked one girl who was more or less upright and coherent why and she said that it was because they couldn't afford to pay the cloakroom attendants in the clubs. It occurred to me that the girls who didn't die from alcohol poisoning would probably die from pneumonia.

Drunk or sober, there's no mistaking the northern sense of humor. On a rare day off, my team—Jim, my assistant; Colin, my driver; and Dave, my motor home driver—decided to drive to Whitby, where we had been told we could buy the best fish and chips anywhere. We found the shop, bought the fish and chips and ate them in the traditional way from their newspaper wrapping while walking around Whitby harbor. We had just rounded a corner—when we stopped, astonished. There, standing on the quayside and staring out into the harbor, was a crowd of about three hundred men dressed as Dracula. They were all shouting in unison, "It's good to talk!" at a small boat bobbing about with two people in it who seemed to be being filmed from a second boat off to one side. We couldn't make head nor tail of it, nor could we see who was in the boat, so we went back to the fish and chip shop owner. He explained everything. Whitby was where Bram Stoker, the Victorian novelist and theater manager, had written his famous story about Dracula. Unbeknownst to us we had come to the town on Stoker's birthday and encountered a whole bunch of Dracula fans who were there to celebrate. Well, that seemed reasonable enough—but what were they shouting and why? That turned out to be simple, too. The boat had contained my old friend Bob Hoskins who was most recently celebrated for his famous TV commercials for British Telecom in which his punch line was, "It's good to talk." You couldn't make it up, could you?

Little Voice was a great success both critically and financially— and for me it confirmed the establishment of my new career. I had needed two miracles, really, to sort both home and career and I was very happy and grateful for one—where, I wondered, was the other one going to come from?

Back from Scarborough, I prowled round my house in Oxford-shire, cooking and gardening and visiting London less and less the further away it got. I scanned every paper looking for my dream house and read the usual bunch of crap scripts and waited for my agent to call. To really consolidate this new phase of my career, I needed a film that would work in America as well as Britain. In 1998 at least one of my prayers was answered with a script for a film version of John Irving's great American classic *The Cider House Rules*. That was a strong enough pedi-gree to hook me in, but the director Lasse Hallström was also very talented, and the cast included Charlize Theron, who would go on to win an Oscar for *Monster*, Tobey Maguire, who would become the hugely successful *Spider-Man*, and my two cohort nurses Kathy Baker and Jane Alexander, both great actresses to work with. I play a doctor who runs an orphanage.

There's an old adage that says actors should avoid working with animals or children, but I've done both and survived. In *The Cider House Rules* it was children and there were about a hundred of them and they were delightful—except for the babies. There are strict rules in movies for working with babies: they can never work for more than half an hour and their eyes must be protected from the bright lights at all times to prevent them from burning their corneas. As a grandfather of two tiny babies, I understand all this, but it makes the acting quite hard work. As the acting time is so short companies usually cast iden-tical twins, which sounds sensible but of the twins I worked with on *Cider House* one never stopped crying and the other never stopped laughing. If that wasn't bad enough there was a strict lady inspector from the authorities looking over our shoulder the whole time.

But I loved the movie—and I loved my part. Given the iconic one-liners from *The Italian Job* and *Get Carter*, I'm always on the alert for lines that will stick in people's minds and in *The Cider House Rules* I thought I spotted one quite early on: every night when I turn out the lights in the orphanage dormitory, I say to the boys: "Good night, you Princes of Maine, you Kings of New England." It's a line I love, and I've been proved right: American men often come up to me and say, "Do you know what I say to my boys just before they go to sleep?" And I have to act surprised.

One of the most enjoyable aspects of getting to my age in movies is watching all the young stars come up, and Charlize Theron is one of the most talented—and beautiful—of them all. She was a pleasure to work with on *Cider House*. We had to play a potentially embarrassing scene together in which my doctor character gives her an obstetric examination with her legs open and up on stirrups. We were all waiting to see how she would handle this and she did it in typical Charlize fashion. When the time came for the shoot, she got up on the stirrups, gave her wickedest smile and opened her legs to reveal the nastiest pair of old man's underpants I have ever seen—although being Charlize, she still managed to look sexy in them!

I have a list of younger actresses that I love to work with and Charlize is right at the top of it, along with Nicole Kidman, Beyoncé Knowles and Scarlett Johansson. They are all brilliantly talented, but they are also funny and they have the same kindness that I see and love in Shakira.

I have always been fascinated by beautiful women. Right from when I was a little boy, I was very aware of female beauty. I know that's true of the majority of blokes, but there's something else I think I respond to. I've met a lot of beautiful women who, if their souls were on their face, would be ugly. I always think that even if Shakira had an ugly face she would be beautiful, because her inner beauty shines out. And that's often the case with female movie stars: some of them are not classically beautiful, but they have this wonderful quality of luminescence.

Of course the reverse is true—I have met beautiful women who have not had that quality and it's what stops them from making it in the movies. To become a really big female star, every man in the audience has to think: I bet she'd go out with me if I met her. Of course Garbo was a big star and no one would ever have thought she'd go out with them, but that's unusual. Even Grace Kelly, who looked aloof, seemed approachable—she had a really warm face and when you looked at her you'd think: I bet she'd talk to me if we met. And it's that warm quality that Charlize has got in spades—although, mind you, she managed to suppress it in her Oscar-winning portrayal of serial killer Aileen Wuornos in *Monster*.

We shot *The Cider House Rules* in the town of Northampton in Massachusetts and it was so cold that Shakira stayed in New York and I fled there to join her at every opportunity. There were other challenges, too, as well as keeping my blood temperature above freezing. As I had when I was filming *The Mandela Story,* I told my dialogue coach confidently that I had no problems with accents. "Go ahead," he said. So I gave him my vintage American accent and he laughed. "It's great!" he said. "But your accent is pure Californian—and you're playing a New Englander in this movie." So it was back to the grindstone and I spent many hours working with him and listening to tapes and just walking round (shivering) and overhearing people talk. In fact the New England accent is actually much closer to an English accent than it is to a Californian accent— it's just a very subtle difference in the vowels. Ironically, while I got a great review for my American accent in *The New Englander* (and they should know), I got poor reviews in the UK papers for sounding "too English." You can't win, can you?

Actually, sometimes you can—because I was nominated for a Best Supporting Actor Academy Award in 1999 for my role in *Cider House*. I had learnt my lesson with my previous Oscar and this time I did turn up for the Awards. And just as well I did—

because I got a long, standing ovation when I won. Time is always the big issue at the Academy Awards and the winner's acceptance speech is always under threat from the music. . . . When the producer thinks you have gone on long enough he starts the music softly and gradually increases the volume until the audience can hardly hear you say good night. I had picked out the other nominees in my category for a remark—Tom Cruise, Jude Law, Michael Clarke Duncan and Haley Joel Osment—and I was aware I was going on a bit long. I needed another minute, so I looked over at the wings to check with Dick Zanuck who was producing that year. He gave me a smile and a thumbs-up and I got that extra minute—which is a gift of pure gold at the Awards.

So there I was, a second Academy Award, another role in a great movie—life, I felt, was great again.

CHAPTER SEVENTEEN

HOME

There's a line in *The Man Who Would Be King* that I've always thought sums up my view of life. I have to ask Daniel Dravitt (Sean Connery) to tell someone that "Peachy's gone south for the winter." And that's always been my creed—Peachy's gone south for the bloody winter. It's always worked perfectly for us, so once again, after the Oscars we went back to our idyllic winter sojourn in Miami. As Shakira and I strolled down Lincoln Road to visit our restaurant the South Beach Brasserie, we became aware of a different atmosphere around the place and it gradually dawned on us that the vast majority of people who were walking round and sitting outside the cafés enjoying the sunshine like us were gay men. There had always been gay men in South Beach and after a lifetime in theater and movies I was hardly unused to this, but I had never encountered so many gay men en masse before.

I had been very conscious of the vicious swathe the HIV virus had cut through the gay community elsewhere and was surprised to see such a fit group in Miami. Fit, bronzed men, their bodies tuned like bodybuilders, were everywhere. One of my friends there, a photographer who was gay, was HIV positive and had looked very ill when I had seen him last. I barely recognized him when I bumped into him on our next visit: he was tanned, fit and muscular. He explained the mystery to me over dinner. Whether or not it was true, he and many of his friends believed that steroids held back the effects of the virus, so they were all pumped and ready to go. Their attitude, he explained, was that they had HIV—and full-blown AIDS in many cases—and they were going to die young, so they were making the best of it. As we left the restaurant he smiled and shook my hand. "It's fun in the sun 'til you're done, hon," he said as he walked away. I knew I would never see him again.

Lincoln Road became a flamboyant nightly parade of happy people either flaunting their love or looking for it. Those on steroids looked a bit like Arnold Schwarzenegger balloons waiting for the pinprick of AIDS to blow them back to reality: I have never seen so many sick people so happy. Eventually, though, the sadness of it all got to us and we decided to sell up, pack up and go home. As we drove back once again over the MacArthur Causeway, what we saw as we looked back seemed like the most glamorous hospice in the world.

Back home in England, miracles were on their way—although, of course, life never goes quite to plan . . . we'd managed to sell our house in Oxfordshire before we had found another one we wanted to live in, so we stored our furniture and moved into the flat in Chelsea Harbor. After the space of Rectory Farm it felt very cramped and, Shakira informed me, I paced round the flat like a caged animal. She was right; that was just what I felt like. In the meantime I looked at every estate agent's brochure in the country, including one for a two-hundred-year-old barn in Surrey, which wouldn't be ready for another year, so I threw that one away.

I continued my search in vain for another couple of weeks until my secretary Tricia turned up one day with a cutting from *The Times*. "Here's one you might like," she said, and handed it to me. It was an advert for the barn conversion job I had already discarded. "I've seen it," I told her and threw it in the waste-paper basket again. She was used to me, so she shrugged and we got on with some other work.

After lunch I was so bored and frustrated that I fished the ad out of the basket and read it again. I had nothing to do, so I decided I might as well go and look at the place. It was in a beautiful valley, named after the River Mole, which ran through it, and quite near Box Hill, where I had gone hiking as a Boy Scout. The site was set in twenty-one acres of the Surrey Hills and had stunning views. All this was, I had to admit, a good start. The barn itself was in good shape for its age and the developers were in the process of putting three stories into the massive space—and that was as far as they had got. As I watched them, it suddenly occurred to me that I might be able to design the place myself. Would this be possible? I asked. The foreman shrugged. He didn't care. "If you buy it," he said, "you can have it any way you like, as long as you pay for any changes to what we've done already." Well, what they had done already didn't amount to much, so I began to get excited: it would be great fun to design a house again, I thought.

I decided to walk around the grounds, which were set on a beautiful sloping hillside. The place had been a barn and busy riding school, attached to the big manor house further up the hill, and so had no garden or cultivation of any kind—it was just virgin fields with a road for delivery trucks. It would be fantastic to design a garden again, I thought, and as I walked round the whole twenty-one acres, I felt excitement welling up inside me at the prospect. Just as I was circling round and back to the building site I saw something that made me certain that this place was right for me and for my family. (Actors are very superstitious people indeed—me included: it's a dodgy profession and you need all the help you can get.) As I stood there, looking out at the view, a flock of about thirty beautiful yellow and green parrots flew over my head. What on earth were they doing in Surrey? When I asked the foreman he told me that they were Brazilian parrots that had escaped years ago from a film set in Shepperton Studios, which wasn't far away. "Which film?" I asked, curious. "*The African Queen*," was the answer—and that was almost all I needed to know. Humphrey Bogart and John Huston? It was a sign. But the ultimate test for me is the "sitting-down test." Just as I had done years before when I was looking at Mill House and invited Mum and Paul to come along, I brought Shakira and Natasha the next day. They loved the setting straightaway, but there was one flaw in my experiment: it was a building site and so of course there was nowhere for them to sit down. I needn't have worried. When I asked them where they would like to go for lunch, they both said they would like to go into town and buy some sandwiches and bring them back to the barn and have a picnic on the grass. I had my answer and I bought the place.

There are a couple of lessons I have learnt in life that applied to buying this house. Sometimes the greatest things that happen to you are out of your control, but they are destined for you anyway. It happened most significantly with Shakira, of course: I only met her because I stayed in one night to watch television. I have no idea what made me do it but not a day goes by when I don't thank my lucky stars for it. It was the same with our new house. I had the house of my dreams in my hand and threw it into the wastepaper basket not once, but twice . . . but something made me rescue the scrunched-up ad, smooth it out and—well, I'm sitting here now!

The house is in the Green Belt, a designated conservation area in which no one is allowed to build. The developer had only got planning permission to do the conversion if he agreed to tear down 46,000 square feet of other buildings on the estate. That had already happened by the time I came along, but I saw the photographs and the old riding school, stables and horses' swimming pool were some of the ugliest buildings I have ever seen. There was also a drive straight up from the main road to the barn. When I bought it as a house, I was told that I couldn't have a gate on the main road and that we would have to go round the back of the property. I was really upset at the time, because I did want to have this great drive up to the front of my house, but in fact it turned out to be the best thing that could have happened. In its place I put a hedge, which cuts the main road off—and now people pass the house without ever knowing it's there, which is brilliant. I'm really grateful to the council for putting these obstacles in my way. Sometimes the things in life you think are bad turn out to be great

We weren't disappointed when we finally moved in ten months later; the house and the grounds were wonderful. But after a brutally cold winter in 2007, we rented a house in Miami to escape the cold after Christmas. It was the perfect place to relax and just enjoy ourselves for a week and wandering round, we found the place had changed again since we were last there. The society around South Beach and Lincoln Road had suddenly become much more diverse. And we discovered that the London restaurant scene had invaded the place: apart from Hakkasan Fontainebleau in Miami Beach, the most enormous Mr. Chow has now been established in the W Hotel in South Beach and Cipriani and Cecconi are due shortly. Nick Jones is building The Soho Beach House, too. The weather, of course, is perfect, and I didn't need much persuading to buy another apartment there. We found one overlooking the ocean, the beach and the cut where the great liners go into the port of Miami, right past my window.

You might think that there is no connection whatsoever between our life in Surrey and our life in Miami but there is. The world is not only strange, it is also small. Not long ago the manor house to which our barn was once attached was sold to a Georgian billionaire called Badri Patarkatsishvili. Shortly after he moved in, he sent his butler down to our house and I happened to open the door to him. "Mr. Badri would like to know how much you want for your house," he said. I was so taken aback I forgot to say $50 million and just said rather pompously, "It's not for sale." Why, I wondered, as I walked back inside, would he want to buy another house so close to his own? I thought it might be for his two doughters, but I later found out that he never stayed in a house for more than one night for security reasons. It was perhaps just as well because I would never have got my $50 million anyway. Mr. Badri, who was a very fit fifty-three-year-old, suddenly died of a heart attack. Our quiet country lane was packed with press and TV vans as limousines with blacked-out windows honked their way through. It turned out that the lane wasn't the only thing that got blocked: there was a big lawsuit over Mr. Badri's will and all his assets were frozen. This didn't mean much to me, until I went to Miami for our winter break and noticed from the window of my apartment that construction on the new block of luxury apartments on Fisher Island on the other side of Government Cut, the entrance to the port of Miami, had come to a halt. I put it down to the credit crunch, but it was in fact due to the death of Mr. Badri, who had owned Fisher Island. So in Miami as well as in Surrey I can look out of my window and see Mr. Badri's former homes. Funny old world.

Our annual escape to Miami usually ends around my

birthday on March 14. I have a big birthday-cum-homecoming party and then my year in England starts. There are all sorts of reasons to celebrate: it's spring and I suddenly become a gardener again, and then the cricket season begins just in time for the April showers. I always think that any country with a drought should send for eleven Englishmen dressed in white, get them to stick three pieces of wood into the ground, then stand back and wait for the rain!

One of the joys of our new house in Surrey was planning and planting the garden. We have twenty-one acres, of which six are cultivated, including an ornamental garden, and I designed and built them all myself. They say that as you grow old you grow into your second childhood—and I think my garden takes me back to the Norfolk farm I was evacuated to during the war. A Chinese friend of mine told me that it was great "Zen" to sow, grow, harvest, cook and eat your own food and that is what I do. Food from my kitchen garden tastes better than anything you can buy in the shops and it makes me very happy, so I guess he's right. I think gardeners are every bit as superstitious as actors. I have a superstition about mulberry trees: if you plant one and it grows it is good luck—but you must never cut it or trim it. So now I have an enormous great mulberry tree blocking a path.

I love the changing seasons in Britain—it's something I missed while we were living in California. My personal first day of summer coincides with the opening of the Chelsea Flower Show, although I know that's really still classed as spring. There's the first day of the Test match cricket season, the first day of the French Open tennis and, of course, Wimbledon. As a sports fanatic, I'm glued to my screen from here on right up to the U.S. Open.

I love the start of autumn, when the trees in my garden change the color of their leaves in one last dazzling display; I planted masses of trees just for their autumn colors—but I hate it when the leaves drop and reveal an endless view of bare twigs. The days get shorter, the clocks go back an hour and although there is the occasional beautifully crisp, sharp, sunny autumn day, the low gray clouds begin to dominate. The only shining light to guide me through the darkness to Christmas is the arrival of the "screeners"—DVDs of the forty top films of the year sent to members of both the American Academy and the European Film Academy, for potential awards. So just as the outside world starts to darken and shrink and the days become impossibly short, we settle down in our own cinema and don't emerge until my favorite festival, Christmas.

Christmas is a very special time for me because it was a time I hardly knew as a child. I have no memory of my first three years, and for the next three years, there was nothing Christmassy to remember. It wasn't until I was six years old and evacuated to Norfolk that I really became aware that Christmas existed—and then we were told there wasn't going to be much of one anyway. Food was rationed, for a start, although we did get the rare treat of an orange and a banana and, wonder of wonders, a bar of chocolate. Sounds extravagant, doesn't it? But there was lots of homemade fun. We made our own paper chains by painting long strips of paper, cutting them into short lengths and then sticking them together with flour-and-water paste—which wasn't very adhesive and meant that you were likely to be suddenly festooned with gluey bits of paper as you walked round the house. There were no presents, toys or cards. There was a Christmas tree, but because the farmhouse we were living in didn't have electricity there were no lights on it. Things were better after the war, but money was always short and we couldn't afford all the traditions and the trimmings that go with a real slap-up Christmas. And then my father died and I became a mostly unemployed actor and so the money was still short. But I already had the fantasy that one day I would have the Christmas of my dreams—and although

I can now afford it, I challenge myself each year to outdo the last one.

Christmas Eve always starts for us with music—and it's always the same song: "So This Is Christmas" by John Lennon. It's a beautiful, haunting melody and it gets us into the mood. It's followed by Bing Crosby singing "White Christmas," Jack Jones's "Sleigh Ride," Sinatra's "Have Yourself a Merry Little Christmas," Nat King Cole's "Merry Christmas" and, during Christmas Eve dinner, a CD of carols from King's College, Cambridge. These songs and carols would probably feature on many people's lists, but two of them have an extra significance for me: I found myself in Hollywood one Christmas in a room with Jack Jones and Frank Sinatra—and they sang those two songs above. It was an extraordinary privilege to be there and hear these great men, and I was both stunned and starstruck—so the memories and emotions I feel on hearing them again are mixed, but deep and happy.

Christmas Eve dinner for us is always roast goose and the evening always finishes watching a midnight mass on TV. On Christmas morning I am up early to cook the turkey. I go for a traditional sage and onion stuffing and gravy, which I prepare in advance, and we always have chipolata sausages and roast potatoes. Shakira, who is a vegetarian, looks at this meat feast with great amusement and is in charge of all the vegetables: traditional Brussels sprouts, sweet potatoes, eggplant and stir-fried vegetables.

We used to start the meal with eggnog, until I saw my cholesterol figures, and now we drink champagne until the lunch is ready. After lunch we pull Christmas crackers and wear funny hats and listen to the Queen's Speech and then we go and open the presents. The whole place is ablaze with light and color and family and food and friends and the best wine I can lay my hands on. Finally, I have made up for those lost Christmases past.

When we have eaten and drunk and laughed and unwrapped until we can manage no more, we go and watch the "screener" that we reckon will be the potential Oscar winner for Best Picture, which we always save for this moment. Dinner on Christmas Night is what is known as "pick and save" in our house: you pick anything out of the fridge that has been saved. I always like to pick and save a tin of caviar. . . . Eventually we retire exhausted, full and happy, knowing that the Boxing Day lunch is still to come. To me Christmas symbolizes the value of the family and close friends who have always been the mainstay of my life—and on Christmas Day I sometimes think I am the happiest man on earth. Last year, drinking a great claret with trusted friends and family and with my new grandchildren safely asleep upstairs, I thought—life doesn't get any better than this. I love Christmas!

CHAPTER EIGHTEEN

THE MAYFAIR ORPHANS

One of the joys of being based back in England is being close to my friends. They mean a lot to me. And while I've lost some good ones along the way—it's inevitable as you get older—it's made me value the rest of them even more. I am often asked if I have any friends from my early days back in the Elephant and the answer is no. The unspoken but immediate assumption is that I dumped all my old friends when I became a movie star, but in fact the exact opposite is true. My old friends all dumped me when I was an out-of-work actor who couldn't afford a round of drinks in the pub.

The one exception to this was Paul Challen, my trusty companion in the London party years and the guy who witnessed my first sight of Shakira, when we stayed in for that life-changing quiet night. I met him when we were both fifteen and I went to the orphanage where he lived (his entire family had been killed in the Blitz) with my drama group from Clubland. It was a terrible, depressing place and I couldn't wait to get outside—where I found Paul waiting for me. He introduced himself and asked if I knew how to get into acting. I didn't, of course, but it was the first time I'd had a conversation with anyone about what I wanted to do and it was the beginning of a friendship that would last forty years. Paul had never been healthy; when I first knew him I'd thought I was thin, but Paul was almost emaciated. First he contracted tuberculosis and had to have a lung removed and then, tragically, he developed multiple sclerosis, gradually becoming weaker and weaker. I knew from very early on that he was never going to make it as an actor; but he didn't have to, because I did. He was my constant and only link to my past in those early years, the only friend who knew me before and after—and my anchor in a strange new sea. I am pleased to have been able to make life as comfortable as possible for him as time went on and I became successful, because he deteriorated very quickly. Paul died over twenty years ago, brave and uncomplaining to the last. He was always with me then, and he's still with me now.

As a young actor I made many friends along the way, but few of them were long-lasting. Some of those actors failed and disappeared; two men I knew—Johnny Charlesworth and Peter Myers—took the failure harder and tragically committed suicide. The life of an actor on the way up is tough and many people just walk away, but if you do stay the course you eventually meet a few people who you get to know, learn to trust and, in some cases, learn to love. I was fortunate enough in my journey to meet a group of friends who fell into this last and most important category. Over the years we have survived the test of friendship and none of us has ever had a row or a falling-out with any of the others; our friendship has been constant. And although our number has been diminished by losses along the way, the survivors remain as tight-knit as we were in our younger days.

The group usually meets for lunch or family dinners, or

even holidays, whenever we can find time in our busy lives. One day in the early '90s, we were all having lunch together at Langan's Brasserie when one of our number, Philip Kingsley, said that it was his mother's birthday; she was ninety-eight. We were of an age where we had assumed that none of us had living parents and indeed all of us, with the exception of Philip, were orphans—and so, because we were eating in Mayfair, and because our parents had all gone, we christened ourselves the "Mayfair Orphans" from then on. Philip was made a probationary member until his mother died.

I met most of the Mayfair Orphans in London during the sixties. It was a fantastic time to be young and right at the center of things. I remember going up to Liverpool in 1959 with Sam Wanamaker's theater company on what, during my leanest period, was a rare job. I was having coffee in a bar where a young group was playing, surrounded by teenage girls, all screaming. When I asked the name of the band that was causing so much excitement, someone said they were called "The Beatles." They're not bad, I thought, downed my coffee and left without a backward glance.

Before the late 1950s there was very little acknowledgment that anyone under twenty-one existed. But gradually the first dance halls and coffee bars began to emerge and although London was hardly swinging, it was beginning to gyrate slightly. The 2 i's coffee bar on Old Compton Street in Soho was where a lot of the music stars of the future used to hang out. Coffee was sixpence upstairs, but half a crown downstairs to listen to the music, which seemed expensive at the time, but in retrospect was a bargain. The very worst thing about the London social scene in those days was that everything shut at 10:30—pubs, theaters, cafés, buses, tube, everything. I once heard a member of Parliament explain that it was to make sure the working classes weren't late for work the next day.

Music wasn't the only form of popular culture that was

booming in those years. The world of drama was changing and with it London's nightlife. Because all the restaurants and pubs closed early there was nowhere for actors to get a meal after a show so they started their own late-night dinner and drinking clubs in defiance of the Establishment's rules. Theater itself was no longer the province of the middle classes; playwrights like John Osborne and the rest of the "Angry Young Men" were transforming it with plays like *Look Back in Anger* and they were being championed by critics like Ken Tynan. Working-class actors like Terence Stamp, Albert Finney, Peter O'Toole and me were blazing a trail, too—and we were all taking full advantage of a much freer attitude to sex and booze, to have the time of our lives.

Peter O'Toole was probably the wildest of us all. During my time understudying him in *The Long and the Short and the Tall* in 1959, my main job was to bring in the drink and find the parties, but I soon learnt to start the evening off with him and then duck out. God knows, I love a party, but I just couldn't keep up. On one Saturday night after the show we were about to set off when he suggested that we line our stomachs first at a fast-food place in Leicester Square called the Golden Egg. This seemed to me to be perfectly sensible and I was encouraged because Peter's diet hadn't to this point seemed to include any food, so I went along. I have absolutely no idea what happened after that because the next thing I remember is waking up in broad daylight in a flat I had never been in before, still wearing my coat. I nudged Peter who was lying next to me and asked him what time it was. "Never mind what *time* it is," he said, "what fucking *day* is it?" Our hostesses, two rather dubious-looking girls I really don't remember having set eyes on before, told us it was Monday and it was five o'clock. The curtain went up at eight. Somehow we got to the theater in time—we hadn't even been sure we were still in London—but instead of being pleased to see us, the stage manager was very cross. It seemed that the manager of the Golden Egg had already been round: henceforth we were both banned. "But what did we—?" I began. Peter nudged me. "Never ask," he said. "Better not to know." The voice of experience. They say that if you can remember the sixties, you weren't there. And this was only 1959. . . .

By the time we actually reached the sixties, I'd wised up a bit. London was buzzing with energy. The Beatles had left that Liverpool café behind and were dominating the charts; the Rolling Stones were unstoppable, Mary Quant had designed the mini-skirt, photographers like David Bailey and Terry O'Neill were chronicling our lives and everything felt new and exciting. Most exciting of all was the feeling that for the first time in British history it didn't matter where you came from. The only thing that mattered was your talent; the young working class were not going to be deferential anymore. A new kind of satire was born and for the first time comedians like Peter Cook and Dudley Moore dared to send up the Establishment—at their club of the same name. For me and for Terence Stamp, my companion in many an adventure in those days, life was a non-stop party, with girls galore and all the time in the world to enjoy them. A far cry from the black-and-white gloom of the fifties: the sixties was an explosion of Technicolor. But the scene was also incredibly fast-moving. By the time I'd finished *Zulu* and got back to London with some money in my pocket, Terry was in love with Julie Christie, Bailey was wooing supermodel Jean Shrimpton and a whole new bunch of music groups—many of them produced by my friend and fellow Orphan, Mickie Most—were dominating the charts. And then, it was all change partners once again. The clubs and discotheques came and went at a dizzying speed, too. This was the era when Orphans Johnny Gold and Oscar Lerman came into their own with Ad Lib, where you could see the Beatles and the Stones on the same dance floor. There was a creative energy around that I don't think has been seen before or since, and it was impossible not to be drawn in and swept along by it. It really did seem as if people could become famous overnight—although as someone who took eleven years to become an overnight success, I've always felt a bit ambivalent about that!

I met the first of the group who would become the Orphans—Roger Moore—in the late 1950s. I didn't know, when he accosted me on Piccadilly and told me that I was going to be a star, that he would also become one of my closest friends. Roger is one of the most genuine and trustworthy people you could ever meet, and very, very funny. He is also a generous man and we spent many fabulous holidays in his beautiful villa on the French Riviera, although sadly those privileges were lost to us when he divorced. As a tax exile, these days Roger has to be classed as an Overseas Orphan and because of that and his many duties as an official ambassador for UNICEF, he's too busy to turn up to many lunches, but he distinguishes our organization in his absence and when he is with us he makes us laugh.

The second Orphan I met was my incomparable agent Dennis Selinger, who gave me such wise counsel in the course of my career and became my guide, confidant and friend. Dennis was diagnosed with cancer in 1998. He would never explain what it was in detail, but he assured us all it was survivable. Dennis—perhaps for the first time in his life—was unfortunately wrong. I had to go to Hollywood to do a film and went to visit him in hospital before I went away. He insisted to me that everything was all right and that he would be out of hospital before I got back. I left and was just walking down the corridor when it suddenly occurred to me that I had not actually said goodbye, which seemed rude. I went back to Dennis's room, opened the door and there was Dennis on his way to the toilet, wheeling his own portable life-support system with needles in his arms and pipes up his nose. "I forgot to say goodbye," I said lamely. He smiled. "See you when you get back," he said. I said goodbye and shut the door. That walk down the passage was one of the longest of my life. I was trying not to cry because I knew I would never see him again. He died while I was still in Hollywood.

It was through Dennis that I met another Orphan, the press agent Theo Cowan. Despite his vast number of show business contacts, his glamorous social life and his great sense of humor, Theo always seemed to me to be a lonely man. There were rumors of an unrequited love affair with the great British screen actress of the 1940s, Margaret Lockwood. Whether or not this was true, he always appeared to be holding some torch for an imaginary woman. Theo's passing was as quiet and measured as his life had been. He had lunch with the rest of us Orphans on the Thursday at Langan's as usual, on the Friday he had a business lunch and then he went back to his office, made a pillow of his hands on his desk to have a little nap and never woke up.

The music scene in London in the 1960s was famously vibrant and one of the greatest icons of the period was one of our Orphans, Mickie Most, who produced records as varied as The Animals' "House of the Rising Sun," Donovan's "Mellow Yellow" and Lulu's "To Sir with Love." Mickie was the fittest of all of us: he regularly ran ten miles a day, whereas most of the rest of the Orphans probably couldn't *walk* ten miles a day. One day at lunch he told us he wasn't feeling great and had had to cut his daily run down to just five miles. We all laughed at the idea of someone who was running five miles a day thinking he was sick, but Mickie was right: he was sick. In fact he had lung cancer. It was a terrible shock; Mickie had never smoked. What was worse was that his lung cancer was the most virulent kind, totally incurable and had come about because of a lifetime of working in a sound studio, where, unbeknownst to anyone, the sound "baffles" were made of asbestos.

The last time I saw Mickie, we had lunch, just the two of

us, and I asked him what they had actually said to him when they told him the bad news. He smiled. "They told me not to send out any dry cleaning," he said, and we both laughed. And then I told him the Henny Youngman joke about the patient whose doctor told him he had only six months to live. When he said he didn't have enough money to pay the bill, the doctor gave him another six months. We were both laughing as we left the restaurant. People must have thought we were having a great time, and the expression "dying with laughter" came to my mind. But as we stood there on the pavement, Mickie said, "Unfortunately, I *can* pay that bill. . . ." We shook hands, walked off in opposite directions, and I never saw my friend alive again.

When the next spring came round, a camellia bush that Mickie had given me for my garden had died. I just couldn't pull it out and throw it away and the following year it came back to life and is now thriving. A horticulturalist would probably give you a perfectly reasonable explanation for this, but, as I've said, actors are a superstitious lot and I know Mickie is out there in my garden every time I go for a walk. He is also with me when I am in one of my favorite places in the whole world: the French Riviera. Chrissie Most, Mickie's lovely wife, who is a great friend of ours, told me that Mickey had asked to be cremated and for his ashes to be scattered in the bay of Cannes, in a spot they could see from their villa in the hills above. Every time I look across that bay, I can see Mickie and feel his presence with us again.

Genius tailor Doug Hayward was known by the rest of us Orphans as the "Buddha of Mount Street" and he became our rock and his Mayfair shop became our base. In fact it was because he would only ever give himself an hour off for lunch that we always had to eat in Mayfair. The rest of us traveled all over the world, but the one place we all came to first when we got home was his shop where we would listen to Doug—who never left London—tell us what had happened while we'd been away, dispense wisdom and tell jokes.

Doug was always as sharp as a needle, so it was a long while after the silent enemy of Alzheimer's had made its permanent base in his brain that we noticed there was anything wrong—and it took a lot longer than that for us to accept it as a fact. Alzheimer's is so slow that you have masses of time to pretend, hope or believe that it's not happening, but it is unstoppable. Eventually he was diagnosed with the disease and we all started our long farewell as we watched him walk slowly away from us. Over a period of three years, one by one we waited for the time when he wouldn't know who we were, and one by one our much loved friend's brain cut us out of his life, leaving us to watch him make that journey to his eventual lonely but welcome end. Like the others, I waited anxiously for the time when he wouldn't recognize me and when it came it was quite a gentle blow—although a blow nonetheless. I had gone up to his apartment above the shop and Doug was watching television as usual. "Michael's here," said Audie, his long-standing friend and assistant who knew him better than anyone else. Doug looked up from the TV and mumbled "Hello," before going back to watching a program he couldn't understand. I stood there stunned as it sank in that he really was gone from my life forever. I waited until I knew I could speak steadily without crying and then I said in a very clear voice, "Goodbye, Doug." He didn't even look up from the TV.

I spoke at Doug's funeral in 2008 and got the chance to say how much I loved him and to say a last quiet "Goodbye, Doug," as his coffin was carried past. He was a man we would never see the like of again. Hayward's, Doug's business, has survived—I still order suits from them—and I feel Doug's continuing presence in the shop, which was sold but which Audie still runs with the same staff. But Doug's death broke our hearts and for a while we didn't want to visit our Mayfair haunts ever again.

The Mayfair Orphans are down, but we're far from out: the group now comprises club owner Johnny Gold, photographer Terry O'Neill, composer Leslie Bricusse, Roger Moore, new recruit Michael Winner, tricologist Philip Kingsley and me— and we make the most of our times together. We've lost Dennis and his wisdom, Theo and his press contacts, Mickie, our link with the world of rock and roll and constant source of free CDs and concert tickets, and Doug, our heart and soul, but we still have Philip, to save us all from going bald, Johnny, our permanent disco and social connection, Terry, our great official photographer, Roger, to lend us some respectability, and Leslie, who knows all there is to know about food and wine. Michael Winner is only an occasional Orphan as he travels constantly, but we're glad to have him around when he turns up, battered and bruised, to recount the havoc he's caused. He's also the only one of us who is capable of being both nice and nasty, and he's the only trained lawyer amongst us, so he's an essential member of the group: if we want anyone or anything done, we send Michael. As for me, I am the joker and the most traveled, so I'm the storyteller. We haven't done so badly.

I first met Terry O'Neill when he took my photograph. By the time we met he had already photographed the Queen in her palace at Sandringham and Frank Sinatra in his palace— the Fontainebleau Hotel in Miami, where he was surrounded by his version of palace guards—and we became firm friends. Terry frightened the life out of us with a bout of colon cancer a few years ago, but he recovered, thank God, and is working as hard as ever.

Leslie Bricusse is another Overseas Orphan like Roger Moore. He, too, has a villa on the French Riviera and he, too, is generous with it. Some of the best times of our year are spent there with him and his wife, Evie. They have just celebrated their golden wedding anniversary, so there are no worries that we'll lose out on another favorite holiday villa in any divorce.

Two-time Oscar winner Leslie is not only the composer of such songs as "What Kind of Fool Am I?" and "The Candy Man," he is also a great wine connoisseur and lover of French food and part-owned the Pickwick, the restaurant where I was eating with Terry Stamp the night Harry Saltzman offered me the leading role in *The Ipcress File*. Leslie had spotted the meeting during the course of the evening and winked at me and gave me the thumbs-up. When I told him later what had happened, it was he who suggested we go on to celebrate at a new disco, the Ad Lib, not far away—and it was there that we met two more people who would become a big part of our life, the Ad Lib's owner and husband of Jackie Collins, Oscar Lerman (who unfortunately would die before we officially named ourselves the Orphans), and his business partner, the incomparable Johnny Gold, one of the great nightclub hosts of all time. Oscar and Johnny went on to open Tramp, one of the most successful discotheques ever, which became the Orphans' shelter for many nights until we started meeting our own grandchildren there.

And so at last the sixties, which had been so good to us and such fun, faded. But that decade didn't die. It lives on in the memories of those of us who were there and especially in the hearts of the Mayfair Orphans who did so much to make it happen. Whether gathered together in our old haunts, sharing holidays together in our favorite places abroad, or just enjoying ourselves sitting round the table in Surrey, for me, home and happiness is all about friends and family.

CHAPTER NINETEEN

A DATE AT THE PALACE

When an actor's been around as long as I have, there's a great temptation to choose a picture for the pleasure of working with old friends, but this can be a mistake. As soon as we had settled in Surrey, I was off again and made three movies in quick succession. In the first one, *Curtain Call*, which was about a camp theatrical couple, my costar was the incomparable Maggie Smith, with whom I had so enjoyed making *California Suite*, and it was also going to be directed by Peter Yates, a good friend of mine. What could go wrong? Well, quite a lot, as it happened. I never actually saw the finished movie—and hardly anyone else did either. . . .

I followed this up with something more serious and dramatic. *Quills* is the story of the Marquis de Sade's descent into madness while locked up in an asylum. Geoffrey Rush played the Marquis brilliantly with all the stops pulled out; Joaquin Phoenix played the Catholic priest who ran the asylum.

Joaquin was a pleasant young man, but somewhat strange. His two brothers were named River and Rain and his two sisters Summer and Liberty. He changed his own name for a while to Leaf (but changed it back again before Autumn came). Joaquin was hard to get to know. He was a combination of enigmatic and explosive, which is a difficult one to understand, but he worked incredibly hard—it made me feel lazy just to watch him prepare for a take—and his labors paid off. Kate Winslet, on the other hand, who played the laundry girl, was much more down to earth. Offscreen as well as on, she is one of the most brilliant and unpretentious actresses I've ever met. I played the man sent by Napoleon to stop De Sade from writing his books, which he had continued to do in the asylum, smuggling them out, rather aptly, in the baskets of dirty laundry. It was a great movie to do, and I took it because I wanted to do something prestigious after *Curtain Call* but it never caught on with the public.

My next film was *Shiner*, in which I played a Cockney gangster. It wasn't a bad film but it seemed as if the public was fed up with gangster films. Although it was more successful than my previous two movies, it still didn't cause much of a stir and so I couldn't have been more pleased when something fantastic came in right out of the blue: *Miss Congeniality*.

Sandra Bullock, who was the producer as well as the star of the movie, wanted me to play the sort of Professor Higgins to her tough, dowdy FBI agent, who has to go undercover as a beauty queen. This picture was a joy from start to finish. Just before we began shooting I had won my Oscar for *The Cider House Rules* and in my acceptance speech I had told Tom Cruise (who was also nominated in this category for his part in *Magnolia*) that he should be pleased that he hadn't won as the dressing room trailers given to supporting actors would be much too small and modest for him. It was a joke and Tom and everyone else laughed, but when I got to the set of *Miss Congeniality* on the first day and was shown to my trailer, it was the biggest and most luxurious accommodation I had ever had on a set. And on the door was pinned a note in Sandra's handwriting. "Welcome to the shoot. This is as big as Tom's." I checked—and it was.

Miss Congeniality was tremendous fun to make. Sandra was fantastic, both as an actress and as a producer. She was always kind and attentive and pleasant and never imposed any problems that she might have been encountering with the production on the rest of us. I never saw her without a smile—and yet I discovered later that just before this movie, her mother had died of cancer. We never knew; she was a true professional. I was so pleased to see her win the Best Actress Oscar for her role in *The Blind Side*. And she has a great sense of humor. The night before winning the Academy Award, she won the Golden Raspberry Award for Worst Actress in a film called *All About Steve*. Typical of Sandra—she turned up to accept it with as much good grace as she showed the next evening at the Oscar ceremony. She's a true star. Candice Bergen, a friend from the past, was also in the movie. We'd last worked together on a terrible film of John Fowles's book *The Magus*, which none of us understood, and neither, it seemed, did the audience. William Shatner was in the movie, too, probably the funniest and craziest actor I have ever met. The romantic lead was Benjamin Bratt and we became good friends. He was going out with Julia Roberts at the time and Benjamin and I were in a car one day together and he phoned her in Las Vegas where she was making a film. During the course of the conversation he handed the phone over to me and said, "Say hello to Julia." I did—and there was no reply. So I tried again. Still no reply. I tried a third time and finally I heard a voice at the other end say, "I can't believe I'm talking to Alfie!" "*Alfie?*" I said. "You're far too young to have seen *Alfie!*" "Have you never heard of television, Michael?" she said. I agreed that I had, indeed, heard of television, told her how brilliant she was in *Pretty Woman* and passed the phone back to Benjamin. I have never spoken to her since—and neither, I think, has Benjamin.

The film was shot in Austin, the capital of Texas. Austin is a very rich town with a massive university and a lot of steak houses. The most famous one at that time was Sullivan's and it was here that the then governor of Texas and his cronies always ate: we saw George W. Bush there every time we went. Everything in Texas is big, including the onion rings. Benjamin and I were at Sullivan's one lunchtime and just about to start eating when we saw a woman approaching us with a smile and a camera. It happens all the time when you are well known: not only is your meal interrupted with the photograph, but attention is drawn to your table and so everyone else thinks it's OK to interrupt you, too. Anyway, as she came over, we both put a brave face on it and prepared to pose, but she completely took the wind out of our outraged sails by saying, "Can I take a picture of your onion rings? The folks back home just won't believe how big they are!"

Austin is a strange town—and the citizens know it. I have a souvenir mug that says "Keep Austin Weird," and they are doing a pretty good job. Sandra was going out with Bob Schneider around the time we were making the film and she took a group of us to see him play. When he came on, the young female fans at the front lifted up their blouses and flashed their breasts at him. Sandra said that they always did that to him as a greeting. It would have made my day back when I was fourteen, but it seems a pretty odd business to me now.

The weirdest thing I saw in Austin was from the window of our hotel, which was on the banks of the Colorado River. Shakira and I arrived back at the hotel late one afternoon and the receptionist told us rather mysteriously to go out onto the balcony of our room at precisely six o'clock and look at the bridge over the river on our right. We did exactly as she suggested and saw that there were crowds of other guests standing on their balconies, too, and a host of people standing below, all with cameras ready, waiting for something to happen. Not wanting to miss anything, I rushed back inside to get my camera and got back just in time to witness one of the most extraordinary sights I've ever seen. At dead on six o'clock, two million bats flew out from under the bridge in their nightly search for food. There's no other word for it—weird.

My next film couldn't have been more different. *Last Orders* was a tiny, low-budget British picture and although I only had a small part and the money was modest, I wanted to do it because not only was the great director Fred Schepisi involved, the cast included actors I liked and admired: Helen Mirren, Bob Hoskins, and from way back in the 1960s, David Hemmings and Tom Courtenay. My character, Jack Dodds, was a battler, just like my dad; playing that character and watching the next generation of working-class actors almost felt like watching the life I could have had play out on-screen.

There couldn't have been a greater contrast to that role than the small part I took for the fun of it in the third Austin Powers movie, *Goldmember*. Again I was playing the father (by now I was getting used to it . . .). The role of Nigel Powers, the rakish super spy, gave me every chance I could ever have wanted to send up the whole business of the 1960s man-about-town, and I adored it. It was an honor to be invited to play a bit part that was really a tongue-in-cheek send-up of my own on-screen image.

I loved *Goldmember* from start to finish. Mike Myers is crazy—but crazy like a fox, because he is a comic genius. For a start, he loves what he does—and he makes sure everyone else has fun, too. At the end of every take, for instance, he played loud rock-and-roll through the speakers and everyone started dancing, which took me completely by surprise the first time it happened, but I soon got into it. And Mike, like me, hates getting up in the morning, so every day we got a later and later start until we were working from noon until midnight. The lines were crazy, too—one of my own favorites was, "There are only two things I hate in the world: people who are intolerant of other people's cultures, and the Dutch," while Mike got to say, when explaining to someone why he had a stiff neck, "I took a Viagra and it stuck in my throat!" No one was going to get an Oscar for this movie, but it was a huge box-office success and a great laugh.

One of the revelations for me in *Goldmember* was the performance of Beyoncé Knowles. Only nineteen at the time of the film, she was still in Destiny's Child. She was quiet, observant, absolutely determined to get her first acting role right and completely professional, with a sensitive regard for the feelings of everyone else on the set. She was famous then, but now of course Beyoncé is one of the top female recording artists in the world, although she once confided to me that she would love to win an Academy Award one day. I am convinced she will.

My working life had felt like a succession of wild changes of tone for a while, but if there could be a greater contrast between my screen role in *Goldmember* and the ceremony I was about to take part in, I can't think what it might be. Receiving a knighthood in the year 2000 was one of the proudest moments of my life. It is not like winning an Oscar—that is for a single piece of work—it is an award for a lifetime's achievement. It means a great deal to me and to my family—but to us alone. I don't expect other people to recognize it or to call me "Sir Michael." The knighthood is for me and for us and what anybody else thinks or says about it is of absolutely no concern to me whatsoever.

You are informed that you have been awarded a knighthood months before the honors list is announced and you are sent some sort of form to fill in if you want to turn it down—which some people do.

My only problem with the whole knighthood business was having to find a morning suit, but fortunately Doug Hayward stepped into the breach again—just as he had done back at the premiere of *Zulu* all those years ago—and lent me his. We were, remarkably, still the same size. Accompanied by Shakira, Dominique and Natasha—all looking incredibly glamorous—I drove to Buckingham Palace. When we got out of the car, we were immediately greeted by an army officer who must have been about six foot five, standing ramrod straight (something I never achieved in my army days) and with a big stick under his arm. He was our own personal usher for the occasion and he led us down the long corridors of the palace at a cracking pace to the ballroom where the investitures were taking place. As we whipped along, I noticed that various doors were half opening along the way as people popped their heads out to watch us go. "Good luck!" some of them whispered as they recognized me, before shutting the doors hastily as our usher glared at them. It was a welcome human touch in such formal and intimidating surroundings. The whole thing was high-tech, too—we were on digital camera for every moment of the ceremony and were told that we could have a photograph of any moment we chose while we were at the palace. Who says the Royal Family is out of touch?

Once Shakira and my daughters were shown to their seats in the ballroom, I was taken to a back room to practice. There was a wooden apparatus with a cushion for kneeling on. "The right knee only!" my usher instructed me firmly. "I know how to kneel," I said. "It's not the kneeling we're worried about," he replied. "It's the getting up again!" He pointed out a rail on one side of the cushion. "This," said the usher—he really did know everything—"is for the older recipients who might have trouble getting to their feet again." He then gave me detailed instructions on the protocol. It seemed enormously complicated and I realized that—unlike the movies—I'd have to get it right first time: there wouldn't be a chance for another take. "When your name is called," he said, "you will walk straight in and turn right on the line directly in front of Her Majesty. You will not at any time speak unless you are spoken to. You will kneel on your right knee until the Queen has knighted you with her sword. You will then stand and again not speak unless spoken to by Her Majesty. She will then stretch out her hand and shake yours and at that point you are done—not another gesture or word— and you will immediately turn right and walk smartly out of the room. Do you understand, sir?" I was reeling by this time, but I told him I did and stood there on my own waiting for my turn. When it came, I did everything I had been told to do and in the correct order (I could sense my usher anxiously watching me from the wings) and stood in front of Her Majesty. "I have a feeling that you have been doing what you do for a very long time," she said. I stifled the temptation to say, "And so have you, Ma'am," and just said, "Yes, Ma'am," went down on one knee and was knighted. I got to my feet, and she put out her hand without another word. I noticed that in her handshake there is a very slight push towards you in case you have forgotten it is over. I turned right as I had been instructed and was met by my usher who seemed very pleased with my performance. As for me, I was walking on air. I was a knight! Just like all those men I had read about in comics and books when I was a kid. I couldn't believe it and I went to join my family for the rest of the ceremony in a daze. I thought of my mother and of my father and of all the generations of their families stretching back behind me over the centuries and I felt that it was for them as well as for myself and Shakira and the girls that I was there.

I watched the Queen as she continued the ceremony, awarding medals and honors of gradually diminishing importance. She was, of course, indefatigable, but she was also incredibly kind. As the grandeur of the honor lessened, she spent more and more time talking to the recipients and putting them at their ease. It was a lovely touch.

A couple of years later I was walking down Piccadilly one day when I bumped into Charlie Watts, of the Rolling Stones. We hadn't seen each other for years and were busy chatting when my phone suddenly went and I took the call. "Who was that?" Charlie asked when I'd finished. "Roger Moore," I said. "He's on the way to Buckingham Palace to be knighted and he's worried about the kneeling bit because he's got a bad knee and he thinks he might get stuck down there and have to ask the Queen to help him up." Charlie looked a bit skeptical, but I explained what I had told Roger. "There's a contraption there to practice," I said, "and a rail a bit like one of those handgrips you get in disabled showers to help you up if you get stuck."

CHAPTER TWENTY

THE QUIET AMERICAN

Just as I was getting comfortable with my leading actor status, along came a film that had, as they say in skating, real "degrees of difficulty"—and I couldn't turn it down. It wasn't just that playing the antihero Thomas Fowler in *The Quiet American* was a challenge that would make greater demands on me than I had faced in some time, it was also—I hoped—a chance to make a film of a Graham Greene novel that the author, who is one of my favorites, would have been proud of.

I was at a table in the Connaught Hotel in London one Sunday evening many years ago, having dinner. We were making a film nearby and I had rushed over between takes. As the only person on the set wearing collar and tie (it was my costume, actually, not my own clothes) and therefore allowed into the place, I was eating alone. Suddenly a shadow fell across my table. I looked up and thought, "Oh, shit!" It was Graham Greene and I was aware that my recent film of his book *The*

Honorary Consul was not very good. He seemed very tall and threatening, but as I stood up to greet him I realized he was only my height. We introduced ourselves and shook hands, and then he said, "I didn't like the film, Michael, but I did like your performance." He was notorious for hating the films of his books, but I think he was probably right about the film—and I was flattered by his assessment of my part in it.

The film—which was eventually and mysteriously released in America in 1983 as *Beyond the Limit*—also starred Richard Gere and Bob Hoskins. I had never worked with Bob before and from the first moment I met him, he was very much "what you see is what you get." We have gone on to make several pictures together since. Richard Gere, on the other hand, is a much more intense actor, although some of the intensity of his concentration during the making of that film may have been down to the appalling dysentery he suffered on location in Mexico. I wasn't surprised when I walked past the café at which he and his girlfriend had eaten—I hadn't seen a plague of rats like it since Korea. Eventually the entire cast and crew fell ill—except me. I had devised the perfect preventative: before every meal I downed a straight vodka and followed it up with wine and finally a brandy (this was in my younger days). I figured that no germ could survive an onslaught like that.

No matter how much I drank off the set, I was always meticulously careful about never being drunk on set; I have too much professional pride for that. I was playing a drunk, too, and that, of course, requires complete sobriety. My character, the Consul, was not only a drunk, but also addicted to aspirins and I was given handfuls of dummy pills to chew. In the first scene I shot, there had been a mix-up and I was handed a fistful of real aspirins. I began to feel very odd, started swaying far more than the Consul was supposed to and eventually collapsed and had to be carried off the set. I recovered back at the hotel and was fine for the rest of the shoot. Maybe my bizarre diet of aspirins and heavy-duty evening drinking stripped my system bare of any rogue germs—I wouldn't recommend it, though.

I felt that justice had not been done to the genius of Graham Greene by *The Honorary Consul* and so in 2001 I leapt at the chance to put things right with *The Quiet American*, which charts the start of American involvement in the Vietnam War. I had waited a long time for this sort of role and I was looking forward not only to a story of this quality, but also to filming in Saigon, or Ho Chi Minh City, as it was named after the war.

It was not exactly how I had imagined it. Shakira and I arrived at the hotel at Sunday lunchtime and we were starving. I asked if we could eat in the restaurant, which I could see from the lobby was doing a roaring trade. The manager was apologetic and told us that there would be a half-hour wait. "It's always packed for Sunday lunch," he said. "What are you serving?" I asked. "Go and see," he said with a smile. "You won't believe it!" We did— and we didn't. Apart from a very few Europeans, the tables were stuffed with Vietnamese families all tucking into roast beef and Yorkshire pudding. "Incredible, isn't it?" the manager said from behind us. "We started it because we get a lot of British visitors and it's just caught on."

After we unpacked we went for a walk. Our impressions of what the streets would look like were all taken from films— mostly French—and featured horse-drawn taxis, vintage cars and locals on thousands of bicycles. We got that one wrong. Ho Chi Minh City has three million motor scooters and not one single traffic regulation or signal that anyone takes any notice of. I later asked a Vietnamese if he had any tips on how to cross a road. "A good start," he said, "is to be a Buddhist."

"Anything else?" I persisted.

"Just step off the pavement," he advised, "and don't catch anyone's eye. If you catch their eye it puts them off and they'll hit you." He seemed to think this was entirely reasonable.

Shakira and I never risked following his advice, but we did come up with a method of our own. We looked for groups of Buddhists, inserted ourselves into the very center of them and crossed when they did. If we were going to be mown down, we would at least be in the right company.

Once we had mastered the art of crossing the road, I noticed that all the young women riding scooters wore full-length evening gloves that reached right up to their armpits: it was a truly bizarre sight. I asked our Vietnamese friend why this was and he told me that middle-class girls did not want sunburnt arms because only peasant women had sunburnt arms.

If we made it safely to the other side unscathed by the scooters, we were ambushed by the small boys who swarmed the streets carrying trays of stuff to sell. Apart from the usual postcards and cigarettes, they also all carried the same three random and at first sight rather puzzling products: David Beckham Number 8 football shirts, pirate DVDs of *Miss Congeniality*, which hadn't even come out in America at this point, and paperback copies of *The Quiet American*.

I was intrigued by all three of these items—not least by how the hell they had managed to smuggle out a black market copy of *Miss Congeniality* so quickly—but it was the presence of the Graham Greene novels I found the most interesting. It turned out that the book had almost iconic status in Ho Chi Minh City. People would point out the window of the room where Greene wrote it in the French-colonial Majestic Hotel. It was possible to sense the decadence, imagine the brothels and almost smell the drugs that had pervaded the city—and Greene's novel. Although the Communist government had cleared out most of the signs of bourgeois decadence, there was one visible reminder of the Saigon Greene writes about so evocatively: portly, elderly European men could be seen everywhere with beautiful young Vietnamese girls on their arms. A couple of the reviews of our film implied that I was too old for the role of

Fowler, but obviously they had never been to Vietnam. I, too, had been a bit worried about taking it on because of the age difference between my character and my young mistress, and when we did the screen test I asked makeup to make the actress Do Thi Hai Yen who was to play Phuong look as old and tarty as they could. It was an impossible task as she was stunningly beautiful—and I needn't have bothered: such was the desperation of many young Vietnamese women to leave the country that they would go out with any foreigner, even one as old and creaky as me.

We finally left the hustle and bustle and the three million motor scooters behind and while the unit prepared to move location, we escaped to the paradise of the Furama Hotel and spa on China Beach, near Da Nang. It was the first free time I had had—I have never worked so hard before or since on a movie—and we were determined to make the most of it. It was also a chance to see the traditional Vietnam—and we weren't disappointed. One night, after a late shoot, we were coming back to the hotel when we suddenly came across a massive vegetable market sprawled across the road for about a quarter of a mile. The car screeched to a halt and we slowly picked our way through the stalls as ladies moved their mats and baskets of fruit and vegetables out of the way. When we finally made it safely to the other side without killing any of the vendors or squashing so much as an onion, I asked our driver, who was a local man, what on earth they were doing holding a market in the middle of the road anyway. He shrugged. "They were there first," he said. "They have been there for a thousand years and weren't going to move, so when they built the road right through the middle of the market they were prepared to change the time of the market to nighttime when there is less traffic." That's what I call tradition!

From there we moved on to the old Communist capital, Hanoi. We encountered the same motor scooters and the same noise—although there didn't seem to be any Buddhists to help us cross the streets there. In fact the whole place and the people we met seemed to be much tougher and I could understand how these people had refused to be beaten by the Americans. Vietnam seemed to me to be almost three nations: the southerners were like the Italians with their great love of life; the ones in the middle were a bit like the Belgians: just anxious to get on with everything quietly and hoping their bigger neighbors would leave them alone; and the northerners were like the Germans—tough, efficient and always on time (Churchill was once asked if the Blitz on London had taught him anything and he said yes, it had—the Germans were punctual!).

There were signs everywhere in Hanoi of the monotonous lives that the Vietnamese had to put up with under the Communist regime. We were driving back late one night through the city and as we passed house after tiny house, all with their doors and windows open and all with the television on, it dawned on me that they were all watching the same program. No wonder—when I asked the driver how many stations they had, the answer was "One." They were also subjected to a relentless diet of propaganda. In an overnight stay in a hotel outside Hanoi, I was woken up at dawn by loudspeakers all over the town blaring martial music at maximum volume before a man came on and began to exhort his comrades to get up and produce even more than they had the day before. It was too noisy to stay in bed, so I got up and went for a walk and by chance passed a small studio with its doors open. Curious, I peeped inside and there was the actual man making the broadcast, screaming his head off. I had nothing to lose (I'd already lost enough sleep!) and I stepped inside and shouted at him to shut the fuck up. He just smiled and waved and carried on. . . .

Eventually it was time to move on from Vietnam and shoot the studio interior sequences, which we did in Sydney, one of the most beautiful cities in the world. It was a relief to get there after Vietnam, and our Australian crew—who were great—were especially happy to be back on home ground.

I showed up for makeup on the first day of shooting feeling very relaxed and happy with life. I sat down and as the makeup lady was getting to work she said to me very casually, "You do know you've got skin cancer, don't you?" I shot out of that chair at about a hundred miles an hour. "Skin cancer?" I said. "Where?" She pointed to a mark on my face that I had thought was just a razor rash. I didn't know what to think, but I was encouraged by how unperturbed she seemed to be—I mean, I know Australians are laid back, but she was a genius. "No worries," she said. "It's very common in Australia—and most of them aren't serious." For obvious reasons I couldn't have an operation while we were filming, so I made an appointment with Sydney's top skin cancer specialist, who scheduled surgery for the very second we finished the shoot, and did my best to put it out of my mind and just get on with the job.

We were operating a more relaxed filming schedule in Sydney, so there was a bit of time to see the sights. We had a fabulous apartment right on the harbor with spectacular views, although the most spectacular of all wasn't there when we went to bed one evening, but in the morning when we woke up it had appeared during the night—there, outside our window, was the QE2. We were invited on board for a tour one afternoon and were shown around by the captain. It is a beautiful and remarkable ship (it was retired in 2008 and is now awaiting refurbishment as a floating hotel) although it has its strange aspects. We were just going past what was obviously the most luxurious apartment on board when the captain put his finger to his lips. "Sssssh," he said. "Our most important guests are probably asleep." It turned out that this couple had actually lived on the ship for several years and traveled all round the world without ever leaving the ship.

When we came back on deck I looked over at the famous

Harbor Bridge and noticed that there was a group of tourists all tied together climbing up the arch. "I'd love to do that," I said, "but it looks a bit scary." "Not at all!" said the captain. "People do it all the time and it's perfectly safe." Not many people can say they were talked into climbing the Sydney Harbor Bridge by the captain of the QE2, so I accepted the challenge and the next day Shakira and I lined up with everyone else. We were given special harnesses to wear that were clipped into a wire that ran all the way up to the top. "That will stop us falling off," I said to the guide rather nervously. "It's not there for that," he said, "it's to stop you jumping off. People lose their nerve sometimes and seem to want to leap!" Not me, I thought, not in a million years, but we took a deep breath and started the climb. It was fantastic—Shakira and I loved every moment and there's a picture of the two of us on the very top, with the block of apartments we were staying in over one shoulder and the Sydney Opera House over the other to prove it.

We were coming to the end of the filming and I knew I was then facing surgery for my skin cancer. I had already been reassured to some extent by my first visit to the surgeon. "If I were going to have skin cancer," he said, "then this is the one I would choose." I nearly kissed him. He did tell me the name of it, which I found unpronounceable, but being a keen gardener and cook there was one syllable I did recognize: "basil"—pronounced in the American way (actually it turns out to have been a "basal cell carcinoma"). So if you are ever unlucky enough to get skin cancer and you hear the word "basil," you are probably OK. In the end, the whole thing was remarkably painless. A lump of skin one inch wide and fourteen stitches long was cut from my neck and I got on the plane to England an hour later and flew all the way home without any discomfort at all. The guy was a genius—there's no sign of any scar at all. In the unlikely event of my ever wanting to have a face-lift, I'll be straight back on that plane!

The Quiet American was first scheduled to be released in September 2001, but because of the tragic events of 9/11, it was postponed for over a year. When it was eventually released—and I had to beg Harvey Weinstein to release it in time to qualify for the Oscars—it got a great critical reception and I was nominated for an Academy Award as Best Actor but I knew in my heart of hearts I was not going to win. I was reminded of something a Hollywood producer—and great friend—I had worked for once said when he had to break some bad news to me about an award. He gave me a hug and whispered, "It's not your turn, Michael." I smiled and pretended not to mind too much. But the capper was, as he walked away, he said, "I am an honest man, Michael. I would only ever stab you in the chest."

A lot of show business is about timing and in this instance the timing was against *The Quiet American* big time. The Americans invaded Iraq on March 20, 2003; the Academy Awards were just four days later on March 24. The night before the ceremony I had dinner at Jack Nicholson's with three of the other four nominees for Best Actor: Jack, for *About Schmidt*, Nicolas Cage for *Adaptation*, Adrian Brody for *The Pianist* (who was a worthy winner). Daniel Day-Lewis, who had been nominated for *Gangs of New York*, was still on a plane and couldn't join us. We were basically deciding whether or not we should go ahead with the ceremony or abandon the whole thing. In the end, we decided to go with movie tradition and the show went on—although it was a very subdued ceremony indeed, only livened up by speeches protesting against the war.

It's always disappointing not to win, but in this case I really felt I had given my best. Phillip Noyce, a great Australian director, guided the film brilliantly and Brendan Fraser, who plays the well-intentioned American, Alden Pyle, for whom my character's mistress Phuong leaves me, gave a great performance. With them, a brilliant new actor I hadn't come across before, Rade Serbedzija, who played Inspector Vigot, and a script by Christopher

Hampton—not to mention the quality of the original novel—I felt I had a chance of getting as close to my own standards of perfection as I possibly could, a chance to reach the limit of my own talent, a chance to improve my work. Great movie actors make themselves and the acting disappear and you only see the character. If you sit there and say—isn't he a wonderful actor?—then he isn't a wonderful actor at all.

CHAPTER TWENTY-ONE

BATMAN BEGINS

During the writing of this book, I traveled to Hollywood to work on a film called *Inception*. I say work, but that's not strictly true—at least not in the way I would normally think of it. I've got two days of filming in Los Angeles, but with no dialogue and I have already done one day's shooting on this picture in London with the star of the film, Leonardo di Caprio. Mine is a tiny role, but I'm doing it as a sort of a good luck gesture for Christopher Nolan, the director of *Batman*, because the Batman films have become for me some of the most important movies I have ever done.

Every so often, something comes along and you just know that it's going to be a turning point. Since *Goldmember* and *The Quiet American* I had done a couple of films, including *The Statement*, which reunited me with old friends like Frank Finlay, with whom I had toured back in 1959 in *The Long and the Short and the Tall*, and Alan Bates, in his last role before he died of pancreatic cancer in 2003. *Secondhand Lions*, which followed, took us back to Austin, Texas, which was still working hard to keep it weird. Although they were fun to do, none of these movies were huge box office hits and so I returned to Surrey and my garden, content to wait.

In the end I didn't have to wait that long. One sunny Sunday morning the phone rang and a voice on the other end introduced himself as Christopher Nolan. I had never met him, but I had seen two of his films, *Memento* and *Insomnia*, and had been very impressed. "I'm restarting the Batman series for Warner Bros.," he said. "The first movie is called *Batman Begins* and I wondered if you would like to play the butler, Alfred." This was something completely different for me— a regular character in a Hollywood blockbuster series—so I suggested he send over the script. "Tell you what," said Chris, "I'll bring it round." It turned out he lived very close and an hour later he was on the doorstep, script in hand. I invited him in, expecting to give him a cup of tea and have a bit of a chat about the film, but he was adamant. "No," he said, "I want you to read the script now. I'll wait."

I was a bit taken aback, but while Chris sat in the kitchen chatting to Shakira as she prepared Sunday lunch, I went to my office and sat down to read. The more I read, the more excited I got. "I love it!" I said, as I came into the kitchen and it was handshakes all round. As he was leaving, Chris asked for the script back; this project was highly confidential and he was very protective of it—he even used the names of his three children as code for each of the films. I handed it over, waved him off and sat down to a delicious Sunday lunch feeling very pleased with myself. Batman had indeed Begun.

A year later, it really did. We started shooting at Shepperton, the studios in which I had appeared in my first movie, *A Hill in Korea*, in 1956. It was extraordinary to walk in there and appear again on the soundstage where I spoke (or rather forgot) my very first lines in a movie. I took this as a very good omen and I was entirely right. The cast that Chris had assembled was brilliant: Christian Bale, the best Batman ever, in my view, Liam Neeson, Gary Oldman, Morgan Freeman, Tom Wilkinson and Cillian Murphy to name just a few.

I decided that Alfred Pennyworth, my butler, was going to be the toughest butler you've ever seen—not the sort of suave English butler that someone like Sir John Gielgud played. I invented a whole backstory for Alfred: he'd been an SAS sergeant who had been wounded and, because he didn't want to leave the army, got put in charge of the sergeant's mess, which is where Bruce Wayne's father found him. So he knows how to serve drinks and all that sort of thing, but he's also a trained killer. I based his voice on the voice of my original sergeant when I joined the British army: it's a very sharp, staccato, military delivery. It's a great role, because I think I get to represent the audience's point of view, to be a point of normality for them, if you like. So just when you're thinking, What's going on? There's a man dressed in a batsuit? I come along and I ask, "What's going on? You're dressing in a batsuit?" It was a very clever move by Chris to keep the audience on its toes but also in the loop.

Chris is a very quiet director, but his sense of authority permeates the whole set. He always wears a coat with a big pocket in which he keeps a flask of coffee that he sips from all day as he watches rehearsals. It's not just hindsight speaking when I say I knew it was going to be fantastic: it was clear from the beginning that we were on to something really special. Chris's whole attitude and demeanor was a big part of it, but the sets, too, were quite spectacular, especially those built in Cardington Hangars, one of two enormous sheds built for the old airships near Bedford. To give you an idea of the scale, our enormous Chicago set fit into one corner. The Bat Cave in particular was incredible. I remember looking up at the ceiling and saying to

Chris, "Those bats in the ceiling, they look almost real—how did you make them?" And he said, "Michael, they are real. They're just asleep. . . ." "Well, whatever you do, don't bloody wake them up!" I said. A journalist later asked me if even at my stage in life I had learnt anything on this movie and I said, "Yeah—to keep my head down and stay away from the bats!"

Unlike blockbuster movies these days, Chris shot most of the amazing stunts in the film with real stuntmen because he wanted a sense of reality. In our movie, when Batman flies, a hook explodes from his sleeve and fixes on a roof and a wire pulls him up. It imparts a sense of the possible rather than being pure fantasy—and it really works. Of course there is some computer-generated imagery—the scene where Christian and I are filmed with a million bats, for instance—but most of the special effects are real.

For the exterior shots we traveled to Chicago. Chris had chosen to film Gotham City in Chicago because although the skyline is as spectacular as New York's, it's not quite as well known. Shakira and I had never been to Chicago and we absolutely loved it. We celebrated my birthday there, just the two of us, and had a fantastic meal at Sullivan's Steak House. We enjoyed every minute of it—especially the birthday special. They bring the biggest slice of chocolate cake you have ever seen with a candle on top and then all the waiters come over to sing "Happy Birthday." But this is a big and very busy restaurant and so they cut the song short: "Happy B'day to you," and sing it in record time—I think the whole thing took less than ten seconds before they rushed back to work!

When I finally got to see the finished film, it was every bit as good as I'd hoped. And then—as always happens—I got sent out on the publicity trail. It kicked off at the Beverly Wilshire Hotel in Beverly Hills and we did what is known as "round tables," in which the cast is split up into pairs and sent from room to room to do twenty-minute interviews with a dozen or so journalists. I was paired with Katie Holmes, which was great, as we had played scenes together and got to know each other pretty well. We were well used to the formula and so we did what we had to do and it seemed to go down OK. We had just finished and were walking out of the pressroom together—when suddenly, outside in the corridor, Tom Cruise appeared. I couldn't work out what on earth he was doing there—but Katie knew all right and she rushed into his arms. I stood there dumbfounded, with the press all crowded behind me. "We're in love," Tom announced to the throng. "I can see that," I said—and that was the first time the news of the relationship broke. I had been with Katie on the movie, been with her on the publicity tour and she had never let on—not for a minute. After that, Tom joined Katie on the publicity tour in New York, London and Paris. They had a ball, we had a ball, but the only problem was they sometimes got more attention than the movie.

After my new outing as a butler, I returned to the role I was beginning to make my own: the father. I played Nicole Kidman's father in *Bewitched* and then went on to play Nicolas Cage's father in *The Weather Man*. Neither movie was a big hit. Although I was a bit miffed not to see my name on the poster for *Bewitched*, when I saw the dire reviews it got I was very relieved. Of course it didn't start out like that. The director, Nora Ephron, had directed *Sleepless in Seattle* and *When Harry Met Sally*. We shot the movie in the old David O. Selznick studio in Los Angeles and it was great to be back in Beverly Hills, and even greater to be working with the person who was responsible for bringing me there in the first place, Shirley MacLaine. It all seemed to augur so well. Why it didn't work is one of those great movie mysteries—although watching it the other day it did occur to me that brilliant though both Nicole and Will Ferrell are individually, there's just no chemistry between them.

Batman Begins, on the other hand, was a huge success and after it came out Chris Nolan called me to suggest another project. We had developed a really great working relationship, so I was pleased to take on *The Prestige*, a movie about magicians in which I played the guy who actually makes the tricks. I was working with Christian Bale again along with Hugh Jackman and Scarlett Johansson. I had never met Scarlett before, but it only took about two minutes of conversation for us to become firm friends: she's talented, clever, funny and beautiful—what more could you want? We were standing together waiting to do a scene when I suddenly realized I was looking down at her from quite a distance. "How tall are you?" I asked. She gave me a funny look for a moment and said, "You mean, how short am I, don't you?" She's five foot four and that's her all over: gets right to the point, with no mucking about!

The Prestige is the ultimate example of cinematic sleight of hand. You watch it, and then you lose the thread and you think, what's going on here? Chris Nolan leads you by the nose right through the movie and then you discover that the whole thing is a trick. It really appealed to me, because it demanded a lot from me as an actor. Of course I'd read the script and I knew what was going to happen and where all the illusions and double meanings lay, but I had to put all that to one side. As an actor you know what's going on, but you have to remain with the character and stay with the reality of his experience. I found it very interesting, because my character was holding the center of the picture together: my job was to explain things (or that's what you're supposed to think).

From all the razzamatazz of a huge international blockbuster movie, I went back into the much quieter world of the British film industry. Well—it was quieter when I went into it, but when we released *Sleuth* in 2007 all hell was let loose. The picture got slammed by the critics in an almost maniacal frenzy of personal attacks on Jude Law, who played the character I had played thirty-five years previously, and its director Kenneth Branagh. I came out of it relatively unscathed.

Perhaps one of the biggest mistakes we made with the movie was not billing it as an original work by Harold Pinter; there isn't a single line of Anthony Shaffer's previous script in the film. (It turned out to be Harold Pinter's last work—which made it all the more special for me as I had been in his first play, *The Room*, at the Royal Court in 1960. Harold died just after the movie was released.) This *Sleuth* is very different from the first version. Ken was always very clear that it wasn't a remake. It was a movie based on the plotline of *Sleuth*, he said, and we happened to have stolen the title, but it's a different concept entirely. Whereas the original was set in an English country house with all those mazes, this was all minimalist marble and glass—it's a much cooler effect. And although I'm playing the role Olivier played all those years ago opposite me, there's a very different feel to that, too. I deliberately didn't go back and watch the movie again—not that I could play the character the way Larry did (I didn't want that little black hairy caterpillar stuck on my face for a start)—but I didn't want any confusion, either. In any case, the Pinter script was so different that the whole movie felt completely fresh to me.

Unlike the critics, I really admired Jude's performance and, having often been mauled by critics myself, I felt great sympathy for him. Jude and Ken have gone on to even greater success. Jude's acclaimed portrayal of Hamlet at the Donmar Warehouse in London's West End in 2009 was, I thought, outstanding, as was Ken's raved-about performance in *Ivanov* at the same venue the previous year, not to mention his BAFTA-winning performance of the Swedish cop Wallander in the Masterpiece Theater production—one of my favorite-ever TV detective series.

After we had all picked ourselves up and dusted ourselves off, I was pleased to know that my next film would be back to the world of the blockbuster. When we had finished *Batman Begins*, I'd asked Chris Nolan what the next one would be like. He's famous for never giving anything away, so all he said was,

"Darker . . . much darker." And how right he was. . . . I thought
the first film was brilliant, but *The Dark Knight*, which finished
filming in 2007, is even better—in fact I think it is one of the
best action movies I've ever seen.

When I read the script for the first time, however, I could
see a problem. Jack Nicholson had been such a fantastic Joker in
the earlier Tim Burton Batman movie that it was difficult to
see how anyone could follow that performance, let alone top it.
But when I called Chris to ask him who he wanted to take the
role and he said he wanted Heath Ledger, I immediately
stopped worrying. Quite what we would get I didn't know—
but I knew it would be something original.

We were back in the big airship hangar at Cardington and
the Chicago set was still standing. The unit had been shooting
since February and it was the end of April by the time I joined
them—I could never get used to the schedules on these enormous pictures—and in fact I actually only shot on this movie
for ten days out of eight months. But for me, one of those days
was unforgettable: it was the first time I came face-to-face with
Heath Ledger's Joker.

The scene was a cocktail party in Batman's flat and as the
butler I was masterminding the event. The flat was enormous—
it was actually the lobby of a grand Chicago hotel—and I was
greeting guests as they came in from the elevator. Eventually a
group of guests were going to arrive and with them would be
the Joker who would terrorize the whole party. I'd never met
Heath before, and I didn't have any dialogue with him during
the scene, but we chatted between shots quite casually, with
me trying not to let him see how disturbing I found his makeup.
Any worries I might have had about him competing with Jack
Nicholson vanished the moment I saw his face: it was truly
horrific—it almost looked as if he was rotting from the inside.
Jack was a great Joker; Heath was not a joke at all—he was a
nightmare. He went in a completely different direction and I

knew from the moment I saw him that it would work. In contrast to his sinister appearance, he was completely charming and so relaxed about his work that I had no inkling of what would happen when those bloody lift doors opened. . . . Alfred thinks he's letting friends in, but instead the Joker has killed them all. I was standing there and suddenly Heath burst out at full throttle and took over not just the party, but almost the entire film. I was so terrified, if I'd had any lines, I'd have forgotten them.

When I'd finished my bit on the film, I packed up and went home to enjoy the rest of the summer of 2007. I knew work was continuing on the movie, but I couldn't have been more shocked to hear the following January that Heath had died of an accidental overdose. It was the most terrible waste not only of a great talent, but of a gentle and thoughtful person. It was hard to go and see the finished film and see all the vitality that Heath exudes, knowing that he was dead, and inevitably much of the publicity surrounding the premiere in July 2008 was centered on the tragedy of his death.

It was a great moment when Heath won a posthumous Oscar for Best Supporting Actor. We had all predicted he would win it, right from his first scenes, and it wasn't just me—everyone on the unit thought he deserved it. It was a standout performance—the opening and closing monologue alone, let alone all his other scenes—and I thought it was very important for his family as well. I was a bit surprised that neither the film itself nor Chris Nolan was even nominated for an Academy Award, though, because *The Dark Knight* is an extraordinary piece of filmmaking. For an action movie it has great depth and real drama—and a serious message, if you want to find it. It's got great comic moments, too. Even Heath, who is playing a complete homicidal psychopath, gets laughs. At one point the Joker sees Maggie Gyllenhaal, and Heath just reaches up and very delicately, almost in a feminine way, brushes back a couple of strands of his stringy hair: it's genius. My butler character gets laughs, too, and I've been discovered by a whole new set of teenage fans who often stop me in the street, but there's real tenderness there between Alfred and Bruce Wayne. It's back to that father figure again: I've gone from Alfie to Alfred; I guess you could say I've become more dignified over the years.

Taking on the role of an old man with Alzheimer's might not be everybody's idea of dignified, but *Is Anybody There?* was one of those challenges I couldn't resist. When I get a script, one of the things I ask myself is: Is this more difficult to do than the last one? And this part certainly was. I drew on my experience of Doug Hayward's dementia and so it was very sad for me—in fact I think it's the saddest film I've ever made. Shakira didn't like it at all because my character actually died of dementia; we persuaded Natasha, who was pregnant at the time, not to see it because we thought it would upset her. My family were reacting like that because it was me lying in that hospital bed, but what I completely forgot to factor in was how harrowing it would also be for an audience to watch—so it didn't exactly do *Star Wars* numbers at the box office. But it got great critical attention and I'm proud to have done it.

CHAPTER TWENTY-TWO

BACK TO THE ELEPHANT

Harry Brown was a movie I just had to do. We filmed on location on a massive council estate that was due for demolition back at the Elephant and Castle. It's my home patch and we were working just round the corner from a mural depicting Charlie Chaplin and me (not that I'd compare myself with the great man, it's just that we came from the same area). I've been in many council flats before in my life, but I had forgotten just how tiny these living spaces are. The flat would hardly have had enough room for a dining table for a family to eat at, something I think is of the utmost importance in bringing up children.

The whole area is now being gentrified and I asked an official I met where they had rehoused the tenants. "As far away from each other as possible," was his rather enigmatic reply. But not everyone was pleased to be getting out. While we were there, we came across a small BBC team filming the last few residents. To my astonishment they said that their documentary was about the terrible loss of community spirit the tenants suffered when they began to pull down the estate. I looked from them and then back at this eyesore and found that hard to believe.

The last time I'd been back to the area I grew up in for professional reasons was in autumn 1985 when Bob Hoskins asked me to take a cameo role in his film *Mona Lisa*. I'd first got to know Bob when we were in Mexico together on *The Honorary Consul* and we'd become great friends—a friendship that had flourished in the slightly less testing surroundings of the Hamptons on America's East Coast, filming *Sweet Liberty* with Alan Alda, earlier that summer. Bob had invited me to his production office to discuss the part but as I sat in the car getting further and further into the depths of the south London streets I'd grown up in, I began to wonder what I was letting myself in for. I knew it was a small-budget movie, but Bob's office—a huge, dark, run-down Victorian building—didn't bode well. "It was a hospital years ago," he said cheerfully as he led me through the maze of corridors, "before it became a lunatic asylum. St. Olave's." I remember stopping dead in my tracks. "But I was born here!" I said. There can't be many movie actors who end up discussing their role in a film in the very hospital they were born in.

I know only too well how tough it is to grow up in an environment like the Elephant and I'm aware that I, too, could easily have gone bad—but I took a different course, and the longer we spent in the neighborhood, the more I wanted to find out why. Quite a bit of *Harry Brown* was shot at night and that gave me the opportunity to talk to some of the gangs of youths—black, white, British-born and immigrant—who were hanging about. I got to know them and began to win their trust a bit. At first I was astonished and then pleased that they were prepared to talk to an old white man on an equal basis. As they opened up, it dawned on me that although we'd had nothing as kids, I had had a life of luxury compared to the young men I was talking to. Our prefab house was small, but it was self-contained: it had a twenty-square-foot garden, a garden fence, a front door and a garden gate. It was the first house I'd ever lived in with electricity and hot water taps and an inside toilet and a bathroom. And this house was only a thousand yards from the monstrous blocks where these boys had grown up.

But the house was only part of it. I had a loving family with a father who stayed with us and a mother who cared for us. Most of these boys came from one-parent families—or none. It's not that single parents can't do a great job raising their children—after all, there were many kids in my generation whose fathers had been killed in the war—but it makes it much harder, and if they are poor as well, it's an extra handicap. I was lucky, too, because I had a good education—at least at Hackney Downs. A lot of these boys were bright but seemed to have opted out of school completely, which is a shame because they would benefit from real education and a sense of possibility. One guy I met told me he likes to build things, likes doing woodwork. It doesn't mean he has to be a carpenter—although that would be a good start: he could be a sculptor, or a woodcarver. Kids need to have a direction for their talents; otherwise they won't know where to go.

And my generation didn't have to deal with drugs and the violence that follows—or at least not on the same scale. Half the time these kids are so drugged up they have no idea what they're doing: there was constant activity from the police while we were filming. I remember one day in particular when we wasted half the day on retakes because every time we finished a shot with dialogue, a police siren would come along and ruin it. But even more than that, these kids had nothing to do and nowhere to go. I had Clubland, the youth club and the drama class and that was where I found the thing I wanted to do more than anything else, the thing that, in the end, set me on my future course.

If it hadn't been for the Reverend Jimmy Butterworth who ran and founded Clubland, I probably would never have made it out of the Elephant. He was a tiny little man—he was only about five foot—and referred to himself as a "little Lancashire Lad," but he was a giant to me. He built that youth club out of nothing but determination and an extraordinary ability to persuade wealthy donors to back the project. It was through this that I met my first real star—Bob Hope. Bob was a very generous man and always gave a lot to charities, but somehow Jimmy had managed not only to persuade him to donate the proceeds of his entire two-week run at the Prince of Wales Theatre to the club, but to come and talk to us as well. He made a great impression on me, but I had no reason to think that he had even noticed a gangly teenager hanging on his every word and I didn't mention it when, years later, I appeared on *The Bob Hope Show* during the publicity for *Alfie*. I should have known better. When I got back to England, my agent called to say he hadn't yet gotten the fee for my appearance. A week later I got a call from Bob himself. He had sent the money straight to Jimmy Butterworth at Clubland. "You owe them," he said. And I do.

On *Harry Brown*, I saw for myself the difference that involvement with something creative can make to the lives of kids who have nothing. The director, Daniel Barber, used a number of the young men who had been watching us on the shoot in the movie. It was late one night and as I stood there watching them rehearse, I thought to myself that he had bought himself some real trouble—I assumed they would get bored very quickly and all be gone by take three, which would mean he would have to reshoot. I was completely wrong. As I watched Daniel directing these kids it dawned on me that here was proof of what was lacking in their lives. They were doing something they really wanted to do, they were interested enough to want to know how to do it well and they were responding to an authority figure who knew what he was talking about and was treating them with the dignity and respect their lives were lacking. By take five, they were completely into it and making their own suggestions—I loved watching the way their confidence grew by the minute. Daniel was happy to let them ad-lib and the only direction I heard him give was, "You can only say 'fuck' twice each and no one can say the 'C' word or you'll get us an X rating!"

The art of directing kids from the street wasn't the only thing I learnt on *Harry Brown*. I was also introduced to the art of ecological filmmaking. There's one scene where I have to take a gun away from a guy and throw it into the canal, which took about five or six takes to get right. Now, I'm used to throwing guns in canals and there's always a diver standing there to go in and get the gun at the end of it. So by the time Daniel called "print," I'd thrown about six guns into the canal and I asked the special effects guy where the diver was. "There isn't one," he said. "Well, how are you going to get the guns back?" I asked. "Ah," he said, "it's a new thing—they dissolve within two hours!" You see? You think you know everything and then they surprise you with dissolving guns. . . .

Harry Brown was a real wake-up call for me and I wanted it to be a wake-up call for others, too. I had gone into the film thinking that we should just lock up these violent offenders and throw away the key, but I completely changed my mind during the course of it. Prison doesn't solve the problems that come with the sorts of backgrounds these kids come from. The fact is that we are failing them. If they are brought up with violence they have no option but to join a gang—most of them join for protection, not because they are naturally violent themselves. I did it myself when I was their age, but although we were rough and tough, compared with the gangs now we were like Mary Poppins.

When it came out, some critics compared *Harry Brown* with *Death Wish*, because the protagonists in both films end up killing the killers of someone close to them. That wasn't our intention, and it's not how I see it at all. Our film is about violence, but it never celebrates violence; Harry Brown never becomes a willing perpetrator, he always remains a victim, and that was very important to me. It works because it's about a fantasy that I think everyone shares to some extent, of being able to scare the people who scare you—and that is what daily life is like on some of these estates.

To me, it's important, always, to remember where you came from. Walking round the Elephant after the last day of filming on *Harry Brown*, I felt no great sense of closure, just a sense of satisfaction that I had made it and gone from there to Hollywood—the place I had always dreamed of. I no longer want to make movies back-to-back as I did in my younger, hungrier days—I'd had eighteen months between finishing *Is Anybody There?* and *Harry Brown*—but the business still fascinates me as much as it did then. If another script comes along that I really want to do, then I'll take it on: if not, I won't. I've always said that you don't retire from the movie business, it retires you—and when it retires me, I tell you now, there won't be any fanfare or public announcement. I'm an old soldier, like Harry Brown, and I will just fade away from my long public life into the embrace of my family. In the end, they mean more to me than the whole lot put together.

CHAPTER TWENTY-THREE

WHAT IT'S REALLY ALL ABOUT

With longer and longer gaps between films I've been able to spend more time on the other pleasures in life—the family, friends, my garden and cooking are just some of these, but one of the greatest has been traveling. I've been all over the world on location and seen some wonderful places (and some bloody awful ones, too), but when you're working you can't be as relaxed about sightseeing as when you're on holiday. So with a less hectic schedule, Shakira and I have been making up for lost time. It's been a chance for us not only to revisit our favorite spots, but to explore some new ones, too—and one of the most exciting for us was the trip we took to India in 2005.

Like everyone else, I had preconceived notions of what India would be like, both good and bad. I thought I would be outraged by the extraordinary wealth of the few and the grinding poverty of the many, but that wasn't the entire story. Yes, we saw examples of extreme wealth and extreme poverty, but this was a country in which many of the richest people really do have a sense of caring for their poorer neighbors and it's a country on the move, with a burgeoning middle class, a highly educated workforce with tremendous technology skills, and a real sense of enterprise.

We were traveling in august company. With us were our friends Olafur Grimsson, president of Iceland, and his wife, Dorrit, there on an official visit, and also Irina Abramovich, the ex-wife of Roman Abramovich, the owner of the Chelsea Football Club. It turned out that my claim to fame in India is as the husband of Shakira—although I did hear a rumor that they have remade *Get Carter* and *The Italian Job* in Hindi, so maybe the next time I go I will have achieved some status of my own.

Because we were with such a high-powered group, we were treated like royalty. Our first dinner was in the penthouse suite in the Taj Palace Hotel in New Delhi as guests of Mrs. Sonia Gandhi, the leader of the Congress Party, and the following day we were invited to have tea with the president, Dr. A. P. J. Abdul Kalam. His palace, which had been built by the British, was unbelievably grand and stood at the end of an enormous boulevard. All I could think of as I gazed at it was what confidence, insanity and conceit the British must have had to build such pompous edifices to an endless future, surrounded, as they were, by some of the poorest people on the face of the earth. Society in India has changed for the better since those days, but buildings like that still look out of place to me.

The president himself was particularly interesting on two counts: first, he is a Muslim, despite the fact that only 20 percent of India's population is Muslim, and second, he is a scientist who played a major part in India's nuclear missile program. After tea he showed us round the enormous rose garden. It occurred to me that it occupied a huge amount of space in a very overcrowded city and, perhaps unwisely, I pointed out the injustice of it. He smiled at me innocently. "Ah," he said. "The British built it." "Ah," I said. "Of course." I was put politely in my place.

The following day we had tea with the prime minister, Dr. Manmohan Singh, and got another surprise: he was a Sikh, the first non-Hindu prime minister of India. Sikhs are an even smaller religious minority than the Muslims and it was a Sikh who had assassinated Mrs. Gandhi. I didn't speak to the prime minister much—it was well above my pay grade—and left most of the talking to Olafur, but I did reflect on the strides India had taken in religious tolerance since independence; the leader of the Congress Party, Sonia Gandhi, is an Italian Catholic by birth, the president of India is a Muslim and the prime minister is a Sikh. And all this in a country where 80 percent of the population is Hindu.

One of the most remarkable days there we spent being shown round the former home of Mrs. Indira Gandhi, who had been killed by her own Sikh guards in her back garden. The house and garden, which are relatively modest, have been kept exactly as they were on the day she died. Only two items on display relate to the tragedy of the Gandhi family: the clothes Mrs. Gandhi was wearing when she was assassinated, and the clothes worn by her son, Rajiv, when he was blown up by a female suicide bomber as she knelt down to kiss his feet in a gesture of respect. After we had been round the house, we were taken out into the garden. The guide led us along a path and then stopped, pointing down to a small bridge with water running under-neath it. At his feet there was a fresh flower. "This," he said, "is the spot where Mrs. Gandhi was shot." And then we walked another twenty or thirty paces further along the path and he said, "And this is where Mr. Peter Ustinov was standing." *Peter?* None of us had ever heard that Peter Ustinov had been there. "What was he doing there?" I asked, completely confused. "He was interviewing her for the BBC," said the guide. "That was why

Mrs. Gandhi had come out to the garden in the first place." I'd had no idea.

My next surprise was the following day. We were visiting the gardens of a temple when a monkey leapt out of a tree and stole the glasses right off my nose. It's a big shock, I can tell you, having your glasses stolen by a monkey, but now I always carry a spare pair just in case there are monkeys around.

After Delhi, we traveled to Agra by car. It took six long hours, but it was extraordinary to see the other side of India gradually unfold as we left the city behind. We did indeed have to drive round a cow that had decided to sit in the middle of the road and we also had to stop at a railway crossing for a train to go by and, yes, people really did travel on the roof and cling on to the sides of the carriages. But all this was just preparation for something I had been looking forward to ever since my father—who had been a soldier in India—had told me tales of it: the Taj Mahal.

Our first evening, Shakira and I strolled out onto the lawn for a look at the Taj Mahal by moonlight. It really was one of the most beautiful sights I have ever seen—and certainly the most romantic. To add to the magic, along a road by the side of the hotel came a wedding celebration, singing beautifully as they processed, with a full band and illuminated by a thousand bright electric lights. Having had some experience with lighting problems back in my first job at Frieze Films, I immediately looked for the source of the electricity and eventually along it came, right at the end of the procession—an elephant pulling a huge electric generator.

The following morning we made our first official visit to the Taj Mahal. You think you know what to expect—after all, it must be the most photographed building in the world—but nothing can prepare you for close-up sight of this monument. It is more breathtaking than any picture could ever capture. For the ladies of the party, Dorrit, Irina and Shakira, there was one place of pilgrimage they were determined to visit: what is now known as "Diana's bench"—the bench on which the troubled Diana sat during her last official visit as Princess of Wales. Each of them sat on it in turn while I took a picture of them, then one of the three of them together and then a passerby took one of all of us. Honor being satisfied, we then walked through the beautiful garden and into the building itself. Its somber atmosphere comes as a surprise, but of course the Taj Mahal is a mausoleum to Mumtaz Mahal, the most loved wife of Shah Jahan, who died in childbirth with their fourteenth child. It was an unforgettable experience.

From Agra, we went on to Jaipur, stopping off at temples every now and again. While the others admired the carvings, I used the opportunity to say prayers of thanks for surviving the journey to the temple and to ask for protection as we traveled on to the next.

Jaipur seems to me to be exactly what India should look like: a big fortress, a grand palace and streets teeming with women in bright, multicolored clothes and elephants everywhere. We were invited to dinner by the then chief minister of Rajasthan, Vasundhara Raje Scindia, a charming woman who invited us to call her "Vasu," much to my relief. She played us a gramophone record of a chant meant to keep you calm in stressful situations, which consisted of a deep-voiced male singer chanting "Oooooooommmm" over and over again. If you do it right, it vibrates right through your body and calms you right down. Shakira was very interested in it and seems keen for me to practice.

The following evening, the former maharajah of Jaipur had invited us to dinner. When we arrived at the palace, we were dropped at the start of the drive up to the front door and got out of the car to find the entire drive lined with a band mounted on elephants and camels decorated with exotic livery, playing the most beautiful music. As we walked through the ancient arch at the end of the drive, we were showered with rose petals by young girls who were seated on the top. It felt as if we were walking through some ancient fable. The dinner was delicious and afterwards we were treated to an extraordinary display of folk dancing in which dancers from all over Rajasthan entertained us—culminating in a finale by a group of tiny women from the mountains who had never before been outside their distant villages. Like most things about India it managed to be both breathtaking and mesmerizing.

Although so much of our time was spent being entertained by the great and the good, I also wanted to get a sense of ordinary lives and the way they were changing in the world's greatest secular democracy. Technological advancement is rushing through India, but it will be a long time coming to most of its population—one wealthy woman I met told me that her electrician didn't have electricity and her plumber didn't have plumbing. In the meantime ordinary Indians muddle through with the enterprise and ingenuity that is on display everywhere. As one person I met there said, "India is living proof that chaos works."

EPILOGUE

Now I'm in the fortunate and luxurious position of only working when I want to. I don't like having to get up early in the morning or spending a long time learning lines, so these days I only work with offers that I really can't refuse. It's very different from the way I used to be. From the age of twenty to the age of twenty-nine, I was obsessed with becoming an actor—and when I finally got to Hollywood, I could never quite believe that I had made it and so I kept on working for fear it would all disappear on me.

These days, I don't think like that at all. I don't see myself as a Hollywood movie star—in fact I don't see myself as anything in particular. I'm aware that I have this image in the media and I have to confess that I quite like it, but of course I'm not allowed to take myself too seriously. I once tried it on Shakira. "I'm an icon," I said. "It says so in the paper." "You may be an icon," she said, "but you'd better take the rubbish out!"

Of course we still go back to Hollywood—it's an incredibly important part of our lives and many of our friends still live there. But the links are loosening. I had thought it was all over in 1992, but it turned out that it wasn't. Now, I think it probably is.

The first hint of this came during a visit to LA last year when we went to a restaurant on Little Santa Monica called Dolce Vita. It was Frank Sinatra's favorite restaurant and as we walked in, I remembered the night long ago when he had first brought us there. As Shakira and I walked to our table, which was right across the room, the faces of friends of ours kept appearing out of the darkness to say hello. When we finally reached the table and sat down, I asked Shakira, "Did you notice anything special about the people who have just greeted us?" "Well," she said, a bit puzzled, "they are all friends of ours. . . ." "I know that," I said, "but they were all women, and they are all widows." I could see at once that she understood: Barbara Sinatra, the widow of Frank, Veronique Peck, the widow of Gregory and Barbara Davis, the widow of our billionaire friend, Marvin.

This time, as soon as we arrived, Shakira and I went for a drive through Beverly Hills, for old time's sake. As we drove around we pointed out to each other the houses of people we had known: Danny Kaye, Jimmy Stewart, Edward G. Robinson, Fred Astaire among others. When we finally got back to the hotel, I had another question for her. "Did you notice anything about those houses we were looking at today?" I asked. This time Shakira had the answer straightaway. "Yes," she said sadly. "The people we knew who lived in them are all dead." Some sort of message was beginning to sink in for us.

The following day, while Shakira had lunch with girlfriends, I had lunch with my Hollywood press agent, Jerry Pam, at The Grill, just off Rodeo Drive, one of my favorite haunts for over forty years. As we sat down, Jerry gave me the news I had been half expecting for some time: he was retiring and leaving

Hollywood for good. He is a sprightly eighty-three, so this wasn't exactly a shock, but given our experiences of the last few days, it was another sign that it was probably time finally to say goodbye to the place I loved so much. After lunch, Jerry and I got to the corner of Rodeo Drive, shook hands, said goodbye— and as I watched him disappear into the groups of Japanese tourists on his way to find his car, I knew it was over.

I didn't hesitate. I went straight into Ermenegildo Zegna and bought myself a shirt. I always do that when I'm a bit depressed. Shopping bag in hand, I wandered back up Rodeo Drive as the memories flooded back. The history of my Hollywood was all around me. I passed the Daisy on my right, once the best discotheque in Beverly Hills, now a clothes shop. The jewelers on the corner had once been the home of Barbra Streisand's hairdresser, Jon Peters, who became the boss of Columbia Pictures. On my left was the site of the Luau, the place to see and be seen by everyone who was anyone in Hollywood. It is now a shopping mall.

By the time I'd got back to the hotel, I'd cheered up. So Hollywood was finally over for me after forty years? It had been great but, I thought, that's the past. I'm going home to my future, to my friends, my family, my home and garden—maybe to another film, if something interesting comes along, but in any case, to everything that really matters—and above all, to the newest and most exciting development in my life—my three grandchildren.

On October 15, 2008, our lives changed forever. I had been delighted by the news of Natasha's pregnancy, and was looking forward to the baby's arrival, but I had no idea of the depth of the love I would feel for my first grandchild. Natasha and her husband, Michael, named their son Taylor and gave him the middle names of Michael and Caine. "You never had a son, Dad," Natasha said, "and now you have one." It was a unique gift. What's more, although both Natasha and Michael have black hair and brown eyes, Taylor has blond hair and blue eyes and people say he looks just like me. I think he is far, far better looking than I ever was and I have decided that I want to live for another fifty years so I can watch him grow up and grow old—as you can tell, I am completely besotted.

Just as Shakira and I were getting used to Taylor and the joy he brought to us, Natasha announced that she was pregnant again. September 2009 was the big month and we were very excited—only to have another surprise when she announced that she was having twins! We went into overdrive: a new bedroom was added, swings and slides adorned the lawn and the living room was turned into a nursery. Our house was a big place for just two people, but it is perfect for visits from our new family—some sixth sense must have been operating when we planned it all!

The twins, Miles and Allegra, were born on September 23, which means for two weeks each year they and Taylor are the same age. They don't look anything like each other: Miles is dark, with brown eyes, and Allegra is blond with blue eyes. I remember Scarlett Johansson introducing me to her twin, Hunter, and being astonished to find that while she is five foot four, with blue eyes and blond hair, Hunter is six foot three and dark. Maybe our twins will be just the same.

The twins, though growing fast, are still babies; Taylor is rapidly becoming a little boy and I love having him just pottering around the room when I'm writing. He's very good at noticing when I'm getting writer's fatigue—which is about every twenty minutes—and he comes over to give me a rest by climbing onto my lap and switching to Mickey Mouse on my computer. It means so much to me to have these precious grandchildren who suddenly appeared in my seventy-fifth year over a period of just over eleven months, an unexpected late joy and one that I could never have imagined would mean so much. They are in my thoughts constantly. I'm planning ahead to Christmas already—the twins were too young to appreciate it last year, although I thought Taylor would enjoy all the lights and the decorations so I pulled out all the stops. He loved it; it was worth everything just to see the look on his face when he came into the room and saw the tree ablaze with lights and piled with presents.

So life moves on and it is now a Monday morning at my home in Surrey as I sit writing this final chapter. Last weekend, the fourteenth of March, was my seventy-seventh birthday and it was such a special one. I had three grandchildren at my birthday for the first time in my life. It was a beautiful sunny day and we picked the first daffodils of spring.

I saw my London friends earlier in the week. We had a dinner at the Cipriani in Mayfair and, appropriately enough, several of the Mayfair Orphans were there to help me celebrate. Johnny Gold, nightclub owner extraordinaire, is now golfer-in-the-Bahamas ordinaire—but he's very happy. Photographer Terry O'Neill is more successful than ever. Philip Kingsley, the trichologist, came along with his wife, Joan, who is a psychiatrist (I've always thought what a great team they would be if going bald was driving you mad) and so did our occasional member Michael Winner, there to enjoy the food for once, not to criticize it. My daughters Dominique and Natasha were there, as well as Natasha's husband, Michael, and Shakira's friend Emile, whom she has known since their early days in Guyana. I was happy to see my old friend the South African hotel mogul Sol Kerzner, whom I first met filming *Zulu*, and his wife, Heather, who shares a birthday with me, and—along with Michael Winner—representing the film world, the movie producer Norma Heyman, with whom I worked on *The Honorary Consul*. I always love Norma's story about her son, David, who told her one day that he wanted to be a movie producer like her and had bought a little children's story to start with. It was called *Harry Potter*. . . .

The departed members of the Mayfair Orphans were represented by Chrissie Most, the widow of our Mickie. It was one of those evenings that we all knew would be good, but which, because of the bond among us all, turned out to be truly special.

And then last Wednesday, I had the third part of my birthday celebrations. Sol Kerzner threw a party at the nightclub Annabel's for Heather and as it was my birthday, too, I was part of the occasion. The first thrill for me was being able to get into the club without wearing a tie—something that would have been impossible when the founder, Mark Birley, was alive. The second was finding it was as full of beautiful, elegant people of all four sexes (maybe even as many as five or six—I haven't been out much lately) as it ever was in my younger days. I didn't recognize any of them, though, which was rather disturbing—although I could tell they were all very important. Shakira saw I was looking a bit puzzled and took pity on me. "They're either from the fashion industry," she whispered, "or so rich we don't know them!" Well—that was a relief. And I was further relieved to find fellow Mayfair Orphan Johnny Gold among the crowd. I stuck to him like a snail, because the music was so loud I couldn't hear anyone introduce themselves. I really am getting old, I thought.

It was a spectacular evening with magnificent food and an incredible cabaret entertainment, including six beautiful dancers. This was followed by the star cast of *Jersey Boys* and then the five of us who had birthdays to celebrate—Heather, me, Sir Philip Green of Topshop fame, Patrick Cox, the shoe designer, and Tracey Emin's boyfriend, photographer Scott Douglas—were all called onstage and presented with chocolate birthday cakes iced with "Love is all you need."

Love wasn't quite what was in the air everywhere, though—just as Heather was making a speech noting, "There's so much love in the room tonight," down in the throng Hugh Grant had called PR man Matthew Freud a stupid shit and Matthew had rubbed his slice of chocolate birthday cake all the way down the front of Hugh's shirt. Hugh hit back with a punch to Matthew's nose, which missed and caught him on the cheekbone. Matthew retaliated by throwing a glass of wine at Hugh, which missed him and soaked Johnny Gold instead. Matthew stormed out of the room clutching his cheek, waiters mysteriously appeared with a clean shirt for Hugh and the party turned into a disco and we danced the rest of the night away. Trust a PR man, though (or, rather, don't trust a PR man) because Matthew Freud had the last word and e-mailed pictures of Hugh Grant's chocolaty shirt to all his friends the next day.

So from a high-octane celebrity party to a small dinner with old friends and then—and happiest of all—to a day at home with three generations of my family—I have had a birthday I'll always remember. It seems to me, too, as I sit here finishing this book, that my three birthdays also reflect the distance I've traveled—from the Elephant all the way to Hollywood and back. It was a tough start, it's had some low moments and it's had incredible highs, but it's been a rich and rewarding journey—and it's not over yet.

MY TOP TEN FAVORITE MOVIES
OF ALL TIME

All my life I have been an avid movie fan, which is why, I suppose, I ended up in the business. I love movies—I can even find something to like in the bad ones—but I do have an all-time Top Ten. Here they are in reverse order.

10. Tell No One, 2006

This is a French film and one of the best thrillers I have ever seen. It's adapted from the brilliant novel by American thriller writer Harlan Coben—who actually appears in the film as the man who follows our hero, Bruno, into the station—and I've always been a bit surprised that it wasn't bought by an American studio. Bruno is played by François Cluzet, who gives it a slight American feel as he looks very like Dustin Hoffman, and the great English turned French actress, Kristin Scott Thomas, costars. The blurb alone is enough to draw you in: "A husband and wife, out together, are badly beaten by a person unknown. The husband survives, but the wife dies. The wife's father identifies her body and they bury her. Seven years later, the husband gets an e-mail from his dead wife saying, 'Meet me in the park in an hour.'" I couldn't resist—the film is stunning.

9. Treasure of the Sierra Madre, 1948

This is a movie involving two of my favorite artists: Humphrey Bogart, whom I never got to meet, and John Huston, who directed me in two of my favorite films, The Man Who Would Be King and Escape to Victory. As

I've said before, I've always thought that if God spoke he would sound like John Huston, a deep voice of experience and wisdom and in this film you can actually hear John's voice. He plays a man who keeps being approached by Bogart's character, who is begging in the street, and John gives him a lecture. I'd listen to a lecture from John Huston any day—his voice is completely mesmerizing. I first saw it when it came out—and I felt it was a metaphor for my own life. It features a load of dumb sods searching for a treasure; and there I was, a dumb sod searching for my own treasure—only in my case, that was a career in the movies. The crazy old man, played by Walter Huston, knows where the treasure is—and fortunately for me, as I went through my life I met my own Walter Hustons. There is a great scene in the movie when Bogart says, "We're never going to find the gold," and Huston starts to laugh and he does this little skip and dance, saying, "You're so dumb, you don't even see the riches you're treadin' on with your own feet . . ." and Bogart and Tim Holt look mystified and then they look down and they are standing on it. . . .

8. *Gone With the Wind*, 1939

This was the first movie in color to win a Best Picture Oscar and, taking inflation into account, it is still the highest-grossing picture ever. The book, by Margaret Mitchell, was turned down by every major Hollywood studio and picked up in the end by the independent producer David O. Selznick. Selznick was a genius at doing movies on the cheap. Apart from using the front door of his own studio as the front door to Tara, he saved money at both ends in the scene of the burning of Atlanta by setting fire to several old sets he wanted to get rid of on the back lot. The first director on the movie was a brilliant, gentle and very sensitive man called George Cukor, and although Selznick fired him and replaced him with Victor Fleming, a brusque, tough, action director, neither Vivien Leigh nor Olivia de Havilland liked the change and continued to seek private direction from Cukor. This was also the film in which Clark Gable said "damn." It had, of course, been said in a film before, but it caused controversy because *Gone With the Wind* was so big. . . . I can watch this movie time and time again without tiring of it. It is a classic.

7. *All That Jazz*, 1979

This is my favorite musical and Bob Fosse, who directed and choreographed it, is my favorite choreographer—he also directed two of my other favorite musicals, *Cabaret*, which won eight Oscars, including one for Bob for Best Director, and *Sweet Charity*, which had my friend and mentor Shirley MacLaine dancing up a storm and featured a great number by Sammy Davis Jr., "The Rhythm of Life." But it is the music and dancing in *All That Jazz* that makes it stand out for me—that, plus the performance of Roy Scheider in the lead. When I was an out-of-work actor I had worked as a stagehand on Bob Fosse's stage production of *The Pajama Game*, but I didn't get to know him personally until he and I and several other actors danced with the Rockettes' chorus line at Radio City Music Hall in 1985. We were lined up in alphabetical order and I was next to Charles Bronson—who turned out to be an unexpectedly great chorus dancer. We were down at one end with the slightly older chorus ladies, who were known as the Dirty Dozen. A bit further down the line, Rock Hudson got the younger, fresher ones—which was a bit of a waste, come to think of it.

6. *The Maltese Falcon, 1941*
This was the first gangster thriller I ever saw, and the first film John Huston ever directed. It was also the first of a series of three films that the then big star George Raft turned down, which consequently turned Humphrey Bogart into an icon. Bogart is fantastic, of course, but he's backed up by an equally strong cast including Sydney Greenstreet and Peter Lorre. I fell in love with Dashiell Hammett's dialogue and started to read his books whenever I could run them to earth in 1950s London. In fact Hammett wrote my favorite thriller line ever: "It was dark—and it wasn't just the night." *The Maltese Falcon* was the start of my love affair with film noir—which continues to this day.

5. *Some Like It Hot, 1959*
This remains one of the funniest films I have ever seen—and the most daring comedy. I had never seen a film where the stars dressed in drag; in the 1950s it was unheard of. Jack Lemmon and Tony Curtis took a real chance with this and with the help of Billy Wilder and his script and the inspired casting of Marilyn Monroe, they made it an all-time great comedy. Many years later I was very close friends with both Irving Lazar and Billy Wilder and Irving told me he was with Billy when he showed the film to the critics for the first time and there was not a laugh during the entire film. After the show they went to Hamburger Hamlet and tough, unsentimental Billy burst into tears. He

should have remembered the old theater adage: "A paper [complementary] house never laughs." I was having dinner with Billy one night and I asked him if Marilyn Monroe had been difficult to work with and he said that she had been. "She was always late," he said, "and she didn't know her lines. But then," he went on, "I could have cast my aunt Martha, and she would have been on time and she would have known her lines, but who the hell would have gone to see her?" A typical Billy Wilder comment. . . .

4. *Charade*, 1963

This is my favorite romantic movie of all time—it is also a great comedy and a great thriller and of course it is set in one of my favorite cities in the world, Paris. It's also, in my view, one of the most underrated movies of all time. The film has a great sense of nostalgia for me as they shot a whole sequence in Les Halles, the old food market where we all used to go in the sixties at two o'clock in the morning after all the nightclubs closed to have French onion soup. The relationship between Cary Grant and Audrey Hepburn is of course the main attraction of the film: they were superb. It's full of brilliant one-liners and these two actors deliver them immaculately. Here are two of my favorites:

> REGINA (AUDREY HEPBURN): "I already know a lot of people and until one of them dies I couldn't possibly meet anyone else."
> PETER (CARY GRANT): "Well, if anyone goes on the critical list, let me know. . . ."

And . . .

> REGINA: "You know what's wrong with you, don't you?"
> PETER: "No. What?"
> REGINA: "Nothing."

Brilliant, isn't it?

3. *On the Waterfront*, 1954

This film was a revelation to me. The script by Budd Schulberg, the direction of Elia Kazan and the performances of the actors took me into a working-class reality in a way that I had never experienced in a movie before. Marlon Brando, Karl Malden, Rod Steiger and Eva Marie Saint were all method actors. There are two main principles: The first is that the rehearsal is the work and the performance the relaxation, so by the time you get to work in front of a camera you should be so familiar with what you are doing it seems effortless. The second principle is that your acting should come from sense memory, finding a moment in your own life to produce a real and instant emotion—I use it to this day, if I am required to cry. Not that I think of some great tragic incident, it's just something that struck me as terribly sad. I've never told anyone— not even Shakira, to whom I am closer than anyone else in the world— what that moment is. If I did, I would then be thinking of her reaction rather than my own and it would lose its power. The result in this film is quite extraordinary—especially in that iconic scene in which Marlon Brando as Terry and Rod Steiger as Charley are in the back of the car and Terry says, "I coulda been a contender. I could have been somebody. . . ." Unforgettable.

2. The Third Man, 1949

Another Graham Greene novel—this time he adapted it for screen himself. And like all great movies, this has a fantastic sense of time and place. Postwar Vienna is an extraordinary setting for what I consider to be the best thriller ever. (Although films like *Psycho, Rear Window, The Usual Suspects* and *Silence of the Lambs* all run it as close seconds.) It was photographed in black and white by Robert Krasker with strange camera angles and a gritty documentary style and it has an unsettling and unforgettable sense of menace. The cast is fabulous—Joseph Cotten and Orson Welles in particular—the first time they had appeared together since *Citizen Kane*. The movie is full of so many memorable sequences it is hard to pull out just one, but perhaps I would point to the scene in which Harry Lime and Holly Martins are at the top of the giant Ferris wheel overlooking Vienna and Martins asks Harry if he has ever seen any of his victims. . . . Harry brushes it off and after they get back down to the ground says to Holly as he's walking away, "Like the fella says, in Italy for thirty years under the Borgias, they had warfare, terror, murder and bloodshed, but they produced Michelangelo, Leonardo da Vinci and the Renaissance. In Switzerland they had brotherly love— they had five hundred years of democracy and peace and what did that produce? The cuckoo clock. So long, Holly." Genius—and this line was written not by Graham Greene, but by Orson Welles himself. Then there's the action climax and the chase through the sewers and the romantic climax where Joseph Cotten is waiting at the cemetery gates as Alida Valli is coming away from Harry Lime's funeral. It's a long walk towards him—will she stop? Or will she walk straight past? I'm not going to tell you. If you haven't seen it, do yourself a favor and get a DVD right now!

1. Casablanca, 1942

Well—what else was it going to be? It should have been just another reasonably successful movie churned out by Hollywood. In fact, it probably shouldn't have worked at all. It started shooting without a finished screenplay, from a play that had never seen the stage called *Everybody Comes to Rick's*. I met Julius Epstein, one of the twin brothers responsible for the screenplay, and he asked me if I knew the traffic light at the bottom of Benedict at Sunset Boulevard just by the Beverly Hills Hotel. I told him I knew it well and I hated it because it always seemed to stay red for about five minutes. He smiled. "It was waiting at that traffic light every day," he said, "that my brother Philip and I wrote a lot of *Casablanca*. . . ."

The studio wanted William Wyler to direct and ended up with Michael Curtiz, who was, apparently, a very irritable and insensitive director. He was, however, responsible for a phrase still used today in English speaking crews all over the world for a non-sound sequence. He was a Hungarian and whenever he wanted to do a scene without recorded sound he would shout out, "Mitt out sound!" which became abbreviated to MOS.

It was another of those three films that Humphrey Bogart was only in because George Raft turned the part down and the studio had changed their mind about the original casting, which was (picture this . . .) Ronald Reagan and Ann Sheridan. There was another problem: Bogart was about two inches shorter than Ingrid Bergman. I can't imagine anyone asking Bogart to stand on a box, so this must have meant very difficult setups. On-screen the two of them had a fantastic relationship, but that wasn't the case offscreen, nor was it the case with the brilliant supporting cast, which includes Sydney Greenstreet, Peter Lorre and, of course, Claude Rains who nearly stole the film as Captain Renault. In fact, as Julius put it, "Nobody burst into tears when the movie finished shooting. . . ."

But in spite of that, the film has gone on to be not only at the top of my list, but at the top of most people's lists. The music is memorable, and of course it contains some of the most often-quoted lines in the whole of the movie business. There are too many to mention here, but Rick's line, "Of all the gin joints in all the world, she walks into mine," stands out as one of the most poignant. And then there's Rick's famous last line, "I think this is the beginning of a beautiful friendship." It wasn't even in the original script. It was written by the producer, Hal Wallis, and dubbed by Bogart later over the shot of him and Claude Rains walking away into the mist. To me this looks like Hal Wallis—who was a very smart producer—hinting at the studio for a sequel. It never happened—and perhaps it's best that we leave it on that note. For me, *Casablanca* will always be number one.

MY OWN FAVORITE MOVIES

I can't help being aware of the image I have in the media, not that Shakira allows me to get away with any movie star behavior, as I've said. She's right of course, but I also know that I have made some films that mean a lot to other people—and they are important to me, too. I can't do a Top Ten of my own movies: it's got to be a Top Thirteen, because there is something about each one of these that means a lot to me. I've never been superstitious about the number thirteen; my passport number for years was 13 13 13—and that got me safely to plenty of places—so here they are, in the order in which I made them, and here's why they matter to me.

Zulu—My first big break. A wonderful introduction to the world of the movies and the first film in which I had a substantial part

The Ipcress File—This was the first movie in which my name was "above the title." Harry Salzman decided to do this even though it was not in my contract. When I asked him why, he said, "If I don't think you're a star, who the hell else will?"

Alfie—The biggest movie of my career to this point and the first movie of mine that was not only a success in the UK but also got a U.S. release. It was also my first nomination for an Academy Award. . . .

Sleuth—The hardest and the best work I had done up until then. It was a two-handed show and the other hand was Lord Olivier, the greatest actor in the world. I was the greatest actor from the Elephant and Castle.

The Man Who Would Be King—A movie costarring Sean Connery, my great and longtime friend, directed by John Huston, my great and longtime idol, in which I played the part intended for Humphrey Bogart, my great and longtime inspiration. . . . As the line in the movie went, "We were not little men."

The Italian Job—Written for me by my friend Troy Kennedy Martin, shot in Italy, costarring Noël Coward—enough said. . . .

Dirty Rotten Scoundrels—The funniest film I ever made—and the happiest.

Get Carter—Based on people I knew in my earlier life (not that they ever found out), this was made partly as a protest against the pornography of violence. And it's about honor, which was every bit as important where I came from as it was for the British aristocracy or the Sicilian Mafia.

The Quiet American—I really feel that this is among my best work. The character I played is the least like me of any characters I have played—but you'd never know. . . .

Educating Rita—Like *The Quiet American*, I was playing another character I had little in common with—and I got an Academy Award nomination for them both.

Hannah and Her Sisters—I was working with Woody Allen, one of my favorite directors, in New York, one of my favorite places. Oh—and I got an Oscar.

The Cider House Rules—Perhaps this character was even less like me—but I got my second Academy Award.

Harry Brown—A beautifully made film by the young first-time director Daniel Barber. It was shot on my home patch, which shocked me when I discovered just how bleak it had become.

INDEX